INTEGRATIVE assessment IN CLINICAL PSYCHOLOGY

Edited by
Andrew J. Lewis, Emma Gould,
Cherine Habib, Ross King

First published in 2010
Australian Academic Press
32 Jeays Street
Bowen Hills Qld 4006
Australia
www.australianacademicpress.com.au

National Library of Australia Cataloguing-in-Publication entry

Title:	Integrative assessment in clinical psychology / edited by Andrew Lewis ... [et al.].
ISBN:	9781921513589 (pbk.)
	9781921513596 (ebook)
Subjects:	Clinical psychology.
Other Authors/ Contributors:	Lewis, Andrew
Dewey Number:	616.89

Cover photograph by © istockphoto.com/studiovision. Cover designed by Maria Biaggini.

Contents

Part II: Child Assessments

Part III: Specialist Assessments

Appendix A

About the Authors

Linda Byrne, PhD is a clinical neuropsychologist and a lecturer in the School of Psychology at Deakin University.

Renee Gedge, PhD is a clinical psychologist and holds a joint appointment with Deakin University Psychology and Eastern Health Adult Mental Health.

Emma Gould is a lecturer in the School of Psychology at Deakin University.

Cherine Habib, PhD is a clinical child and family psychologist and was previously senior lecturer in Clinical Psychology at Deakin University.

Marina Haywood, PhD is a neuropsychologist and a lecturer in the School of Psychology at Deakin University.

Ross King, PhD is a clinical psychologist and a senior lecturer in the School of Psychology at Deakin University.

Andrew J. Lewis, PhD is a clinical psychologist and an associate professor in the School of Psychology at Deakin University.

Caroline Long is a research fellow in the School of Psychology at Deakin University.

Helen Mildred, PhD is a clinical psychologist and a senior clinical academic in the School of Psychology at Deakin University.

Jane McGillivray, PhD is a clinical psychologist and an associate professor in the School of Psychology at Deakin University.

Nicole Phelps is a graduate of the Master of Psychology (Clinical) in the School of Psychology at Deakin University.

Petra Staiger, PhD is a clinical psychologist and an associate professor in the School of Psychology at Deakin University.

James Vess, PhD is a forensic psychologist and senior lecturer in the School of Psychology at Deakin University.

INTRODUCTION

Integrative Clinical Psychology: Linking Assessment and Treatments

Andrew J. Lewis, Emma Gould, Cherine Habib and Ross King

When the only tool you have is a hammer, every problem begins to resemble a nail.

Attributed to Abraham Maslow

Clinical assessment is a process that extends from the point of referral to the formal commencement of treatment. Its aim is principally to appraise the patient's core life issues, to accurately diagnose psychopathology and to apply the relevant factors in a recommendation of the most effective and efficient treatment regime. Within these broad parameters, assessments take place in a wide variety of clinical circumstances. Assessments also address diverse referral questions. In some cases the referral question is made by a well-informed professional who is seeking a very specific determination from a clinical psychologist about psychopathology, risk issues, intellectual or personality function. In other cases, and increasingly as clinical psychologists take on less specialised roles in the mental health system, assessment might be requested by the patient or intake system and takes the form of a general assessment of mental health and indicated treatment.

This book contains chapters that demonstrate a wide variety of different types of clinical assessment. The presenting problems and diagnostic categories have been chosen to reflect the assessment tasks that clinical psychologists are typically required to undertake in the Australian mental health system. Each case report is accompanied by a commentary discussing the assessment techniques, choice of assessment measures and a commentary on unique aspects of the case. The aim is to produce a reference work that will aid in both the practice of clinical assessment and the reporting of such assessments. Each chapter also provides an opportunity to examine the complexities of a specific case, the most current assessment techniques, treatment planning and consideration of current research findings on the assessment of an individual case.

Cases presented in the book are based on actual clinical material but each case has been carefully 'fictionalised' to ensure there are no issues of confidentiality or privacy. The aim is to present clinical material that might be used for demonstration and discussion purposes. The cases also demonstrate the use and integration of multiple sources of information derived from clinical interview and the selection and application of commonly used standardised measures.

One of the unique contributions that clinical psychologists can make within the mental health system is to combine information derived from clinical interview with that derived from carefully selected psychological measures. Each chapter of the book demonstrates the combination of both sources of information and also discusses the clinical decisions the assessors used to make the choice of instruments. The chapters provide a demonstration of the clinical application of the most common standardised tests currently used by clinical psychologists including the Weschler instruments, Millon and MMPI. In addition, a number of new instruments are introduced and some quite specialised instruments are also included.

The chapters have been organised according to broad diagnostic categories. The assessment of each case demonstrates an integrative approach to clinical assessment and treatment planning. This approach is based on the assumption that assessment must determine the diagnostic, client and common factors that indicate the preferred treatment options. Mental health disorders are caused by multiple interacting factors operating across different levels of analysis: genetic, neurobiological, cognitive, affective, social and psychosocial (Kandel, 1998; Lewis, 2008). Accordingly, case formulation requires an integrated appraisal of these different aetiological processes and their systemic and developmental interactions. In the integrated model, interventions need to be tailored to address a range of such factors, rather than offering a 'one size fits all' intervention. Therefore, the integrative model places greater emphasis on rigorous assessment as one of the core clinical skills and distinguishing features of clinical psychology.

Applying the Evidence to Assessment and Treatment

Given the rapid pace of change in the science of psychology and its application to clinical practice there is a continual need to both reappraise and update clinical practice. Not least among these changes is the movement towards evidence-based practice, which gained considerable momentum across the health sector in the 1990s and is now widely seen as a logical extension of the scientist-practitioner approach within psychology (Goodheart, Kazdin, & Sternberg, 2006). There remains a lively debate as to the manner in which empirical science ought to be used to develop, test and inform health practices, although the bulk of this discussion in clinical psychology is focused on psychological therapies rather than assessment practices. As Kendall notes, the empirical basis of clinical psychology is one of the profession's key distinctive features (Kendall, 1998) and it sets a high standard for the profession. The fact that clinical psychology is so well informed of and by the scientific evaluation of treatment ensures that it will remain at the centre of the mental health system. However, science is an ongoing investigative process based in a creative and regenerative development of ideas, theories and instruments of measurement. One of the hallmarks of the scientific attitude is a certain degree of scepticism regarding propositions and a critical examination of the evidence put forward to support assertions. So, clinical psychologists need to be cautious in endorsing particular interventions or assessment practices as a 'gold standard'.

The most recent American Psychological Association Presidential taskforce reported in 2005 on evidence-based practice and redefined it as 'the integration of the best available research with clinical expertise in the context of patient characteristics, culture, and preferences' (American Psychological Association Task Force on Evidence-Based Practice, 2006). The APA taskforce defines clinical expertise as 'Assessment, diagnostic judgement, systematic case formulation, treatment planning, interpersonal expertise, clinical decision making, treatment implementation, monitoring of patient progress, evaluation and use of research evidence, and understanding the influence of individual, cultural and contextual differences on treatment' (p. 276). To be noted is the emphasis on the integration of research and expertise. In this context, research findings are most effectively applied by considering their relevance to clinical data derived from careful and skilled assessment. Individual patient characteristics need to be considered and so too the patient's preference and suitability for the increasing number of psychological interventions that are supported by adequate evidence.

Treatment planning is the major goal of the assessment process. Recommendation of intervention requires considerably more than simply consulting the latest evidence for the principal diagnosis. The methodology used to evaluate treatments produces studies with robust design that maximises internal validity, but this often comes at the expense of external validity. Outcome trials are typically conducted by screening out complex cases of comorbidity in order to maximise homogeneity of diagnosis within the patient group (Kazdin, 2008; Westen, Novotny, & Thompson-Brenner, 2004). Drew Westen and colleagues question the four basic assumptions underlying the use of RCT methodologies to validate psychological therapies, namely that psychopathology is highly malleable, that most patients can be treated for a single problem or disorder, that psychiatric disorders can be treated independently of personality factors unlikely to change in brief treatments and that experimental methods provide a gold standard for identifying useful psychotherapeutic packages. In a widely cited paper, Martin Seligman took the argument one step further to suggest that efficacy studies of homogeneous patient groups using RCTs omit most of the crucial elements of real clinical practice, such that they are of limited value when applying evidence-based criteria to treatment selection within an individual assessment (Seligman, 1995).

As the chapters presented in this book show, the planning of intervention needs to be informed by the available evidence. However, given these limitations within the evidence base for psychological therapies, clinical psychologists are in a position to make good use of that evidence in clinical assessment and treatment planning without becoming enslaved by it. There are many factors to be considered in assessment such as the suitability of treatment, the patient's communicative, information processing and interpersonal style. There are also factors particular to the service setting such as the available expertise in a given intervention. In addition, the current evidence base for intervention has a limited application to complex patient presentations.

Applying Integration at a Clinical Level

The integrative approach implies that clinical psychology training needs to broaden the curriculum to encompass a range of theories of psychological change and therapies as they might be applied across a diverse range of patient groups (Wachtel & Wachtel, 1997). Training models are considerably underresearched and this critically important aspect of clinical psychology demands considerably more attention (Kazdin, 2000). However, broadening the skill base and the treatment options also requires clinical psychologists to assess a broader range of patient functions and characteristics. In addition to diagnostic factors, evidence supports the role of client factors and common factors as equally important considerations in outcome (Groth-Marnat, Roberts, & Beutler, 2001). Therefore, a comprehensive and integrative assessment ought to consider all these factors in order to tailor individualised treatment plans with the maximum likelihood of success (Wampold, 2001).

A good deal of clinical practice, especially private practice consists of addressing repetitive maladaptive interpersonal patterns, problematic personality dispositions, dysfunctional ways of regulating negative emotions and externalising pathology (Westen, 2002). These categories do not often fit neatly within DSM categories but can be conveyed within a skilfully constructed formulation. Problems in interpersonal and personality styles, as distinct from fully fledged disorders, are a common feature of clinical presentations that might otherwise meet diagnostic criteria for eating, mood, anxiety or substance abuse disorders. It is arguably the case that these more pervasive and often enduring patterns, that are subclinical according to the DSM, if targeted in psychological therapy will produce more lasting change. For example, assessment of personality styles has suggested differences in responsiveness to psychological treatments. Results from the NIMH Treatment of Depression Collaborative Research Project, suggest that 'depressed patients with higher levels of social functioning do better in brief interpersonal therapy, while depressed patients with higher cognitive functioning do better in brief cognitive–behavioural therapy' (Blatt & Felsen, 1993, p. 245). Such research supports the assertion that clinical psychologists need to be able to assess differentially for patient characteristic that have been shown to predict responsiveness to different treatment approaches.

This book aims to demonstrate an integrated model of clinical psychology practice where disorders are understood as the outcome of multiple interacting factors across different levels of analysis; biological, psychological and psychosocial. The integrated approach to clinical assessment is a prerequisite to an integrated approach to psychological therapy. Increasingly, clinical psychologists are able to employ integrated forms of psychological therapy as the field comes to accept both the strengths and limitations of cognitive, behavioural, humanistic, psychodynamic and systemic approaches. Integration in contemporary approaches such as Mentalisation-Based Therapy (MBT), Acceptance and Commitment Therapy (ACT) or Schema Focused Therapy (SFT) are good examples of the blending and integration characteristic of contemporary practice. No doubt this trend towards hybridisation and integration will continue to shape intervention models and influence the emergence of integrative assessment in clinical psychology.

References

American Psychological Association Task Force on Evidence-Based Practice. (2006). Evidence-based practice in psychology. *American Psychologist, 61*, 271–285.

Blatt, S., & Felsen, I. (1993). Different kinds of folks may need different kinds of strokes: The effect of patients' characteristics on therapeutic process and outcome. *Psychotherapy Research, 3*(4), 245–259.

Goodheart, C.D., Kazdin, A.E., & Sternberg, R.J. (2006). *Evidence-based psychotherapy: Where practice and research meet.* Washington, DC: American Psychological Association.

Groth-Marnat, G., Roberts, R., & Beutler, L. (2001). Client characteristics and psychotherapy: Perspectives, support, interactions, and implications for training. *Australian Psychologist, 36*(2), 115–121.

Kandel, E.R. (1998). A new intellectual framework for psychiatry. *American Journal of Psychiatry, 155*(4), 457.

Kazdin, A.E. (2008). Evidence-based treatment and practice: New opportunities to bridge clinical research and practice, enhance the knowledge base, and improve patient care. *American Psychologist, 63*(3), 146–159.

Kazdin, A.E. (2000). Evaluating the impact of clinical psychology training programs: Process and outcome issues. *Clinical Psychology: Science and Practice, 7*(4), 357–360.

Kendall, P. (1998). Empirically supported psychological therapies. *Journal of Consulting and Clinical Psychology, 66*(1), 3–6.

Lewis, A.J. (2008). Neuropsychological deficit and psychodynamic defense models of schizophrenia: Towards an integrated model. In J. Gleeson, E. Killackey & H. Krstev (Eds.), *Psychotherapies for the psychoses: Theoretical, cultural and clinical integration* (pp. 52–69): New York: Routledge.

Seligman, M. (1995). The effectiveness of psychotherapy: The Consumer Reports study. *American Psychologist, 50*, 965–974.

Wachtel, P.L., & Wachtel, P.L. (1997). *Psychoanalysis, behavior therapy, and the relational world* (1st ed.). Washington, DC: American Psychological Association.

Wampold, B. (2001). *The great psychotherapy debate: Models, methods, and findings.* Mahwah, NJ: Lawrence Erlbaum Associates.

Westen, D. (2002). Manualizing manual development. *Clinical Psychology: Science and Practice, 9*(4), 416–418.

Westen, D., Novotny, C.M., & Thompson-Brenner, H. (2004). The empirical status of empirically supported psychotherapies: Assumptions, findings, and reporting in controlled clinical trials. *Psychological Bulletin, 130*(4), 631–663.

PART I

ADULT ASSESSMENTS

CHAPTER 1

The Clinical Assessment of a Client With Alcohol Dependence and Co-Occurring Anxiety Symptoms

Caroline M. Long and Petra K. Staiger

This case describes a common presentation of clients with an alcohol use disorder who recognise they have a problem, but would not regard themselves as dependent or 'addicted'. They therefore require education about recommended levels of alcohol use, harm reduction strategies, and need assistance in understanding the link between their cognitions and their behaviours (e.g., not recognising that their alcohol expectancies do not match the actual outcomes of binge drinking or the interaction between their emotional state and their substance use, as with the client described in this chapter). Such clients often self-refer for symptoms or outcomes from their substance use rather than for the substance use itself. An effective method of facilitating engagement and creating hope is to provide clients with a framework for conceptualising their substance use and to utilise therapy that integrates clients' stage of change, their strengths and priorities. The transtheoretical or 'Stages of Change' model (Prochaska & DiClemente, 1982) is particularly helpful in this regard because of its focus on understanding each individual client's perspective.

This assessment occurred in a drug and alcohol outpatient treatment centre. It was undertaken to assist the clinician to develop a relevant treatment plan that addressed both the client's requirements and the service's capacities. Because of the nature of the service, the initial focus was the client's substance use issues; however, assessment of alcohol or other substance use disorders, using an evidence-based approach to guide case formulation and treatment planning (e.g., Green, Worden, Menges, & McCrady, 2008; Rohsenow, 2008; Tucker, Vuchinich, & Murphy, 2002), requires more than assessing the patterns and consequences of use. High-prevalence mental health disorders such as depression, anxiety spectrum and posttraumatic stress at clinical or subclinical levels, are sufficiently routine in the majority of substance use presentations to be viewed as expected, rather than exceptional (Green et al., 2008; Minkoff & Cline, 2004). This service recognised the significant impact of mental health issues on substance use (and vice versa) therefore assessment of comorbid issues was considered a recommended component of a comprehensive assessment.

The prevalence of dual diagnoses is consistently high across Australia, the United Kingdom, the United States and Europe, with prevalence estimates ranging from 30% to 50% of clients who have a substance use disorder also having a significant mental health issue, with alcohol being the most often implicated (e.g., Crome, 2004; Regier et al., 1990). While there are clients who present with substance use disorders independent of any underlying mental health pathology, these are less common. This forthcoming case example of 'Sara' exemplifies a presentation within which mental health issues are inextricably linked with the alcohol/drug use. Assessing and treating the substance use without concurrently considering the mental health issue substantially reduces the likelihood of a lasting positive outcome for the client.

One example of this is that the client's capacity and/or motivation for treatment may be impaired if they have a thought or mood disorder (Allsop, 2008), thus the pace of change is slower and symptoms may be misattributed, leading to components in the treatment plan being inappropriate from the client's perspective. In addition, clients with co-occurring disorders have poorer outcomes generally (e.g., Mueser, Noordsy, Drake, & Fox, 2003). Ignoring such relevant context denies the client's reality; for example, that substance use is frequently an inadequate but compelling means of temporarily moderating unpleasant mental states. Reduction of the drug or alcohol use removes that 'self-medication' and therefore the client needs to develop alternative methods of managing their problematic mood state. It is essential for these alternatives to become well integrated as coping strategies in order to confidently anticipate abstinence or moderate alcohol use as a long-term choice. Ideally, this support would be created using evidence-based interventions such as cognitive–behaviour therapy (CBT; Mueser et al., 2003) and incorporating such techniques such as mindfulness, wherein the client learns to manage negative emotions and to tolerate rather than act on craving for alcohol (Witkiewitz & Marlatt, 2007; Witkiewitz, Marlatt, & Walker, 2005).

This case example considers many of the issues described above. As is typical of such clients, Sara self-referred with concerns about her behaviour when she was intoxicated and her lack of a stable boyfriend. Mental health issues appear to underlie her substance use. Sara expressed doubts about her ability to achieve desired outcomes through counselling, because she had seen four therapists previously for short periods of time. In each case she abandoned therapy after two or three sessions. The reason given was that each of the therapists 'insisted' on relating her drinking to past issues with her father, who abandoned the family when she was much younger. Sara was emphatic that this was not relevant and she requested that her intervention deal more directly with her unwanted behaviour, in particular, the disinhibition that occurred when she was inebriated.

The Case of Sara Wolfe

CLINICAL PSYCHOLOGY ASSESSMENT[1]
PRIVATE AND CONFIDENTIAL

NAME:	Sara Wolfe
ADDRESS:	23 Ironbark Rd, Pemberton, NSW
AGE:	35
DOB:	August 14, 1971
REFERRED BY:	Self
DATES SEEN:	August 1, 8 & 12.

Presentation

Sara is a single, 35-year-old marketing manager who self-referred for counselling in a drug and alcohol treatment service, to address her concerns about problematic behaviour while drinking, and her lack of a life partner. Sara indicated she was seriously worried about the side effects of her alcohol use, but did not consider herself an alcoholic because she did not experience cravings to drink. She described a 12-year history of increasing alcohol abuse, more recently leading to blackouts, distressing behaviour, hangovers and intensely self-critical thinking.

Her primary fear was that this behaviour was beginning to be talked about in the workplace. As a result, she had concerns she was in danger of losing her job. She also thought it may be interfering with her ability to retain a long-term boyfriend. Sara expressed no apprehensions about addiction or the cumulative harm of alcohol on her body. She described several situations where her 'personality changed' when she became intoxicated. She indicated she usually presented as self-contained and controlled, but after a few drinks she became flirtatious, uninhibited, 'aggressive and childish'. She noted that drinking after work was an expected part of the workplace activity and she did not see how she could control her intake under the circumstances.

Sara's comments about herself overall reflected self-critical and rigid thinking, in which she represented herself as continually failing to meet her own standards. She was employed in marketing and sales and described working long hours to satisfy her need to be viewed as a high-achieving businesswoman, and an ongoing pervasive concern that she was not performing well and would not be promoted or given more challenging projects. Much of her socialising involved work. She noted that she felt 'fired up and tense' when she got home and would use alcohol as a facilitator for relaxation and sleep. She described routinely arriving home late and feeling tired, so she would sit and drink approximately three-quarters to one bottle of wine in front of the television before going to bed. Three to four nights a week she would go to a bar with her co-workers, drinking five to eight cocktails or mixed drinks, and either dancing or talking. Occasionally, she would drink up to 12 or more drinks in a night. Sara noted she had a reliable memory until she had consumed a few drinks, and then her recollections became uncertain. On occasion she had no memory of how she returned home after an evening out. She commented that there had been 'a couple of times' when she had woken up next to someone she did not remember, and this profoundly distressed her. Sara's alcohol use had not yet escalated to the point where she believed had been overtly harmed by it, although she could not recall if she had had unprotected sex or not. Sara displayed some insight into her potential for harm should her drinking increase. She tended to use problem-diminishing language when referring to her consumption, saying that 'Other people drink a lot more than I do' and 'I only ever drink at night'. She indicated she was careful not to drive while intoxicated and never took sick days or was late to work due to hangover.

Background Information

The following information was obtained in a client interview: Sara is Australian-born and educated to university level, the first member of her family to have achieved this. She was the oldest of two children born in a small rural community and retained close links with her mother, brother and maternal grandparents, all of whom still reside there. She did well in school and was known by her teachers as 'the bright one' of the family. Her mother was described as a self-effacing housewife. Sara's father was a physically large and dominating man, but was punitive, and used ridicule and demeaning language to control the family, while never resorting to actual physical abuse. At the age of six, her father left the family unexpectedly to live with another woman, resulting in severe financial hardship until the children were old enough to work. Sara's mother 'always talked about it' and become depressed for years afterwards. Sara has little clear recollection of her father, other than remembering he was 'big and loud' and she had been afraid of him.

Sara was told by her mother that Sara's father had been a heavy drinker and that his biological family, with whom they had no contact, had a history of alcoholism. His own father and grandfather died of alcohol-related illness. Sara's brother, Simon, is a carpenter who is divorced with a young child. He was described as 'a bit of a boozer', drinking heavily on the weekends, but Sara said that was usual behaviour among his friends and colleagues. She observed that he had lost his licence twice for drink-driving, and alcohol was implicated in his divorce.

Sara described multiple brief relationships since her teenage years, but only one relationship of any duration. This was with Ian, when she was aged 22, and it lasted 12 months. The relationship ended when she decided she did not want to settle down and chose to move interstate to concentrate on her career. Her subsequent lack of a stable partner was of significant current concern to her and Sara said she often regretted not marrying at the age of 22, because 'at least I would have children'. On the other hand, she expressed satisfaction at having moved away from what she predicted would be a routine and unremarkable future and said that at the time she had been confident about the decision.

Sara reported generally good health apart from chronic difficulty falling asleep and a tendency to wake in the early hours of the morning with 'my head full of things I need to get done'. She noted this often prevented her from getting back to sleep and impacted on her alertness at work. She attends a gym three times a week and goes running on the weekends, stating that she likes to keep fit and finds exercise a helpful way of dealing with stress. Sara eats regularly, although she describes a tendency to rely on convenience food such as frozen meals, takeaways or bar snacks. Most of her time is spent at work or in solo activities such as running, gym work and watching DVDs at home. She confirmed that she had suffered 'culture shock' when she moved interstate and 'never really got the hang of the city', but her opinion was that being in a relationship would solve that difficulty.

Psychiatric History

There was no history of diagnosed mental health issues, although Sara agreed she had always been a 'worrier' and was like her mother and brother in this regard. She spoke of symptoms including chronic sleep disturbance, nail biting and difficulty relaxing. She also identified some compulsive behaviours including extensive list-making at work and home, having preferred ways of doing things that she was uncomfortable modifying, and repetitive checking behaviour with locking her home and her car. Finally, Sara acknowledged a high level of longstanding negative self-talk.

Family Psychiatric and Substance Abuse History

There was no family history of diagnosed mental illness, although Sarah commented that her mother had probably been clinically depressed after her father left, but 'never did anything about it'. As indicated, there was significant alcohol abuse history with respect to her father and his family, and her brother, Simon. Her mother did not drink.

Mental State Examination

Appearance, attitude, activity. Sara was a well dressed woman who appeared her stated age. She was of average height with a muscular build and seemed an intense person, who stared attentively at the interviewer and never relaxed her posture, sitting very upright throughout the sessions. After an initial abruptness that dissipated as the first session progressed, she was cooperative and friendly and she appeared eager to hear what the clinician had to say. She attended every session punctually.

Mood and affect. Sarah described her mood as 'quite nervous' and 'restless'. Initially, her affect was confident, but brittle and brusque; for example, she began her first session with a description of what she did and did not want from therapy. This mirrored her self-image, with positive, hopeful ideas balancing a strongly pessimistic perspective. As sessions continued, she appeared more relaxed, punctuating her comments with brief laughter that was appropriate to content. When discussing her drinking or her personal attributes, she would look down and appear weighed down.

Speech and language. Sara's speech was fluent and grammatical, with normal rhythm but was rapid in rate.

Thought process. Sara tended to interrupt both herself and the clinician, but her thinking remained on topic and relevant. No loosening of associations, blocking or other phenomena were noted.

Thought content. Sara's thought content centred on her drinking and its impact on her behaviour. It was solution-focused, self-critical regarding perceived failures to meet her own standards, and pessimistic despite Sara's generally positive presentation. She tended to focus her attention on stage-of-life issues relating to where she 'should' be at this point in her life. No suicidal or homicidal ideation or plans detected.

Perception. No perceptual disturbance was observed or reported.

Cognition. Sara appeared alert and fully oriented. She was able to sustain attention throughout interview and according to her report, her long- and short-term memory appeared intact, except for alcohol-related blackouts.

Insight and judgment. Insight was largely good; Sara had sought assistance for her problematic behaviour while intoxicated and was aware of the potential for harm if her drinking escalated. Likewise, her judgment was largely good. She does not drink-drive or miss meals; however, it seemed likely that she had engaged in unprotected sexual activity while under the influence.

Assessment

1. General

- Semistructured clinical interview
- Mental State Examination (MSE)
- The Stages of Change Readiness and Treatment Eagerness Scale (SOCRATES; Miller & Tonigan, 1996).

2. Substance Use

- Drug use history
- Alcohol Use Disorders Identification Test (AUDIT; World Health Organization [WHO], 2001)
- TimeLine Followback (TLFB; Sobell & Sobell, 1992)
- Alcohol Use Diary (once treatment had commenced)

3. Mental Health

- State-Trait Anxiety Inventory for adults (STAI; Spielberger, Gorsuch, Lushene, Vagg, & Jacobs, 1983)
- Patient Health Questionnaire–9 (PHQ-9; Spitzer, Kroenke, & Williams, 1999)
- Generalised Anxiety Disorder (GAD) section of the Anxiety Disorders Interview Schedule Anxiety Disorder Inventory (ADIS-IV; Brown, DiNardo, & Barlow, 1994)

The assessment consisted of three phases occurring over three sessions: (1) The first phase consisted of a standard semistructured clinical interview comprised of a mental state examination, family mental health and drug use history, level of readiness to change, previous personal history (i.e., social, occupational, educational, life events, family history) and Sara's past experience of and personal goals for treatment. (2) The second phase of the interview consisted of questions regarding the context of alcohol use, full drug use history (i.e., frequency, quantity and category of drugs used both current and lifetime), supported by standardised questionnaires (i.e., AUDIT, TLFB and later, an alcohol use diary). (3) The final phase of the interview was an assessment of anxiety and depression.

In the first phase of the interview it became apparent that there were recurring references to stress, persistent worrying and insomnia, all of which are indicative of a potential anxiety disorder. For this reason formal assessment of Sara's present and past anxiety levels and its impact on her substance was conducted (i.e., Anxiety Disorder Inventory, State-Trait Anxiety Inventory and clinical interview) together with a screening tool for depression (PHQ-9).

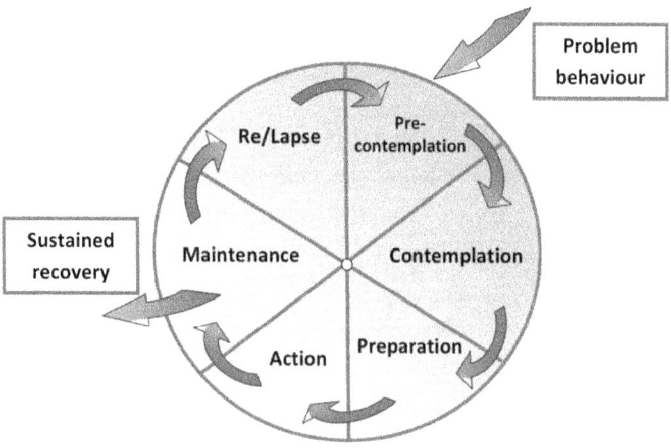

Figure 1.1

Stages of change model (Prochaska & DeClemente, 1983).

Phase 1: Semistructured Clinical Interview and Readiness to Change Assessment

A semistructured clinical interview was used in the first session to elicit the necessary elements of Sara's personal and family history and to obtain the information for the mental state examination. In addition, the 'stages of change' model (Prochaska & DiClemente, 1983) was used to assess Sara's motivation to make changes to her substance use. This is a circular model that defines the different stages an individual may experience when making a decision to change an aspect of their life and is often used in the context of alcohol/drug treatment. The stages occur serially, the length of time spent in any stage can vary from minutes to years and clients may regress at times.

The stages are 'Precontemplation', 'Contemplation', 'Preparation for change', 'Action', and 'Maintenance' (see Figure 1.1. Clients may subsequently lapse or relapse and, after a period of time, may begin the cycle again. In order to establish where on the continuum Sara functions with her alcohol use, she was asked to complete the Stages of Change Readiness and Treatment Eagerness Scale (SOCRATES; Miller & Tonigan, 1996). The results indicated that Sara was currently in the Contemplation stage for her alcohol use. She is unsatisfied with outcomes of her use and was aware she needed to make some changes but had not yet identified successful strategies. Sara had some ambivalence about the need for changing her alcohol behaviours, because alcohol helped her to fall asleep and was perceived as a necessary part of her networking for work. She was in the Action stage for relationship change, but her actions to change this (internet dating sites, adult education classes) were not offering her the outcomes she desired.

In the course of the interview Sara made numerous references to high levels of stress, feeling criticised, feeling pressured at work and other anxiety-related language. When asked if she had ever sought assistance for stress and anxiety, she mentioned that she had spoken to her medical practitioner on a number of occasions regarding her difficulties sleeping. She said this was because she wakes in the middle of the night and has trouble falling back to sleep due to racing thoughts and preoccupations with work and her lack of an intimate relationship. She reported that at different times she had used sleeping tablets and had discussed medication for stress with her doctor.

Finally, Sara said candidly that she was not feeling very confident about coming for therapy because of her lack of success in addressing her behavioural concerns with four therapists in succession. In the recent past, she has had no success in moderating her drinking and no ideas about how to manage her behaviour otherwise.

Phase 2: Semistructured Assessment of Substance Use

The second phase of the clinical interview focused specifically on detailing a full substance use history. This included completing a chart of any drugs Sara had experience of, her age at first use, the route and frequency of use and a ranking of her level of concern for each. It also included questions about her past experience of treatment and coping strategies. Sara said she had begun drinking when she was 13 and stole alcohol from the living room cabinet and at her friends' family homes. She remembered that it made it 'easier to cope' when she felt stressed and was a useful way of getting to sleep. She noted her drinking did not seriously escalate until she left home.

The Alcohol Use Disorders Identification Test (AUDIT) was used to assess the level of severity of alcohol misuse. Sara obtained a score of 27 out of a possible 40, indicating a high level of risk and possible alcohol dependence. 'Drinking in the morning' was the only item she did not endorse.

The TimeLine Followback (TLFB) was included as a memory aid to review Sara's substance use over the previous weeks up to three months prior. She had difficulty recalling her consumption on specific days, so she was asked about her usual pattern of drinking (i.e., whether she tended drink more at different times of the week, such as, proximal to pay day or on the weekend and whether she usually drank more when she was with others or alone). Her alcohol use escalated during the week with the highest consumption on the weekend. Sara commented that it became 'harder to get it together for work' as the week progressed and she was often very hung over on Sunday and Monday morning. She was also asked about special occasions and spoke of regular work functions, which were particularly risky events for overuse of alcohol. In addition, there were questions about what she drank in a typical week (discussing time of day and weekly activities) and she was asked if there was anything different about each week. This technique revealed that Sara very rarely had an alcohol-free day.

Sara was asked about use of other substances over the same time frame and how this interacted with her alcohol use. Using this method, Sara was able to add further detail and provide a clearer picture of how alcohol and other substance use fluctuated according to her activities and stress levels. This brought to attention her occasional use of Ecstasy (methylenedioxymethamphetamine; MDMA), which she had not referred to earlier. Approximately once a fortnight, Sara would go out 'clubbing' with friends and she described occasional use of 'E's' (Ecstasy). She noted that when she thought she needed a break from drinking, she would take an E instead, but that was only satisfactory when she was out at clubs with friends. She did not consider this harmful behaviour because she 'only ever took one' and 'everybody does it'.

While discussing the TimeLine Followback, Sara recalled that she had successfully given up smoking six months previously. She achieved this abstinence without external assistance by stopping overnight and maintaining an intensive exercise regime for several weeks. She had implemented this herself and expressed surprise at her ease in accomplishing it, but noted that 'it wouldn't surprise me if I started smoking again'.

Phase 3: Assessment of Anxiety

Phase 3 of the assessment focused specifically on eliciting further information about Sara's experience of anxiety, because in the early stages of her assessment it became clear that this was likely to be the underlying motivation for her alcohol consumption. That is, her preoccupations with her coworkers' opinions of her, her concerns about her work performance and relationship history were interfering with her sleeping. Alcohol was a significant method of muting these concerns and relaxing, but it then led to further concerns about behaviour while intoxicated, and the alcohol itself disturbed her sleep cycle (while alcohol does have an initial sedative effect, it suppresses rapid eye movement (REM) sleep and disrupts the sequence and duration of the sleep cycle [e.g., Roehrs & Roth, 2001]). Unlike depressive disorders, which are characterised by extreme variation in mood with related symptoms, anxiety is complex to assess because it manifests in multiple behavioural and psychological ways. Dependent on the primary expression, anxiety can manifest as obsessive–compulsive behaviours, panic attacks, agoraphobia, specific phobias, posttraumatic stress, acute stress or generalised anxiety.

The trait section of the State-Trait Anxiety Inventory (STAI) for adults was administered in order to estimate Sara's general level of anxiety. Sara's score of 69 placed her in the severe range of trait anxiety; that is, her anxiety was not a function of current events, but was a pervasive and established pattern of thinking. This indicated that more detailed assessment would be beneficial.

Sara described a tendency to focus on detail and rules, and possessing a strong need to feel in control. While this behaviour causes Sara to work late and to 'overdeliver' at work, it does not prevent her from completing tasks or delegating to achieve deadlines, and she derives significant satisfaction from being seen as a careful, conscientious professional. Overall, her perfectionism suggests obsessive–compulsive personality traits but not a personality disorder. Sara's most disabling symptoms were persistent worry that she was unable to control, and sleep disturbance as a consequence of her 'head being too busy' and being unable to calm down. She struggled to find effective ways to calm her mind, with alcohol and exercise being used for this purpose. Her symptoms were indicative of a generalised pervasive anxiety. For this reason, Sara was administered the generalised anxiety disorder (GAD) section of the Anxiety Disorders Interview Schedule (ADIS-IV; Brown, DiNardo, & Barlow, 1994). The score of 4 represents the clinical cut-off, and Sara rated a score of 6, placing her in the 'severe' category. Her responses were consistent with GAD, with uncontrollable worrying being her primary symptom, together with sleep disturbance, muscle tension, irritability and difficulty concentrating.

Finally, Sara completed the Patient Health Questionnaire (PHQ-9) as a screening measure for depression. Sara's score of 7 was below the cut-off for major depression and her score related to difficulty sleeping (scored 3/3), feeling bad about herself (scored 2/3) and difficulty concentrating (scored 2/3). This indicated that depression was not a key issue for Sara at this time.

Case Formulation

Sara is an independent, professional, 35-year-old, Australian woman who presented with concerns about symptoms relating to problematic alcohol use and relationship issues. From her own account, it seems that Sara's experience of her father and of his abandoning the family in her childhood is likely to have impacted on her self-esteem and confidence and to have exacerbated a predisposition to anxiety. The emotional abuse within the marital relationship was likely to have triggered maternal depression, probably impacting on Sara's mother's parenting, which had implications for Sara's attachment to her mother. This in turn was compounded by a family history of alcohol abuse; thus in her family-of-origin alcohol was an available escape and excessive drinking was modelled to the children from an early age. Sara began to make use of alcohol to manage her negative psychological states at or near puberty and when she relocated interstate at 23. The loss of her personal support network and the isolation brought on by that and her long working hours amplified her drinking. She was sufficiently disciplined and insightful to successfully give up smoking, but had made no serious attempts to moderate her drinking, probably as a consequence of having no adequate alternative means of managing her anxiety and limited recognition of the potential for her drinking behaviour to cause harm.

Sara's symptoms included chronic worrying, which interfered with her sleep and contributed to a work–life imbalance, perfectionism, excessive alcohol use leading to harmful and distressing consequences, and a reduction in intimate relationships. A comprehensive assessment confirmed a longstanding GAD complicated by alcohol dependency. Importantly, the diagnosis of GAD provided Sara with a better understanding of how poor social and work functioning was related to a pervasive and enduring difficulty with anxiety. This knowledge enabled her to reframe her life history and to begin to directly address her anxiety and understand the relationship that this had with her alcohol use.

Despite her previous failed attempts at therapy Sara's prognosis is good. She is a conscientious woman who has successfully stopped smoking and maintained some limits on her drinking in order to restrict the impact on her work. She has demonstrated proactive behaviours, including persisting with treatment despite failure, regular exercise, a strong work ethic and avoidance of drink-driving. In addition, she demonstrates high motivation for change and a capacity for psychological insight. Other protective factors include regular employment, stable accommodation and a good relationship with her doctor. Without undertaking a neuropsychological assessment, it is not possible to fully dismiss the possibility of alcohol-related brain injury, particularly in the light of a nutritionally impoverished diet; however, Sara reports no indication of any memory or other intellectual impairment, and her reported alcohol use and age do not indicate the probability of liver dysfunction. Her chronic pessimism and some mild resistance would be important to address early on in treatment.

Diagnosis

Axis I	300.02	Generalised Anxiety Disorder
	303.90	Alcohol Dependence
Axis II	None	Obsessive–compulsive personality traits
Axis III	None	
Axis IV		Poor relationship history and limited social supports
Axis V	GAF	52 (current) 60 (highest)

Treatment Plan

Individual Psychological Therapy

Cognitive–behavioural treatment was indicated for Sara's anxiety (Butler, Chapman, Forman, & Beck, 2006; Chambless, Ollendick, & Thomas 2001; Gould, Otto, Pollack, & Yap, 1997; Rygh & Sanderson, 2004). It is an evidence-based treatment that can directly target the maladaptive thoughts that fuel her anxiety and result in unhelpful behaviours such as binge drinking, drinking to assist with sleep onset and working long hours. The initial contract was for 12 sessions. The initial focus of treatment was the reduction of alcohol use and cognitive therapy addressing the anxiety symptoms.

Components of the alcohol treatment consisted of:

- clarification of client life goals, drinking goals and priorities
- focus on alcohol abuse as the symptom rather than the primary issue
- harm reduction education about recreational drugs and alcohol use
- weekly exercises including self-observation and drinking diary.

Further Assessment as a Psychoeducational Technique

Sara was asked to record her drinking behaviour over a 3-week period using a drink diary. She was asked to record the following information for each episode of drinking: the date and time, alcohol choice, how many drinks consumed, location, who she was with and her mood prior to drinking. Sara and the clinician agreed she would record this information in the evening as soon as practicable after she returned home and she would bring it with her in to future sessions. If she had not completed one or more days of recording her use, she was asked to do so retrospectively. The purpose of this activity was to obtain a more accurate picture of how Sara drank and a tool for her to better comprehend factors that may affect her consumption, particularly in understanding how anxiety may influence her alcohol use.

Components of the treatment for linking alcohol and anxiety were:

- provision of a model of alcohol use that links it with anxiety. Drinking is a temporarily effective and easily accessible way of quieting a strident inner critic and a perfectionist nature; however, it leads to an increase in worry and sleep disturbance, with the potential for longer-term negative outcomes such as alcohol dependence, liver dysfunction and acquired brain injury.

- to examine the cycle of anxiety and alcohol use with the therapist, to model more constructive thinking and provide opportunities for skills development.

Techniques addressing anxiety included using:

- CBT to identify, challenge and practice techniques for reducing Sara's unhelpful cognitions
- practical strategies to manage anxiety, such as relaxation and mindfulness training.

Sara's initial priorities in attending therapy were to not engage in embarrassing behaviours while inebriated, to acquire an intimate partner, and to create a more balanced life. When discussing her desired outcomes, it became clear that there were good reasons to modify her priorities to achievable interim therapeutic goals, notably to increase harm reduction strategies for her drinking behaviour and to moderate some of her maladaptive thinking. These, in turn, would move her towards her desired outcomes, including improving her work–life balance, avoiding embarrassing behaviours and improving her social network, thereby increasing her opportunities for finding a life partner.

Assessment Commentary

When an individual presents with alcohol misuse, it is essential that the clinician conducts a full substance use assessment and, in addition, screens for comorbid mental health symptoms. This case illustrates a common presentation of an underlying high-prevalence mental health disorder triggering alcohol misuse, which consequently developed into a significant dependency.

Choice of Assessment Methods

The assessment occurred in stages to create an iterative process of building and extending the hypothesis of alcohol dependence co-occurring with an anxiety disorder. The first phase of Sara's assessment involved a semistructured clinical interview to provide context for her current concerns and understand the relevant developmental issues. During this interview, the clinician also elicited information to complete a mental state exam. This is not a formal instrument, but a format for reviewing a client's presentation and level of functioning that addresses salient, observable features of possible psychiatric disturbance.

This was followed by The Stages of Change Readiness and Treatment Eagerness Scale (SOCRATES) to ascertain Sara's current level of motivation and preparedness for changing her behaviour. This is a 19-item scale that specifically enquires about the client's perception of their alcohol or other drug use, providing scores for 'ambivalence' (precontemplation/contemplation), 'recognition' (contemplation/preparation) and 'taking steps' (preparation for change/action). In addition, Sara was questioned about her previous experience of treatment and her goals in attending for this assessment.

The second phase consisted of a thorough assessment of substance use. A number of standardised tools were used to inform the assessment process. The Alcohol Use Disorders Identification Test (AUDIT) is a well-established, reliable and efficient assessment tool with good psychometric properties, developed by the World Health Organization for the assessment of problem alcohol use. In it, respondents are asked to respond to ten items about their drinking using a 5-point scale that is scored from 0 (*Never*) to 5 (*Answer depends on the question*). Questions include items about frequency, quantity, drinking behaviour and dependence and consequences of drinking. It is easily scored and each section is scored independently and as a part of the total (out of 40) to provide scores of consumption (maximum score of 12), dependence (maximum score of 12) and alcohol-related problems. The two supplementary items are not scored, but provide clinical information about the client's perspective on their alcohol use. A total score of 16 or more indicates harmful or high-risk drinking.

The TimeLine Followback (TLFB) was included as a memory aid to obtain further detail about the quantities of alcohol consumed from week to week over the previous 3 months. It was originally developed for the assessment of alcohol but adapted for use with other drugs. Clients are asked to think about the context in which they use alcohol and use that information as memory aid. In this way, clients provide improved (or confirmed) recall of their weekly substance use and build a more complete picture of their substance use, which guides the clinician in the creation of a relevant treatment plan. Sara was asked to begin by considering what alcohol she had drunk in the last couple of days, then in the previous week and beyond. This recent information is expected to be the most reliable. Special occasions, significant days (e.g., holidays, pay day), patterns, and alcohol/drug combinations are used to prompt the respondent's recall and develop a more intricate and contextual picture of substance use. Any lack of recall may indicate excessive consumption, combination use of different drugs, brain impairment or trauma.

The final phase of the assessment was focused on the anxiety. It became apparent during the clinical interview that Sara suffered from significant issues with anxiety and further information was required to better understand her experience. The STAI was used as a preliminary assessment to determine if Sara had an anxiety disorder and if more intensive assessment was required. This is a self-report measure comprising two subscales of 20 items for trait and state anxiety respectively. Resulting scores range from 20 (*Almost never anxious*) to 80 (*Almost always anxious*) for each subscale. For the purposes of this assessment, only the trait subscale was used.

The GAD section of the Anxiety Disorders Interview Schedule (ADIS-IV) was selected to further investigate Sara's current experience of anxiety, given her high score on the STAI and her references to chronic worrying and difficulty sleeping attendant on that symptom. The ADIS-IV is a structured interview based on DSM-IV criteria, which assesses a number of anxiety and related disorders. It offers a functional review of symptoms and provides a clinical rating of severity ranging from 0 to 8 that indicate the degree of impairment and distress. This tool was selected because it provides a comprehensive review of DSM-IV criteria, enabling a clinician to determine if a diagnosis of GAD is warranted. Anxiety disorders vary substantially and this interview provides sufficient specificity to determine a diagnosis. The interview can be used in its entirety to distinguish between the full spectrum of anxiety disorders. In this assessment, the clinician had collected sufficient information in the course of a clinical interview to have a high degree of suspicion that this client had a diagnosable GAD. To save time and confirm the diagnosis, the relevant subsection of the ADIS-IV was used. If the results had not supported GAD, additional sections or the full interview could have been added to the assessment schedule for further clarification.

Mood disorders often co-occur with anxiety, therefore the Patient Health Questionnaire (PHQ-9) was selected to screen for depression. The PHQ-9 is a widely used, 9-item, self-report tool in which clients indicate how often they experience nine key symptoms of depression, followed by a single item that indicates the level of impairment. It is quicker than the Beck Depression Inventory and Functions as a basic screen. Given Sara's results did not indicate the presence of depression and her symptoms did not suggest further investigation was warranted, no other measure of depression was used.

A moderately conservative approach to assessment was used here, whereby a clinical interview was used to elicit from the client the context for her current circumstances and key symptoms were followed up by relevant screening tools and more diagnostic assessment measures, as appropriate. This enables the clinician to identify the critical symptoms and causal factors and avoids more hypothesis-driven approaches. Furthermore, it enables each psychological issue to be intensively considered before a formulation is achieved.

Comment on Treatment Approaches

This client made it quite clear that she preferred a practical solution-focused approach to manage her concerns and, given her self-perceived recent 'failures' of therapy, it was important to focus on strategies with good face validity and some more immediate outcomes. Once Sara experienced some positive results from therapy, she and the therapist would have more freedom to consider how to build on the changes she made, including considering more intensive work on anxiety. This flexibility in the treatment plan is particularly helpful when working with clients who have experienced past treatment failure. Early successes may make the difference between the client persisting with therapy or not. Sara's assessment was formulated to enhance engagement and the results provided a framework for her to understand the dynamics of her problematic behaviour. Later, at the end of the assessment, she referred to the sense of hope that the formulation elicited.

Assessment should be viewed as a work in progress, in which the clinician uses structured interviewing, validated instruments and clinical judgment to build a comprehensive picture of the individual at this stage in their life. It is not essential to have uncovered every possible diagnosable issue for a client, because a healthy component of subsequent therapy is to review progress at intervals and determine if the original formulation continues to fit what is revealed over time. As therapy continues, new material can lead to diagnostic revisions or modifications. New issues may come to light as the client progresses in treatment, or when compensating behaviours (such as binge drinking) diminish as the effects of treatment are felt. Substance use may modify the expression of different mental illnesses or may mask underlying issues. An example of this is that clients with severe drug dependence may not acknowledge or be fully cognisant of traumatic experiences until they cease to use the drug to shut down difficult memories or other symptoms. In some cases, clients may not disclose sufficient information to enable the therapist to accurately identify disorders until they have developed a high level of trust. Therefore, it is valuable for assessment to be ongoing. Any one assessment episode is not expected to be definitive. If new symptoms come to light, or progress in treatment suggests that there was overlooked material in the original assessment, the clinician is able to review the earlier results and augment them with further measures and/or interviewing, perhaps with other diagnoses or formulations in mind.

This revisionist approach to assessment is paralleled in treatment. In the course of a lifetime, an individual is likely to work on one or more issues at different times, building on their experience of therapy by formal (e.g., counselling, therapy groups) and informal means (e.g., self-education via bibliotherapy or online). This is particularly useful to keep in mind when working with chronic conditions such as GAD, which can be difficult to eradicate, but is certainly possible to diminish as the client increases their expertise in managing the condition over time. The advantage of this orientation is that it reduces the pressure to achieve all desired outcomes at any one point, and it acknowledges the benefits of building on success.

This therapist's core goal in working with Sara was to provide a comprehensive assessment that considered both the client's formulation and the therapist's, the latter grounded in reported and observed symptoms and more objective assessment measures. The resulting synthesis of information provides a solid basis for creating a treatment plan that is most likely to create an experience of hope and of success for the client. It increases the opportunity of her remaining in treatment sufficiently long to begin to experience improvement in her cognitive and behavioural outcomes. Without this, the client may have only been treated for alcohol misuse, perhaps with some therapeutic work to target the relationship concerns. The likelihood of a substantial and successful outcome with such limited focus for intervention would have been low. The starting point for a good outcome was to adopt a rolling model of assessment in which each stage arose out of the previous one, ensuring that relevant material was attended to. The clinician could then devise a formulation that enlightened the client and allowed the treatment to be firmly based on evidence from the outset.

Endnote

1 This case assessment is fictional and is to be used for the purposes of demonstration only. Any resemblance to persons known is entirely coincidental.

References

Allsop, S. (Ed.) (2008). *Drug use and mental health: Effective responses to co-occurring drug and mental health problems.* Melbourne, Australia: IP Communications.

Brown, T.A., Di Nardo, P.A., & Barlow, D.H. (1994). *Anxiety Disorders Interview Schedule for DSM-IV (ADIS-IV).* San Antonio, TX: Psychological Corporation/Graywind Publications Incorporated.

Butler, A.C., Chapman, J.E., Forman, E.M., & Beck, A.T. (2006). The empirical status of cognitive–behavioral therapy: A review of meta-analyses. *Clinical Psychology Review, 26*(1), 17–31.

Chambless, D.L., Ollendick, T.H., & Thomas, H. (2001). Empirically supported psychological interventions: controversies and evidence. *Annual Review of Psychology, 5*, 685–716.

Crome, I.B. (2004). Comorbidity in young people: Perspectives and challenges. *Acta Neuropsychiatrica, 16*, 47–53.

Green, K., Worden, B., Menges, D., & McCrady, B.S. (2008). Alcohol use disorders. In J. Hunsley & E.J. Mash (Eds.), *A guide to assessments that work* (pp. 339–369). New York : Oxford University Press.

Gould, R.A., Otto, M.W., Pollack, M.H., & Yap, L. (1997). Cognitive behavioral and pharmacological treatment of generalized anxiety disorder: A preliminary meta-analysis. *Behavior Therapy, 28*, 285–305.

International Society for Traumatic Stress Studies. (2001). *Traumatic stress and substance use problems* (ISTSS public education pamphlet. Northbrook, IL: Author.

Miller, W.R., & Tonigan, J.S. (1996). Assessing drinkers' motivation for change: The Stages of Change Readiness and Treatment Eagerness Scale (SOCRATES). *Psychology of Addictive Behaviors, 10*, 81–89.

Minkoff, K., & Cline, C.A. (2004). Changing the world: the design and implementation of comprehensive continuous integrated systems of care for individuals with co-occurring disorders. *Psychiatric Clinics of North America, 27*(4), 727–43.

Mueser, K.T., Noordsy, D.L., Drake, R.E., & Fox, L. (2003). *Integrated treatment for dual disorders: A guide to effective practice.* New York: The Guilford Press.

Prochaska, J.O., & DiClemente, C.C. (1982). Transtheoretical therapy: Toward a more integrative model of change. *Psychotherapy: Theory, Research & Practice, 19*(3), 276–288.

Regier, D.A., Farmer, M.E., Rae, D.S., Locke, B.Z., Keith, S.J., Judd, L., & Goodwin, F.K. (1990). Comorbidity of mental disorders with alcohol and other drug abuse: Results from the epidemiological catchment area (ECA) study. *Journal of the American Medical Association, 264*(19), 2511–2518.

Roehrs, T., & Roth, T. (2001). Sleep, sleepiness, and alcohol use. *Alcohol Research & Health. 25*(2), 101–109.

Rohsenow, D.J. (2008). Substance use disorders. In J. Hunsley & E.J. Mash (Eds.), *A guide to assessments that work* (pp. 319–338). New York: Oxford University Press.

Rygh J.L., & Sanderson W.C. (2004). Treating generalized anxiety disorder: Evidence-based strategies, tools, and techniques. New York: Guilford.

Sobell, L.C., & Sobell, M.B. (1992). Timeline Follow-back: A technique for assessing self-reported ethanol consumption. In J. Allen & R.Z. Litten (Eds.), *Measuring alcohol consumption: Psychosocial and biological methods* (pp. 41–72). Totowa, NJ: Humana Press.

Spielberger, C.D., Gorsuch, R.L., Lushene, R., Vagg, P.R., & Jacobs, G.A. (1983). *Manual for the State-Trait Anxiety Inventory.* Palo Alto, CA: Consulting Psychologists Press.

Spitzer, R.L., Kroenke, K., & Williams, J.B.W. (1999). Validation and utility of a self-report version of PRIME-MD: The PHQ primary care study. *Journal of the American Medical Association, 282*(18), 1737–1744.

Tucker, J.A., Vuchinich, R.E., & Murphy, J.G. (2002). Substance use disorders. In M.H. Anthony & D.H. Barlow (Eds.), *Handbook of assessment and treatment planning* (pp. 415–452). New York: Guilford Press.

Witkiewitz, K.A., & Marlatt, G.A. (2007). Therapist's *guide to evidence-based relapse prevention in the series practical resources for the mental health professional.* San Diego: Elsevier Inc.

Witkiewitz, K., Marlatt, G.A., & Walker, D.D. (2005). Mindfulness-based relapse prevention for alcohol use disorders: The meditative tortoise wins the race. *Journal of Cognitive Psychotherapy, 19*(3), 221–228.

World Health Organization. (2001). A.*U.D.I.T: The Alcohol Use Disorders Identification Test: Guidelines for use in primary care* (2nd ed.). Retrieved from http://whqlibdoc.who.int/ hq/2001/ WHO_MSD_MSB_01.6a.pdf.

CHAPTER 2

The Clinical Assessment of a Patient With Major Depression and Complex Personality Features

Renee Gedge and Helen Mildred

This case presents some of the challenges encountered in the assessment of a patient with a major depressive disorder complicated by personality disorder features. It is not unusual that a person presenting with a mood disorder and suicidality, such as in this case of Mr Smith, gradually reveals a history of dysfunctional relationships and unresolved interpersonal conflict. Such clients rarely come to the attention of clinical mental health practitioners, except at times of acute crisis. Further, while such clients may appear to willingly participate in the assessment process, it is very difficult to engage them in an ongoing therapeutic process that may challenge their views and beliefs about themselves (McMurran, Huband, & Overton, 2009; Paris, 2009).

Mr Smith was referred to the primary mental health team by the general practitioner (GP) to whom he had disclosed suicidal ideation. He was seen in a crisis assessment by the consultant psychiatrist who was unsure about some aspects of Mr Smith's complex diagnostic presentation. Specifically, in addition to the immediate concerns about Mr Smith's mental state, the consultant wanted a more comprehensive assessment of Mr Smith's psychosocial history and context, as well as some of his personality (Axis 2) features that may have contributed to and/or precipitated his presentation in crisis at this time. The clinical psychologist was asked to undertake a full clinical and personality assessment of Mr Smith. The assessment would then be used by the multidisciplinary team to develop and provide a comprehensive service plan for him. Such a plan could include: a crisis plan to monitor and respond to risk; medication review and management by the doctor; increasing social connectedness and assisting with enlisting council services, such as in-home domestic support by the social worker (should that be required); and the provision of therapy by the psychologist. Once completed, a copy of the assessment report is sent to the GP, and the team would also provide ongoing liaison and consultation to the GP to support her in her work with Mr Smith.

Predominantly, it is Mr Smith's suicidality that has led to a mental health referral. Given his current social isolation, he is at moderate risk of attempting suicide and this could increase rapidly if circumstances deteriorate. His suicidality is complex as he has made threats in front of his GP, including a specific plan and, while he denies any current intention, does not rule it out as an option. More specifically, he threatened to suicide once he had written a blaming letter to his wife, which added a more vengeful motivation to his ideation.

In addition to his depression, Mr Smith suffers a number of serious and chronic physical health issues. He also demonstrates some problematic personality features in that his narcissistic traits lead him to blame those around him for his situation, his antisocial traits indicate a desire to punish those who he perceives as having wronged him, and his many relationship disruptions are consistent with borderline traits. In conjunction with his mood disorder, these additional features make both the assessment/formulation as well as the implementation of a treatment plan difficult.

Mr Smith's presentation indicates a tendency to avoid discussion of difficult or unpleasant questions and issues, and it can be difficult in such interviews to elicit the necessary clinical information to guide treatment. Given his tendency to externalise blame, it may be hard for Mr Smith to imagine that he is suffering from a mental health problem that may contribute to his ongoing difficulties. Further, the manner in which he spoke of the 'breakdowns' suffered by his previous partners indicate that he sees mental health problems as a weakness (not an illness) from which he then distances himself. So the psychological formulation and solutions a clinician offers may well be at odds with Mr Smith's perceptions of what the problems are (i.e., other people) and what possible solutions to these problems there may be (e.g., start a new relationship).

Indeed, Mr Smith has a long history of severed relationships — with his siblings, partners and children. He attributes these relationship splits as being largely due to the instability or unreasonableness of the other party. Despite not being on speaking terms with many family members, he shows limited insight into his potential role in these broken relationships. He is now at an age where there has been an accumulation of lost relationships (and associated grief) that is potentially very painful for him. His construction that his relationship difficulties are purely other people's fault may also be increasingly difficult to maintain.

Given his history, it is unlikely that this is Mr Smith's first episode of depression. It is possible, however, that he is now more isolated than at previous times of personal crisis. Certainly his presentation and reported suicidality indicate that his usual coping strategies are overwhelmed and that his social roles (as an engineer and husband) are impaired. Careful and frequent monitoring of Mr Smith's mental state and risk will be a crucial part of his ongoing care.

When assessing clients with complex mood and physical ill-health, as well as personality issues, it is even more important than usual to try to build and maintain rapport throughout the assessment. Such clients are extremely sensitive to potential negative evaluation from others, and their usual history of severed relationships can make the therapeutic alliance particularly difficult to establish. It is, therefore, necessary for the clinician to take extra care to ensure the client feels they are being listened to and their point of view understood and respected. It is important to show genuine curiosity through open questioning about the client's construction of their difficulties. Challenging such clients, even gently, in the assessment process can alienate them from continuing to access assistance. It may be useful to have breaks in the interview if you detect that the client is uncomfortable or frustrated by the process. It is also useful to highlight to them that you may say things that they find irritating or upsetting, and establish an agreement on how you will both deal with that situation if it arises. In conclusion, in addition to a careful clinical interview, such cases require regular risk assessments, liaison with providers of physical health care, as well as clinical and psychometric evaluation of mood, anxiety and their personality profile.

The Case of Mr Bob Smith

CLINICAL PSYCHOLOGY ASSESSMENT[1]
PRIVATE AND CONFIDENTIAL

CASE FILE NUMBER:	157624
NAME:	Mr Bob Smith
ADDRESS:	35 Oak St
AGE:	62
DOB:	September 11, 1945
REFERRED BY:	Dr R.B. Warren, Consultant Psychiatrist
CLINICIAN:	Dr Helen Wilson, Clinical Psychologist, Oaktree Primary Mental Health Team
DATES SEEN:	March 4, 2010, (Initial interview); March 11 (Assessment interview followed by administration of the Hospital Anxiety and Depression Scale (HADS) and the Minnesota Multiphasic Personality Inventory (MMPI-2); March 18 (Feedback and treatment planning).

Presenting Problems

Mr Smith is a 62-year-old Australian man who lives alone since his wife left him three months ago. He has two adult children from an earlier marriage with whom he has no contact. He is currently on extended sick leave from his job as an engineer with a telecommunications company and believes he will be made redundant shortly. He was referred by the consultant psychiatrist on the mental health team to the psychologist within the team for assessment and treatment. The consultant had reviewed Mr Smith following disclosure of suicidal ideation to his GP. He reports a sense of hopelessness, feeling depressed and lacking in motivation most days, anger towards his wife and her family, generalised worry about the future, severe sleep problems and physical health problems. There is no record of any suicide attempts in the past.

History of Presenting Problem and Previous Treatment

Mr Smith's recent suicidal ideation followed his separation from his second wife in December, and family problems related to this separation. The referral was precipitated by Mr Smith telling his GP that he planned to kill himself, probably by hanging, after sending his wife a letter blaming her for his death. His wife, to whom he had been married for six years, left him abruptly after being told he had made a sexual suggestion to her 17-year-old granddaughter at a family function. Mr Smith denies that this occurred and says the girl is lying as part of a plot by his wife's family (particularly his wife's son) to separate them. Mr Smith claims he has been subjected to harassment by members of his wife's family, including late night and early morning phone calls.

Mr Smith has experienced difficulty sleeping since his wife left and has been feeling very depressed and anxious. He says his relationship with his wife was previously 'very good' and believes they could sort things out if she would agree to speak to him. He fears the financial consequences of another divorce, stating he lost most of his assets in the previous divorce. He has not been to work for the past six weeks, stating that he cannot cope with work, as he is unable to concentrate and feels exhausted and stressed all the time. He said his employer advised him to take leave as he was arriving late and not completing tasks due to his stress. He has since been informed by a work colleague that the company is now restructuring and he will almost certainly be made redundant. Mr Smith states that he has never been treated for any psychiatric disorder in the past. However, he states that his first wife was hospitalised following 'a breakdown' some 20 years ago and that he became 'rather depressed' at that time.

Family History

Mr Smith was born in Melbourne and was the eldest of three boys. He states that his mother married only because she was pregnant with him and that she resented him as a result. He believes she always favoured his two younger brothers over him. Both of his brothers are still alive, but he has very little contact with them and spoke disparagingly of them. Mr Smith believes his parents' marriage was loveless, in particular that his mother disliked and resented his father. He describes his father as a tough man, but fair to all the children. His father worked as a butcher for all of his working life

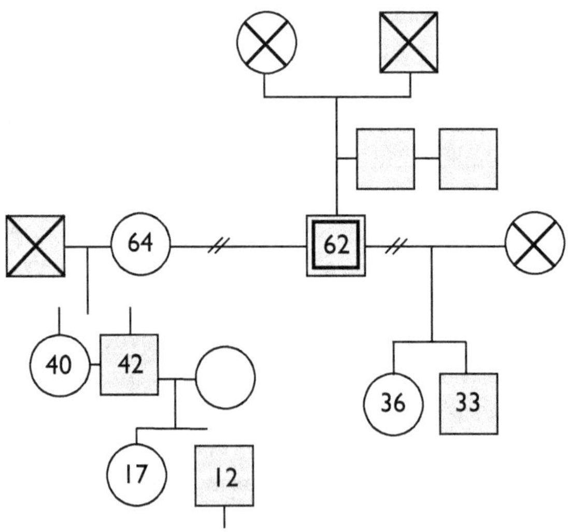

Figure 2.1
Family genogram.

while his mother undertook home duties. The family had very limited social contacts and he describes his childhood and the family home as 'pretty miserable'.

He first married at 21 and had two children, a son and a daughter. His wife had what Mr Smith described as 'a breakdown' some years after the birth of their second child and was hospitalised for several months in a psychiatric hospital. This marriage broke down when his wife later left him after 22 years of marriage, an event which Mr Smith attributed to his job that he said involved very long hours and some travelling. Mr Smith's first wife has since died. He has no contact with his children and appeared unconcerned by this. He states that he became estranged from them many years ago following disagreements over his relationship with a woman who moved into his home. He states that this woman also had what he described as 'a breakdown' after a few years and she then moved out. However, Mr Smith stated that he has had contact with this woman recently and wonders if they may resume an intimate relationship.

Mr Smith married his current wife six years ago after meeting her as a neighbour. She was a widow at that time. She left the family home abruptly after the accusations of sexually inappropriate behaviour towards her granddaughter and has had no contact since. Mr Smith's view of the situation is that his wife's son is trying to break them up and states that everything would be alright if he could talk with his wife. This view is directly contradicted by his wife, who contacted the family GP and stated she never wants to see him again. She stated that she believes her granddaughter is telling the truth and that it is consistent with other deceitful behaviour, which she had become increasingly concerned about during their marriage. She did not elaborate on what this behaviour was, but reiterated that he was 'completely untrustworthy'. Mr Smith appears socially isolated, but states he has a few friends, including a male neighbour he chats to sometimes and one work colleague who has rung a couple of times to see how he was. He has, until recently, been quite a keen gardener and enjoyed building model aeroplanes, but says he has lost all interest in these activities over the past few months. He does not smoke and states that he is a 'social drinker' only, which he explains as drinking a few glasses of wine with a meal when dining out.

Family Structure

Mr Smith's adult family life has been characterised by complete dislocations, with multiple instances of unresolved conflict and intimate relationships ending abruptly and in distressing circumstances.

Medical History

Mr Smith suffers from hypertension, cardiovascular disease and chronic respiratory disease and is currently on multiple medications for these conditions. He has been prescribed anti-anxiety and antidepressant medication but has chosen not to take these at present.

Developmental History

Mr Smith's developmental history is unclear as he reports that he remembers little of his childhood and none of his developmental milestones. However, he reports doing well at school and enjoying maths and science. Mr Smith reported feeling unloved and unwanted by his mother, whom he said favoured his brothers. There is a general sense of an unhappy family home, with little warmth or affection between the parents and possibly considerable sibling rivalry between the three brothers that, without counterbalancing affection and guidance from parents, may have resulted in considerable ongoing resentment. Mr Smith reported no significant friendships at school or as a young man. His wives/partners have apparently formed his major emotional support throughout his adult life.

Educational History

Mr Smith completed Year 10 at school and then left to work in an electronics retail business. After a few years, however, he undertook training in electronics and has worked in this field up until the present time.

Mental State Examination

Appearance, attitude, activity. Mr Smith is a 62-year-old man who appears his stated age, and is of short stature and medium build. He presented as well groomed and appropriately dressed in casual clothing. Throughout the interview, he maintained an upright posture but was breathless and complained of breathing difficulties. He made occasional eye contact, while at other times he looked around the room or down at his hands. He appeared to be of average intelligence or above, and was engaged, cooperative and appeared willing to disclose personal information.

Mood and affect. Mood was anxious and depressed; he described severe sleeping problems over the past few weeks and made remarks such as 'What's the use?' and 'What's the point of anything now?' When questioned further, he denied having any current suicide plan, but refused to rule out suicide as an option if things got 'too difficult'. Affect was anxious, quite labile, but generally appropriate. Any allusion to his wife's absence resulted in him becoming tearful, while he became agitated and irritable when discussing the accusation against him, or the actions of his wife's family.

Speech. Speech was fluent, grammatical, coherent and at a normal rate and volume.

Thought process. Mr Smith's thought process was largely normal, although at times he became somewhat circumstantial and tangential when talking about the past. There was no other evidence of thought disorder or other psychotic phenomena.

Thought content. Mr Smith's thought content centred on the theme of perceived injustice of his current situation; he appeared incredulous that his wife has left him without giving him an opportunity to defend himself. He blames the situation on a plan by her son to break up his marriage and was highly derogatory towards him. Overall, there was a sense of considerable anger towards others in many of his responses. In an odd aside when referring to his model aeroplane collection, he stated that he got a large number of these for next to nothing from an old man whom he described as a 'sucker' who didn't know their proper value. He acknowledged suicidal ideation and a vague plan to hang himself but denied any homicidal ideation.

Perception. He denied experiencing hallucinations or other disturbances of perception and none were detected.

Cognition. He was oriented to time, place and person and able to attend and concentrate throughout most of the interview, although he appeared somewhat distracted at times. Details of past events were vague at times. Mr Smith also seemed to have minor difficulty recalling some recent events.

Insight and judgment. Mr Smith demonstrated limited capacity for insight, but acknowledged he was depressed. He tended to avoid and evade difficult issues rather than reflect on them. His judgment was somewhat impaired by depression and anxiety, as reflected by suicidal ideation.

Psychological Testing

Given Mr Smith's complex presentation, psychological testing was undertaken. In particular, two issues were of interest. First, to gauge the extent of his anxiety and depressive symptomatology, independent of his physical health issues; second, to investigate the presence of more longstanding personality issues that might be interacting with his presenting problems. Observations during completion of the psychological tests suggested that Mr Smith became somewhat impatient and irritable when completing some items on the MMPI-2. He frequently shifted in his seat, muttered under his breath and made occasional audible remarks to himself commenting on the 'stupidity' of the question.

Tests Administered

- Hospital Anxiety and Depression Scale (HADS; Zigmond & Snaith, 1983).
- Minnesota Multiphasic Personality Inventory-2 (MMPI-2; Butcher, Dahlstrom, Graham, Tellegen, & Kaemmer, 1989).

Test Results and Interpretation

HADS. This scale was used to assess intensity of both anxiety and depression symptoms. The HADS is a 14-item self-administered scale of depressive (7 items) and anxious (7 items) symptoms, each rated from 0–3. The possible range of scores for both subscales is 0–21, with higher scores representing higher levels of depression or anxiety. Mr Smith scored in the severe range on both anxiety and depression, endorsing many items at their highest level, including feelings of panic, worrying thoughts, and lack of enjoyment.

MMPI-2. The MMPI-2 was administered to assess personality function. This is a self-report questionnaire consisting of 567 items with a true or false format. Responses are scored to create a profile consisting of ten basic clinical/personality scales and several validity scales. A large pool of additional scales have also been developed that allow the clinician to add to this basic profile. These include the Personality Psychopathology Five Scales (PSY-5), developed to assess a more pathological range of personality functioning.

Mr Smith took approximately 1 hour and 40 minutes to complete the items, which is within acceptable limits for the test. His pattern of responses indicated a consistent and careful manner. However, there were some indicators that he may have been motivated by a desire to present himself in a more positive light or may see himself in an unrealistically positive way. Overall though, the results were considered to reflect a valid assessment.

Mr Smith scored within the clinical range on many of the basic scales, particularly those associated with social alienation, depression and anxiety. His responses are indicative of multiple psychological symptoms and problems, including stress, anxiety and depression and indicated he is unable to cope with many of the ordinary demands of life at present.

Mr Smith's profile suggests that he has a resentful and cynical attitude towards people in general. He tends to blame others for his problems and shows little awareness of his own role in creating or maintaining any of his difficulties. He feels it is generally safer not to trust others and feels alienated from most people. His interpersonal difficulties are most prominent in his own family, where he feels he has been let down and victimised. The recent trauma associated with the breakup of his marriage and the likely loss of his job is reflected in raised levels of traumatic symptoms and in recent suicidal ideation. Mr Smith also experiences considerable anxiety about his health, with somatic symptoms in both respiratory and neurological areas and he has concerns about chronic weakness and lack of energy. Interestingly, he did not endorse any items regarding past sexual behaviour causing trouble, although there was some indication of moderate levels of impulsivity in some responses. Overall, Mr Smith's response pattern was consistent with, and suggestive of, a Cluster B personality disorder, with a longstanding pattern of maladaptive social interactions and behaviours. This interpretation is given further weight by the examination of the PSY-5 scales, which were somewhat elevated on the aggressiveness, negative emotionality/neuroticism and disconstraint scales. An elevated aggressiveness scale suggests higher than average levels of antagonism, grandiosity and desire for power. The elevated disconstraint scale is consistent with some degree of impulsiveness and possibly antisocial attitudes, while elevated negative emotionality/neuroticism is seen when there is a wide range of negative emotions such as irritability, anxiety and dysphoria.

Formulation

Mr Smith presented initially as a very sad and bewildered man, whose wife had recently left him and who felt harassed by her family after allegations of an inappropriate sexual remark made to his wife's teenage granddaughter. His symptoms included lowered mood, poor concentration and low motivation most days for several weeks, a recent suicide threat, difficulty sleeping and frequent tearfulness. In addition to his depressive symptomatology, he also displayed high levels of anxiety and irritability. All of these symptoms are exacerbated by serious health issues that limit his physical activity and cause him considerable physical distress.

However, personality factors appear to be highly relevant to understanding his situation, with the gradual emergence of a history of interpersonal conflict and estrangement and an apparently diminished capacity for empathy. His wife's belief in the accusation of sexually inappropriate behaviour and her unequivocal statement that he was completely untrustworthy suggest a relationship that, far from the positive way Mr Smith portrayed it, was already severely compromised. Mr Smith appeared motivated largely by self-interest in the current situation, lamenting the likely financial consequences of divorce and mentioning a possible resumption of a previous intimate relationship, rather than expressing concern for his wife or her granddaughter. Similarly, he expressed no interest in, or concern for his estranged children or siblings, with his primary emotion appearing to be resentment and self-pity. This preoccupation with his losses and lack of expressed concern or empathy for others are suggestive of narcissistic, or possibly antisocial personality traits. There is also some evidence of antisocial traits in his description of tricking an elderly man for financial advantage. However, his current depression and threat of committing suicide after sending an accusatory letter to his wife are more suggestive of borderline personality disorder (BPD) traits. His personal history of alienation from his children and his siblings, at least three failed marriages/defacto relationships and the lack of any significant friendships are all suggestive of a longstanding and pervasive pattern of impaired interpersonal functioning that would be expected in the Cluster B personality disorders.

However, his responses are not entirely consistent with any one particular disorder belonging to this cluster. For example, there is no evidence of the antisocial disorder traits of conduct-disordered behaviour in youth, or high levels of impulsivity or aggression. His sense of entitlement and self-absorption are more typical of narcissistic than antisocial traits, particularly in light of his current feelings of anxiety and depression. This is a relatively common presentation in the narcissistic personality, in which a growing sense of emptiness and despair develops as multiple relationship failures build up over a lifetime. Major depression is also a common response to loss and difficulty in those with BPD, and Mr Smith's childhood may have been responsible for the development of some of these maladaptive personality traits. He felt unwanted and maltreated by his mother, which may have contributed to unconscious motivations in his relationships including anger, fear of abandonment and ambivalence towards women. It is noteworthy that all three of his long-term wives/partners eventually left him, apparently in situations of crisis.

Mr Smith is very vulnerable due to his combined lack of family or friendship support networks, ill health and probable imminent retrenchment. Should his situation worsen, this lack of support, combined with Mr Smith's personality traits and depressive symptoms, would place him at serious risk of further suicidal ideation and intent. Mr Smith's personality traits would be difficult to change given his age and lack of insight. However, he does have a number of protective factors. He appears to be of above average intelligence and has been quite receptive to treatment for his anxiety and depressive symptoms. Even though his intimate relationships have generally ended acrimoniously, he also demonstrates an ongoing willingness to initiate and engage in such relationships, and has expressed an interest in resuming a relationship with a previous partner.

Diagnosis

Axis I	296.35	Major depressive episode
Axis II	310.9	Personality Disorder Not Otherwise Specified (PD NOS). Narcissistic, antisocial, and borderline traits.
Axis III		Hypertension, cardiovascular disease, chronic respiratory disease.
Axis IV		Psychosocial stressors included separation from wife, and ongoing conflict with her family.
Axis V	GAF	40 (current)

Differential Diagnosis

Axis 1. 309.28

Adjustment disorder with mixed anxiety and depressed mood.

Mr Smith has a clearly identified stressor in his wife leaving him and the emergence of symptoms within three months. Furthermore, it is likely that this event precipitated his depression and anxiety. However, this diagnosis is not given due to the severity of symptoms meeting the criteria for major depression.

Treatment Plan

Crisis Plan

While he denies immediate intent, Mr Smith must be considered a serious suicide risk. He has multiple risk factors, being a recently separated male with an agitated depression, suicidal ideation and a partially formulated plan (hanging himself after writing a letter to his wife). He has chronic health issues, is currently not working and has an extremely limited support network. His imminent retrenchment could be a time of particular crisis as he would not only lose income, but also possibly role, status, a sense of competence and social connectivity. His mental state requires regular and careful monitoring to detect any deterioration from current levels and Mr Smith will therefore be seen at least weekly. The clinic psychiatrist will be asked to review Mr Smith's mental state, consult with Mr Smith's GP and again explore the possibility of Mr Smith taking medication. In addition, Mr Smith has been given the phone numbers of a number of 24-hour crisis lines including the hospital psychiatric triage should he need additional support after hours. At this stage, he has agreed to telephone these if he becomes more suicidal. In his current situation, if Mr Smith continues to stay at home with no social contact, his self-care may deteriorate. If this occurs, given his significant physical health issues, a referral to the Crisis Assessment and Treatment Team would then be made to offer more intensive outreach support.

Short-Term Management (Approximately 8 Weeks)

- Cognitive–behavioural (CBT)-based treatment for depression and anxiety, including monitoring of suicidal ideation should be commenced immediately. Mindfulness meditation training may also assist Mr Smith with relaxation and insight.
- As Mr Smith has been experiencing severe sleep difficulties, a sleep program involving education, monitoring and

development of personal strategies should be commenced such as *Sleep Better Without Drugs* (Morawetz, 2001).

- Medication may be useful for both anxiety and depression, although Mr Smith is currently averse to taking medication.
- Exercise and relaxation training may also be useful for depression and anxiety.
- Once his mood is improved, if there is remaining evidence of some memory problems and minor difficulties with attention and concentration, formal assessment of memory functioning should be conducted.

Long-Term Management: Individual Psychological Therapy

Insight-oriented psychotherapy may be most effective to address conflicts surrounding his history of broken relationships, marital breakup and allegations of sexually inappropriate behaviour. However, despite Mr Smith's apparent willingness to engage with clinical staff, considerable challenges exist in maintaining a long-term therapeutic partnership. Once Mr Smith's mood has improved it is possible that such therapy will become unappealing to him as it inherently involves self-exploration and the contributions one makes to the relationship dynamics that evolve in friendships, partnerships and families. Further, there may be a difficulty establishing a trusting relationship given Mr Smith's personality traits and the allegations of sexually inappropriate behaviour. Mr Smith may feel unable to reveal sexually inappropriate impulses and behaviour in the therapeutic situation for a variety of reasons including not wishing to be seen poorly by the therapist, as well as the possibility of this information being permanently recorded in his file. Overall, however, it is unlikely that the therapist would be able to establish the veracity or not of the allegations made against him by his wife's family unless Mr Smith admits such behaviour.

Assisting Mr Smith to regain his emotional equilibrium in the short term through CBT may enhance the possibility of him trusting the therapist and engaging in longer-term work. The careful building of a therapeutic relationship may then allow Mr Smith to confront his behaviour. As there is no collateral information in this assessment other than that of the GP, the focus of the longer-term psychotherapy would need to be comprehensively explored with Mr Smith before commencing such therapy.

Dr Helen Wilson, Clinical Psychologist, Oaktree Primary Mental Health Team, March 20, 2010

Commentary on the Assessment

Overview

Several issues are relevant to an assessment such as that described in this case. First, when a client has active suicidal ideation, their safety is the first and primary concern and assessment should begin with a comprehensive risk assessment (Bryan & Rudd, 2006). Following this, important clinical information can be derived from psychometric measures of the anxiety and depression that commonly underlie suicidality. Serious medical problems can complicate this clinical picture and care needs to be taken to discriminate between symptoms of physical versus psychological origin. Finally, no assessment is complete without an understanding of basic personality functioning and this is of critical importance where there is current suicide risk.

Personality disorders are frequently associated with other disorders, including anxiety and depression, as illustrated in this case. However, clients with personality disorder may evade questions or present a highly biased view of their circumstances and serious depression can alter and obscure underlying personality function (De Fruyt, Van Leeuwen, Bagby, Rolland, & Rouillon, 2006; Watson, Sawrie, Greene, & Arredondo, 2002). Psychometric instruments can highlight aspects of a client's personality functioning that may be difficult to evaluate through interview alone and thereby increase understanding of both suicide risk and helpful treatment approaches. However, it is important to always emphasise the unique qualities of every client and their situation. Psychometric test results are never the measure of a person and a careful and empathic series of clinical interviews is always the primary instrument of assessment. In addition, further information should be sought from family, friends and other health professionals wherever possible, and particularly where doubt exists as to premorbid functioning. At times, a remarkably different account of the person will emerge. Where personality disorder is being considered as part of the diagnostic picture this is vital, as by definition, this must be a longstanding and pervasive pattern of behaviour.

The Cluster B personality disorders — histrionic, narcissistic, antisocial and borderline — are considered by many people to be highly pejorative. Antisocial personality disorder in particular is closely linked to criminality. It is therefore crucial that such diagnoses are not made lightly and are made primarily for the purposes of understanding and informing treatment options rather than a desire to categorise or label an individual.

Choice of Measures

Working with a client such as Mr Smith, with labile affect, lowered mood and irritability, it is important to minimise test burden and to explain and justify the use of measures in a way that maximises his motivation to complete them accurately. Careful consideration must also be given to the form and content of feedback from personality tests as some terms and descriptions generated from standard interpretations can be offensive and threaten the therapeutic alliance (Graham, 2000).

Depression and Anxiety Assessment

In the case of clients with significant medical issues, it is vital to reduce or eliminate the confounding of symptoms arising from medical illness rather than depression or anxiety. As many standard psychometric tests include questions concerning fatigue, sleep problems, difficulty breathing, weight loss or gain and appetite changes, it may be necessary to either interpret the score very cautiously or apply an instrument specialised for use with a medically ill population. Mr Smith has serious health conditions with symptoms including breathlessness, fatigue and disturbed sleep due to respiratory problems. It was therefore decided to use tests that can be applied when physical ill health may confound standard test results. In a review of instruments to measure depression in the medically ill, Sellick and Crooks (1999) recommended the Hospital Anxiety and Depression scale (HADS), the Beck Depression Inventory (BDI), and the General Health Questionnaire (GHQ). However, the BDI and GHQ do contain several somatic indicators of depression, whereas the HADS has none. According to Stark and colleagues (Stark et al., 2002), the most accurate screening questionnaires for anxiety in the medically ill are the trait scale of the State–Trait Anxiety Inventory (Spielberger, Gorsuch, Lushene, Vagg, & Jacobs, 1983) and the HADS. While the STAI would have been appropriate as a measure, the HADS was chosen as it combines an anxiety and depression instrument and it is readily available. Its anxiety subscale also has seven questions compared to the STAI's 20, therefore representing a reduced response burden.

Recent comprehensive reviews of the HADS indicate that it has good validity and reliability characteristics with the medically ill population, both in hospitalised and outpatient populations (Bjelland et al., 2002; Olsson, Mykletun, & Dahl, 2005). Internal consistency was demonstrated with a mean Cronbach's alpha of .83 for the anxiety subscale and a mean Cronbach's alpha of .82 for the depression subscale. Test–retest stability is well established, and sensitivity and specificity of the HADS is generally considered adequate.

Personality Assessment

Given that personality issues can have such a major impact on treatment choice and that suicidality was a major concern, it was important to supplement clinical interviews with other objective measures of personality functioning. The MMPI-2 was chosen for this purpose due to its availability to the clinician and extensive use in clinical practice (Friedman, Lewak, Nichols, & Webb, 2000). The MMPI-2 was originally developed by Hathaway and McKinley in 1940, and continues to undergo extensive development based on research findings (Binford & Liljequist, 2008). With a total of 567 items, the MMPI-2 is a lengthy assessment. However, computerised versions do reduce both administration and scoring time considerably and, provided the client is informed and prepared, its length is generally acceptable. The MMPI takes an empirical approach, in which patterns of responses are compared to standardised samples to generate descriptions of personality functioning and psychiatric symptoms. The Personality Psychopathology Five Scales (PSY-5) assess a more pathological range of personality functioning (Harkness, McNulty, Ben-Porath, & Graham, 2002; Saulsman & Page, 2004), and the MMPI-2 validity scales are particularly important where personality pathology such as narcissism or antisocial traits are suspected. Overall, the MMPI-2 is psychometrically quite robust with good internal consistency and moderate test–retest reliability across all scales ranging from .58 to .92 (Groth-Marnat, 2009).

While it is vital that MMPI scores are examined in the overall context of the profile rather than individually, valuable clinical information can often be obtained from standardised interpretations provided for the clinical scales and for code types based on the two highest scale elevations. However, many profiles are less well-defined and should be interpreted by considering all elevated scales and integrating their meanings — often a complex exercise (Graham, 2000). In this case, Mr. Smith did not have a well-defined profile based on only two elevated scales, but rather many of the clinical scales and the PSY-5 scales were moderately elevated.

Choice of Treatment

A combination of CBT and mindfulness training was chosen as the initial treatment approach. Depression and anxiety are the two most prominent presenting problems and CBT has been identified as an effective short-term therapy for depression and anxiety (Chambless & Ollendick, 2001). A considerable research base has now established the efficacy of mindfulness training for both anxiety (Kabat-Zinn et al., 1992) and depression (Segal, Williams, & Teasdale, 2002), particularly when used as an adjunct to CBT. A meta-analysis of studies using mindfulness training for patients with a variety of medical conditions found both health and wellbeing benefits (Grossman, Niemann, Schmidt, & Walach, 2004).

Treatment for Cluster B personality disorders, on the other hand, is notoriously difficult, with frequent and major issues surrounding motivation for change and the development of an effective therapeutic alliance (Binks et al., 2006; Livesley, 2003). However, mindfulness training has been incorporated into a number of treatment approaches for personality disorders, including Dialectical Behaviour Therapy for BPD (Linehan, Cochran, & Kehrer (2001) and more recently Acceptance and Commitment Therapy (Binks et al., 2006). Given the limited evidence for any empirically based treatments for Personality Disorder Not Otherwise Specified (PD NOS) with Cluster B traits (Verhuel & Herbrink, 2007), the treating clinician hoped that mindfulness training may provide opportunities for Mr Smith to develop greater awareness of his emotions and cognitions.

There are some risks with mindfulness training that must be considered. In particular, mindfulness meditation can precipitate anxiety or even panic in some people when they are required to sit quietly and take an observational stance to their mental and emotional experience. Others will become irritated or angry as a defence against awareness of inner experience that is unpleasant or unpalatable to them. In training the client in mindfulness, the clinician needs to both encourage a nonjudgmental stance, but also ensure the client feels free to stop any mindfulness practice if the level of discomfort is too high.

Endnote

1 This case assessment is fictional and is to be used for the purposes of demonstration only. Any resemblance to any persons is entirely coincidental.

References

Binks, C., Fenton, M., McCarthy, L., Lee, T., Adams, C.E., & Duggan, C. (2006). Psychological therapies for people with borderline personality disorder. *Cochrane Database of Systematic Reviews, 25*: CD005652.

Binford, A., & Liljequist, L. (2008). Behavioral correlates of selected MMPI-2 Clinical, Content, and Restructured Clinical Scales. *Journal of Personality Assessment, 90*(6), 608–614.

Bjelland, I., Dahl, A.A., Haug, T.T., & Neckelmann, D. (2002). The validity of the Hospital Anxiety and Depression scale. An updated literature review. *Journal of Psychosomatic Research, 52*(2), 69–77.

Bryan, C., & Rudd, D. (2006). Advances in the assessment of suicide risk. *Journal of Clinical Psychology*, 62(2), 185–200.

Butcher, J.N., Dahlstrom, W.G., Graham, J.R., Tellegen, A., & Kaemmer, B. (1989). *The Minnesota Multiphasic Personality Inventory-2 (MMPI-2): Manual for administration and scoring.* Minneapolis, MN: University of Minnesota Press.

Chambless, D.L., & Ollendick, T.H. (2001). Empirically supported psychological interventions: Controversies and evidence. *Annual Review of Psychology, 52*, 685–716.

De Fruyt, F., Van Leeuwen, K., Bagby, R.M., Rolland, J.P., & Rouillon, F. (2006). Assessing and interpreting personality change and continuity in patients treated for major depression. *Psychological Assessment, 18*(1), 71–80.

Friedman, A., Lewak, R., Nichols, D., & Webb, J. F. (2000). *Psychological assessment with the MMPI-2.* Mahwah, NJ: Erlbaum.

Graham, J.R. (2000). *MMPI-2: Assessing personality and psychopathology* (3rd ed.). New York: Wiley.

Grossman, P., Niemann, L., Schmidt, S., & Walach, H. (2004). Mindfulness-based stress reduction and health benefits. A meta-analysis. *Journal of Psychosomatic Research, 57,* 35–43.

Groth-Marnat, G. (2009). *Handbook of psychological assessment* (5th ed.). New York: Wiley.

Harkness, A.R., McNulty, J.L., Ben-Porath, Y.S., & Graham, J.R. (2002). *MMPI-2 Personality Psychopathology Five (PSY-5) scales: Gaining an overview for case conceptualization and treatment planning.* Minneapolis, MN: University of Minnesota Press.

Kabat-Zinn, J., Massion, A.O., Kristeller, J., et al. (1992) Effectiveness of a meditation-based stress reduction program in the treatment of anxiety disorders. *American Journal of Psychiatry, 149,* 936–943

Linehan, M.M., Cochran, B.N, & Kehrer, C.A. (2001). Dialectical behavior therapy for borderline personality disorder. In D.H. Barlow (Ed.), *Clinical handbook of psychological disorders: A step-by-step treatment manual* (3rd ed., pp. 470–522). New York: Guilford Press.

Livesley, W.J. (2003). *Practical management of personality disorder.* New York: Guilford Press.

McMurran, M., Huband, N., & Overton, E. (2010). Non-completion of personality disorder treatments: A systematic review of correlates, consequences, and interventions. *Clinical Psychology Review, 30,* 277–287

Morawetz, D. (2001). *Sleep better without drugs: A four to six week self-help program* (Book and three audio cassettes). Melbourne, Australia: Sleep Better.

Paris, J. (2009). The treatment of borderline personality disorder: Implications of research on diagnosis, etiology, and outcome. *Annual Review of Clinical Psychology, 5,* 277–290.

Olsson I., Mykletun, A., & Dahl, A.A. (2005). The Hospital Anxiety and Depression Rating Scale: A cross-sectional study of psychometrics and case finding abilities in general practice. *BMC Psychiatry, 5,* 46.

Saulsman, L.M., & Page, A.C. (2004). The five-factor model and personality disorder empirical literature: A meta-analytic review. *Clinical Psychology Review, 23*(8), 1055–1085.

Segal, Z.V., Williams, J.M.G., & Teasdale, J.D. (2002). *Mindfulness-based cognitive therapy for depression.* New York, NY: Guildford Press.

Sellick, S., & Crooks, D. (1999). Depression and cancer: an appraisal of the literature for prevalence, detection, and practice guideline development for psychological interventions. *Psycho-oncology, 8,* 315–333.

Spielberger, C., Gorsuch, R., Lushene, R., Vagg, P.R., & Jacobs, G.A. (1983). *Manual for the State–Trait Anxiety Inventory.* Palo Alto, CA: Consulting Psychologists Press.

Stark, D., Kiely, M., Smith, A., Velikova, G., House, A., & Selby, P. (2002). Anxiety disorders in medical patients: their nature, associations, and relation to quality of life. *Journal of Clinical Oncology, 20*(14), 3137–48.

Verheul, R., & Herbrink, M. (2007). The efficacy of various modalities of psychotherapy for personality disorders: a systematic review of the evidence and clinical recommendations. *International Review of Psychiatry, 19*, 25–38.

Watson, P.J., Sawrie, S.M., Greene, R.L., & Arredondo, R. (2002). Narcissism and depression: MMPI-2 evidence for the continuum hypothesis in clinical samples. *Journal of Personality Assessment, 79*, 85–109.

CHAPTER 3

Integrative Assessment of Eating Disorders: A Case of Anorexia Nervosa

Ross King

This case report illustrates the complexities associated with the assessment of individuals with an eating disorder, particularly those with anorexia nervosa. The setting for this particular assessment is a multidisciplinary outpatient specialist eating disorders service located within the public mental health sector. However, the assessment described would be similar to that which might occur as part of the admission process to an inpatient eating disorders unit.

Given the medical complications associated with anorexia, as well as the extreme dietary restraint, the psychological assessment constitutes just one component of the assessment. Both a thorough medical (Crow & Swigart, 2005) and nutritional assessment (Rock, 2005) are also required. Furthermore, given the age of onset is usually adolescence, involvement of parents in the assessment process as well as an assessment of the family itself typically required (le Grange, 2005). The aim is to provide a comprehensive and integrated assessment of the client that will guide the delivery of treatment specifically tailored to the needs of the individual (Keel & McCormick, 2010).

A further complication in the assessment process is the tendency for the individual to deny the presence of an eating disorder or the seriousness of the problem and to be reluctant or actively resistant to involvement in the assessment or treatment process (Vitousek, Watson, & Wilson, 1998). The adoption of a motivational interviewing approach in the assessment and early therapy phase that is matched to the individual's readiness to change can help boost the engagement of the person (Feld, Woodside, Kaplan, Olmsted, & Carter, 2001; Treasure & Schmidt, 2008).

The following case depicts an 18-year-old female with anorexia nervosa, Samantha. This is a fictionalised case, drawing on elements of several clients seen by the author. However, the case illustrates many of the typical aspects of such assessments.

The Case of Samantha George

CLINICAL PSYCHOLOGY ASSESSMENT[1]
PRIVATE AND CONFIDENTIAL

CASE FILE NUMBER:	100908
NAME:	Samantha George
ADDRESS:	19 Jordan St
AGE:	18
DOB:	April 14, 1991
SERVICE:	TEWKESBURY EATING DISORDERS SERVICE
REFERRED BY:	Dr Susan Walker, GP
DATES SEEN:	November 11, 2009, November 15, 2009, November 22, 2009

Identifying Information

Samantha (Sam) is an 18-year-old white female who lives with her parents Helen and David and younger sister Gemma and brother Luke. She is currently a Year 12 student at a coeducational private school in Tewkesbury. She was referred to the eating disorders service by her GP, Dr Susan Walker, for assessment and development of a treatment plan following an eight-month deterioration in her eating behaviour and associated significant weight loss. She attended all interviews with her mother but was seen separately for a proportion of each session.

Presenting Problem

Sam initially stated that she was at the service only because her parents and GP had made her come. When asked why she felt they wanted her to come, she stated, 'They think I have an eating disorder and that I have lost too much weight but it's not that bad. I just decided to eat healthier and exercise more'. Consistent with a motivational interviewing style, the clinician responded with an amplified reflection of this lack of concern ('So they really have no reason to be concerned at all? Everything's okay?'). In response, she replied, 'Maybe not'. Asked what concerns she had, she became tearful and said she was sick of feeling sad and tired, and that she was having trouble concentrating, lacked motivation and was worried that this was affecting her studies. However, she felt this was largely due to stress associated with studying Year 12. While she acknowledged that her eating patterns and weight preoccupied her, the focus of concern was on gaining more regulation over the amount she ate and a desire to lose weight.

History of Presenting Problem

Given Sam's denial regarding the presence of an eating disorder, the history was supplemented by information supplied by her mother Helen and the letter of referral from Dr Walker. Helen stated that she noted a change in Sam's eating in the first term holidays of Year 12. She reported, and Sam concurred, that she had been very anxious about achieving high marks in her senior studies but was finding some subjects such as maths harder than previous years. At the same time, she was subjected to bullying by two other girls in her grade, involving social exclusion, name-calling (e.g., 'fat bitch') and cyber-bullying via the computer. While she kept this hidden from her parents for approximately two months, an episode of tearfulness led to a disclosure. While subsequent meetings at the school led to a cessation of the bullying, both Sam and her mother indicated that, combined with the stress regarding her schoolwork, her self-esteem was severely affected.

It was during the term break that Helen stated that Sam began to diet with the intention to become healthier. Initially, the changes were positive in nature, with elimination in junk food coupled with walking three times a week. Sam lost approximately three kilograms over the break and she received positive comments from both family and school friends. Sam stated that this made her feel better about herself and more in control. Helen stated that over the next three months, Sam began to become more restrictive in her eating, largely excluding meat and full-fat dairy products from her diet, and insisting that her mother not cook foods in oil. Helen stated that she had become 'inflexible and obsessive' over meal and exercise routines, becoming angry or anxious if she was obstructed. She would repeatedly ask her mother whether there was any fat or sugar in the food. However, at other times Helen would find food missing from the pantry and evidence of vomiting in the bathroom. Sam increased her walking to five kilometres every day and began attending aerobics classes four times a week. At the same time, she had become more irritable with family members and had become withdrawn from friends, stating she did not feel like going out or that she had school or exercise commitments. She complained of the cold constantly and on two occasions almost fainted. Her weight loss had become more rapid and by October 2009 she was clearly underweight. However, when challenged by her concerned parents she denied that she was underweight and stated that she just wanted to lose another two kilograms then she would be happy.

At this time, her mother took her to Dr Walker for an examination. Her letter of referral to the service noted that at that time Sam was 165 cm and weighed 44 kg, giving a Body Mass Index (BMI) of 16.2, or in the extremely underweight range. Physical examination indicated that she was mildly dehydrated and had postural hypotension. An electrocardiogram indicated bradycardia with a heart rate of 45 beats per minute but no arrhythmias or other abnormalities. Blood tests revealed anaemia and mild hypokalaemia due to low levels of phosphorus. She had been amenorrhoeic for four months but was unconcerned by this. She denied laxative abuse or intentionally inducing vomiting but stated that if she ate fatty food it made her feel bloated and nauseous and that this had caused her to vomit. Sam also denied being underweight, stating that a lot of friends were this weight and that she wanted to lose more weight. Given her physical status and denial of any concerns, she was referred to the eating disorders service for a more comprehensive assessment.

David, an accountant, and Helen, a teacher, met through a mutual friend in their final year of university, then dated for several months before moving in together and eventually marrying. In recent years, their relationship had been, in Helen's words, 'rocky'. Sam described them as constantly arguing and stated that David was always in a bad mood. Sam felt that he was constantly critical of her and that, despite her efforts, her marks were never good enough for him. In contrast, she described her relationship with her mother as very close, though she added, 'She treats me like a child and always questions what I am doing. She always has done this'. Therefore, the family environment could be conceptualised as one of high levels of expressed emotion. The relationship between Gemma and Sam was a jealous, rivalrous one; Sam was jealous of her more extraverted socially adept sister and

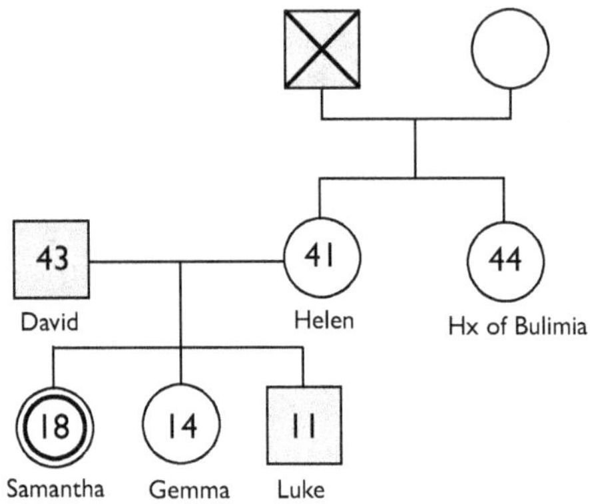

Figure 3.1
Family genogram.

verbal fights between them were common. Helen reported that she often had to settle disputes between them in order to 'keep the peace and not upset David'.

From a family psychiatric history, the only relevant factor was a prior history of bulimia in Helen's older sister when she was a young adult. Helen stated that while the family suspected the sister was bingeing and vomiting for some time, her sister only confirmed this after been caught vomiting by their mother. She was seen by the GP and referred to a psychologist whom she saw for approximately a year with good results. Sam was aware of her aunt's eating disorder (see genogram in Figure 3.1).

Developmental History

Sam's mother described a normal pregnancy and labour. There were some difficulties with feeding in infancy; she described Sam as a 'fussy eater' as well as being messy and that she was often reluctant to allow her to feed herself.

She achieved her milestones in normal timeframes and was described by Helen as 'a good child; polite, considerate but a little anxious and withdrawn at times'. At kindergarten, prep and primary, Sam was conscientious and high-achieving, as well as well-behaved and liked by teachers. She had a firm, small number of close friends throughout her primary school years.

The transition to high school was somewhat unsettling as only two of her friends went to the same school. Sam struggled with the larger school environment and was more withdrawn socially.

With respect to schoolwork, Helen stated she was very perfectionistic and obsessive, and very focused on achieving high grades.

Past Psychiatric History

No history of psychiatric disorders was noted.

Medical History

Sam's prior medical history was unremarkable. She suffered the usual childhood illness, and apart from a ruptured appendix at age 12, she had never been hospitalised.

Substance Abuse History

Sam stated that she had previously gone to parties or nightclubs with friends but denied being drunk on any more than a couple of occasions or any use of illicit drugs. Her mother reported she had no evidence of any substance abuse.

Mental State Examination

Appearance, attitude, activity. Young adult White female, appears stated age but emaciated in appearance. Dressed in oversized casual clothes that obscure actual body size. Face gaunt with sunken cheeks, skin dry and hair thin, brittle and lacking lustre. Eye contact at times overly maintained but avoids when topics centre on food and weight issues. Attitude unengaged and resistant; expresses a desire to leave interview on several occasions but agrees to remain. Becomes hostile when asked about eating behaviour and weight but is more cooperative as interview progresses. Improves as interview progresses. Posture upright, sits turned away from mother, arms folded and continually jiggles leg.

Mood and affect. Initially, mood tersely described as 'fine', but later admits 'I'm struggling, like I'm falling into a black hole'. Affect reactive and broad in range from anxious to sad and tearful to somewhat guarded, angry and sullen when eating behaviour discussed.

Speech and language. Speech fluent and grammatical with normal rate and prosody. Volume alters with affect; lowered when sad or sullen, raised when angry. Comprehension intact.

Thought process. No loosening of associations, blocking or other phenomena noted.

Thought content. Content centred on preoccupation with need to restrict intake and adhere to strict rituals with regard to eating and exercise. Stated that unless she did so, 'I will lose control and get fatter than I am already'. Denial of her emaciated state held with near-delusional intensity stating 'I can see myself in the mirror, I know what a disgusting fat pig I am'. Depressive themes regarding perceived failure to sufficiently restrict eating and increasing struggle to adhere to exercise and maintain school study patterns and grades. No suicidal or homicidal ideation or plans.

Perception. Illusion of self as overweight despite emaciated state. No other abnormalities noted.

Cognition. Alert and fully oriented. Largely able to sustain attention but at times distracted and needing to have questions restated. Long- and short-term memory appear intact but not formally assessed.

Insight and judgment. Insight partial; acknowledges current distress regarding mood but unwilling to admit to suffering an eating disorder and risk to health of current level of emaciation. Judgment also impaired; continues to engage in restrictive eating despite physical impact and resistant to suggestion that need to increase weight.

Assessment Methods

- Eating Disorders Examination
- Eating Disorders Inventory-3
- Anorexia Nervosa Stage of Change questionnaire
- Decisional Balance scale
- Food monitoring sheets
- Structured Clinical Interview for DSM-IV–Mood Disorders Module
- Beck Depression Inventory-II

Eating Disorder Symptomatology

As part of the assessment process, Sam was administered the Eating Disorders Examination, a semistructured interview designed to assess eating disorder psychopathology across four key areas (restraint, eating concern, shape concern and weight concern) as well as frequency data on two key behavioural features (overeating and extreme methods of weight control) over the previous 28 days. On each of the four key areas, Sam scored in the clinical range.

On the Eating Disorders Inventory-3, Sam approached the test in a consistent manner and did not attempt to present herself as either experiencing extreme or negligible levels of symptoms. Therefore, her responses were considered a valid indication of her current state. Sam's Eating Disorder Risk Composite was in the elevated clinical range, reflecting serious levels of eating symptoms and concerns. Compared to a sample of anorexia nervosa binge–purge type adults, her preoccupation with weight, fear of weight gain and concern with dieting was in the elevated clinical range, exceeding 73%

of this comparison group. Similarly, her tendency to think about and engage in uncontrolled overeating exceeded 75% of this group. Her level of body dissatisfaction with the size and shape of her body was in the typical clinical range, exceeding 62% of the comparison group.

A food monitoring diary completed between sessions 2 and 3 indicated the extent of her dietary restriction, compensatory behaviour, and associated cognitions. A section of this is shown in Figure 3.2.

Together, these assessment tools indicate a significant pattern of disturbed eating, excessive exercise, weight concern and body image disturbance. Combined with her significant weight loss to a BMI of 16.2 and the presence of amenorrhea, a diagnosis of anorexia nervosa, binge-eating/purging type is warranted.

Comorbid Conditions

Sam's presentation during the interviews, as well as the common comorbidity of depression with anorexia, indicated the need to assess for this in addition to the eating disorder. Examination with the mood disorders module of the SCID-IV, a semistructured diagnostic interview indicated the presence of a depressed mood coupled with loss of interest in pleasure that had persisted for the past two months. Additional features, such as sleep disturbance in the form of initial insomnia, impaired concentration and sense of worthlessness, were also present. Suicidal ideation was denied. Loss of appetite and weight loss were also acknowledged but clearly overlap with the anorexic symptomatology. Episodes of manic-type symptoms were denied.

Her score on the Beck Depression Inventory–II indicated a moderate level of depressive symptoms consistent with the SCID-IV. On the two critical items concerning hopelessness and suicidal ideation, her scores were at the mild level. High scores were obtained on items concerning loss of appetite, energy, concentration difficulty, as well as worthlessness and self-criticalness. Moderate scores were obtained on items pertaining to sadness, guilt and self-dislike. On the basis of this, a diagnosis of major depressive disorder was warranted.

Eating Disorder-Related Psychological Features

The EDI-3 also assesses for nine psychological features associated with eating disorders. On many of these, Sam scored in the elevated clinical range. With regard to her sense of ineffectiveness, she indicated extreme feelings of personal insecurity, inadequacy and ineffectiveness; a pervasive sense of emotional and aloneness, emptiness and of things being out of control. Interpersonally, she felt discomfort in social situations, especially concerning expressing thoughts and feelings as well as feeling a sense of distance, estrangement and lack of trust in relationships. She felt that she did not experience understanding or love from others. With respect to overcontrol, Sam expects extremely high standards of performance from herself; any failure to achieve perfection

Food Diary

Time	Food	Place	Binge	V/1	Comments
10.00	Coffee (skim milk)	Kitchen			Will not binge — must lose weight. 47kg. So what out of proportion. Must lose weight off stomach & thighs
12.30	Salad sandwich 5 slices bread with marg+++ & vegemite, 12 pieces chocolate	Lounge	Y	V	Why do I do this to myself!!! I'm such a failure!
6.00	Coffee	Lounge			Threw out tea, calorie intake too high.

Figure 3.2

Food monitoring diary.

results in severe self-criticism. Coupled with this, she placed great value on self-denial, self-sacrifice and control of bodily urges as well as guilt and shame if she experiences pleasure.

Readiness to Change

Consistent with her presentation, Sam's responses on the Anorexia Nervosa Stage of Change questionnaire indicated a low motivation to change. She was in the precontemplation stage with respect to weight gain and eating behaviour and use of weight control strategies. However, she was in the preparation stage with respect to addressing relationship, emotional and psychological issues. Overall, she was in the contemplation stage. Furthermore, her responses on the Decisional Balance scale indicated greater perceived benefits to continuing her current behaviour than perceived burdens.

Formulation

Sam is an 18-year-old female with an eight-month history of restrictive eating, excessive exercise and associated weight loss, compensatory behaviour, fear of weight gain, body image disturbance and amenorrhea consistent with a diagnosis of anorexia nervosa, binge-purge type. A pattern of lowered mood consistent with major depressive disorder was also present.

Sam's anorexia appears to have arisen within the context of a number of predisposing factors such as a family history of eating disorders, being of female gender, early feeding difficulties and personality characteristics such as perfectionism, low self-esteem and a poor capacity to express emotions and anxiety regarding interpersonal relationships. The onset of the anorexia appears to have been precipitated by not only her adolescent age but the experience of bullying and increased challenges in managing to maintain high school grades, leading to intensification of feelings of inadequacy and of being out of control. Once initiated, the eating disorder was perpetuated by the positive attention received by Sam for her weight loss, coupled with an increased sense of control, pride in her capacity to deny bodily urges to eat and a sense of specialness, as well as a fear of weight gain. The high levels of parental expressed emotion and her jealous rivalrous relationship with her younger sister were additional perpetuating factors. Her lack of insight into her condition and readiness to alter her eating patterns also act as perpetuating factors. Protective factors included the recent onset of the anorexia and her intelligence.

Diagnosis

Axis I	307.1	Anorexia nervosa, binge-eating/purging type
	296.21	Major depressive disorder, single episode, mild
Axis II	V71.09	No diagnosis
Axis III	263.0	Malnutrition, moderate
Axis IV		Parental discord, high parental expressed emotion
Axis V	GAF	45 (current)

Treatment

This integrative assessment of Sam provides important information that can be used in treatment planning. The most important initial consideration is whether she requires medical stabilisation and nutritional management in an inpatient setting. Established clinical guidelines exist to assist in such decision-making (American Psychiatric Association, 2006; Royal Australian and New Zealand College of Psychiatrists Clinical Practice Guides Team for Anorexia,

2004). On the basis of her current BMI and physical status, it would seem that hospitalisation is probably unnecessary at this point. Ongoing monitoring by her GP and oral phosphorus supplementation would be sufficient; however, if her BMI was to decrease to 13.5 or her cardiac functioning, postural hypotension and hypokalaemia were to deteriorate further, hospitalisation would be warranted. Additionally, given her comorbid depression, the GP or the team psychiatrist could assess whether a low-dose SSRI antidepressant could be instituted. Nutritional management on an outpatient basis should commence through the development of a dietary plan by the treatment team's dietitian.

With respect to psychological treatment, two evidence-based treatment alternatives appear most appropriate. First, given her age and the fact that she is still residing with her parents, family-based treatment using the Maudsley model approach (Eisler, Lock, & le Grange, 2010; Lock, le Grange, Agras, & Dare, 2001) could be considered. However, given the existence of high levels of parental expressed emotion, the separated version of this approach should be adopted, with the parents seen separately from Sam.

The alternative approach would be lengthy individual CBT. This could either be CBT with a particular focus on enhancement of motivation and engagement (Pike, Carter, & Olmsted, 2010; Pike, Devlin, & Loeb, 2004) or the broad version of Fairburn's (2008) enhanced CBT (CBT-E) with a particular focus on addressing Sam's perfectionism and low self-esteem.

Dr Ross King B.A., PhD (Clin Psych), Clinical Psychologist, Tewkebury — Eating Disorders Service

Commentary on Assessment

Anorexia nervosa (AN) presents several challenges for the clinician undertaking an assessment.

First, while anorexia is a psychological disorder, starvation as a result of restrictive eating, excessive exercise and purging behaviours can have a significant physical impact on the individual, including a risk of death. Anorexia has the highest mortality rate of all psychiatric illness (Sullivan, 2002); the overall mortality rate for AN is five times that of the same aged population in general; with death from natural causes such as complications from starvation and sudden death more than four times greater (Agras, 2001; Beumont, 2000). Anorexia affects virtually every system of the body and comprehensive assessment of the individual's physical status by a medical practitioner is critical (Pomeroy, 2004). Severe weight loss and overall physical health (e.g., presence of arrhythmias, electrolyte disturbances) will determine whether hospitalisation for medical stabilisation and refeeding is needed as the first component of an integrated treatment.

Second, unlike psychological disorders such as depression or anxiety, the symptoms associated with anorexia are typically viewed by the individual as egosyntonic; that is, they provide a solution to perceived problems rather than a source of distress and impairment. Therefore, at least in the early stages of the condition, those with anorexia are unlikely to present to health professionals of their own accord. Rather, they may reluctantly attend as a result of pressure from concerned others such as parents. Consequently, resistance or denial may impact on their engagement in both the assessment and subsequent treatment (Vitousek et al., 1998). This is of importance as readiness to change predicts treatment outcome (Ametller, Castro, Serrano, Martinínez, & Toro, 2005; Geller, Drab-Hudson, Whisenhunt, & Srikameswaran, 2004; McHugh, 2007). Therefore, the use of eating disorder-specific measures of transtheoretical or stages of change model (Prochaska & DiClemente, 1983) constructs such as readiness to change (Rieger, Touyz, & Beumont, 2002), self-efficacy to recover (Pinto, Guarda, Heinberg, & DiClemente, 2006) and decisional balance (Cockell, Geller, & Linden, 2002) as part of the assessment process is warranted.

Third, anorexia is associated with significant psychological comorbidity; particularly anxiety disorders such as social anxiety and obsessive–compulsive disorder (Altman & Shankman, 2009; Gotard, Flament, Perdereau, & Joammett, 2002), mood disorders, and personality disorders such as obsessive–compulsive, avoidant, dependent and borderline (Sansone, Levitt, & Sansone, 2005). In addition, a quarter of all mortality in anorexia is due to suicide with the risk of successful suicide being 32 times that of the same aged population (Beumont, 2000; Pompili, Mancinelli, Giradi, Ruberto, & Tatarelli, 2004). As a result, the clinician must carefully assess for the presence of comorbidity.

Fourth, pre-existing personality features such as perfectionism and obsessive–compulsive traits (Cassin & von Ranson, 2005) as well as cognitive abnormalities such as set-shifting difficulties or inflexibility (Roberts, Tchanturia, Stahl, Southgate, & Treasure, 2007) and a bias towards details rather than an integrative processing of information or weak central coherence (Lopez, Tchanturia, Stahl, & Treasure, 2008) may act as risk factors for the development of eating disorders. Furthermore, these factors may be exacerbated by the eating disorder and can impact on the individual's ability to alter their behaviour patterns during treatment. Therefore, a thorough assessment should consider these areas as well.

Lastly, the use of well-validated and reliable measures such as the Eating Disorders Examination (Fairburn, Cooper, & O'Connor, 2008) and the Eating Disorders Inventory-3 (Garner, 2004) provides the clinician with continuous data regarding eating-related symptomatology for both behaviour and attitudes. These serve both as valuable tools to guide case conceptualisation and treatment planning (Sysko, 2008) and as excellent outcome measures with which to evaluate the impact of therapeutic interventions over time (Pike, 2005).

Endnote

1 This case assessment is fictional and is to be used for the purposes of demonstration only. Any resemblance to persons known is entirely coincidental.

References

Agras, W.S. (2001). The consequences and costs of the eating disorders. *Psychiatric Clinics of North America, 24*, 371—379.

Altman, S.E., & Shankman, A.A. (2009). What is the association between obsessive–compulsive disorder and eating disorders. *Clinical Psychology Review, 29*, 638–646.

American Psychiatric Association. (2006). Practice guideline for the treatment of patients with eating disorders third edition. *American Journal of Psychiatry, 163*(Supp), 5–54.

Ametller, L., Castro, J., Serrano, E., Martinínez, E., & Toro, J. (2005). Readiness to recover in adolescent anorexia nervosa: Prediction of hospital admission. *Journal of Child Psychology and Psychiatry, 46*, 394–400.

Beumont, P. (2000). Anorexia nervosa as a mental and physical illness: The medical perspective. In D. Gaskill & F. Sanders (Eds.), *The encultured body: Policy implications for healthy body image and disordered eating behaviours* (pp. 80–94). Brisbane, Australia: Queensland University of Technology.

Cassin, S.E., & von Ranson, K.M. (2005). Personality and eating disorders: A decade in review. *Clinical Psychology Review, 25*, 895–916.

Cockell, S., Geller, J., & Linden, W. (2002). The development of a decisional balance scale for anorexia nervosa. *European Eating Disorders Review, 10*, 359–375.

Crow, S., & Swigart, S. (2005). Medical assessment. In J.E. Mitchell & C.E. Peterson (Eds.), *Assessment of eating disorders* (pp. 120–128). New York: Guilford.

Eisler, I., Lock, J., & le Grange, D. (2010). Family-based treatments for adolescents with anorexia nervosa: Single-family and multifamily approaches. In C.M. Grilo & J.E. Mitchell (Eds.), *The treatment of eating disorders: A clinical handbook* (pp. 150–174). New York: Guilford.

Fairburn, C.G. (Ed.) (2008). *Cognitive behavior therapy and eating disorders.* New York: Guilford.

Fairburn, C.G., Cooper, Z., & O'Connor, M. (2008). Eating Disorders Examination (Edition 16.0D). In C.G. Fairburn (Ed.), *Cognitive behavior therapy and eating disorders* (pp. 265–308). New York: Guilford.

Feld, R., Woodside, D.B., Kaplan, A.S., Olmsted, M.P., & Carter, J.C. (2001). Pretreatment motivational enhancement therapy for eating disorders: A pilot study. *International Journal of Eating Disorders, 29*, 393–400.

Garner, D.M. (2004). *Eating Disorder Inventory-3: Professional manual.* Lutz, FL: Psychological Assessment Resources.

Geller, J., Drab-Hudson, D.L., Whisenhunt, B.L., & Srikameswaran, S. (2004). Readiness to change dietary restriction predicts outcomes in the eating disorders. *Eating Disorders: The Journal of Treatment and Prevention, 12*, 209–224.

Gotard, N., Flament, N., Perdereau, F., & Joammett, P. (2002). Comorbidity between eating disorders and anxiety disorders: A review. *International Journal of Eating Disorders, 32*, 253–270.

Keel, P.K., & McCormick, L. (2010). Diagnosis, assessment, and treatment planning for anorexia nervosa. In C.M. Grilo & J.E. Mitchell (Eds.), *The treatment of eating disorders: A clinical handbook* (pp. 3–27). New York: Guilford.

Le Grange, D. (2005). Family assessment. In J.E. Mitchell & C.E. Peterson (Eds.), *Assessment of eating disorders* (pp. 150–174). New York: Guilford.

Lock, J., le Grange, D., Agras, W.S., & Dare, C. (2001). *Treatment manual for anorexia nervosa: A family-based approach.* New York: Guilford.

Lopez, C., Tchanturia, K., Stahl, D., & Treasure, J. (2008). Central coherence in eating disorders: A systematic review. *Psychological Medicine, 38*, 1393–1404.

McHugh, M.D. (2007). Readiness for change and short-term outcomes of female adolescents in residential treatment for anorexia nervosa. *International Journal of Eating Disorders, 40*, 602–612.

Pike, K. (2005). Assessment of anorexia nervosa. *International Journal of Eating Disorders, 37*, S22–S25.

Pike, K., Carter, J.C., & Olmsted, M.P. (2010). Cognitive-behavioral therapy for anorexia nervosa. In C.M. Grilo & J.E. Mitchell (Eds.), *The treatment of eating disorders: A clinical handbook* (pp. 83–107). New York, NY: Guilford.

Pike, K., Devlin, M.J., & Loeb, K.L. (2004). Cognitive–behavioral therapy in the treatment of anorexia nervosa, bulimia nervosa, and binge eating disorder. In J.K. Thompson (Ed.), *Handbook of eating disorders and obesity* (pp. 130–162). New York: Wiley.

Pinto, A., Guarda, A., Heinberg, L., & DiClemente, C. (2006). Development of the Eating Disorder Recovery Self-Efficacy Questionnaire. *International Journal of Eating Disorders, 39*, 376–384.

Pomeroy, C. (2004). Assessment of medical status and physical factors. In J.K. Thompson (Ed.), *Handbook of eating disorders and obesity* (pp. 81–111). New York: Wiley.

Pompili, M., Mancinelli, I., Girardi, P., Ruberto, A., & Tatarelli, R. (2004). Suicide in anorexia nervosa: A meta-analysis. *International Journal of Eating Disorders, 36*, 99–103.

Prochaska, J.O., & DiClemente, C.C. (1983). Stages and processes of self-change in smoking: Toward an integrative model of change. *Journal of Consulting and Clinical Psychology, 51*, 390–395.

Rieger, E., Touyz, S., & Beumont, P. (2002). The Anorexia Nervosa Stages of Change Questionnaire (ANSOCQ): Information regarding its psychometric properties. *International Journal of Eating Disorders, 32*, 24–38.

Roberts, M.E., Tchanturia, K., Stahl, D., Southgate, L., & Treasure, J. (2007). A systematic review and meta-analysis of set-shifting ability in eating disorders. *Psychological Medicine, 37*, 1075–1084.

Rock, C. (2005). Nutritional assessment. In J.E. Mitchell & C.E. Peterson (Eds.), *Assessment of eating disorders* (pp. 129–147). New York: Guilford.

Royal Australian and New Zealand College of Psychiatrists Clinical Practice Guidelines Team for Anorexia Nervosa. (2004). Australian and New Zealand clinical practice guidelines for the treatment of anorexia nervosa. *Australian & New Zealand Journal of Psychiatry, 38*, 659–670.

Sansone, R.A., Levitt, J.L., & Sansone, L.A. (2005). The prevalence of personality disorders among those with eating disorders. *Eating Disorders: The Journal of Treatment & Prevention, 13*, 7–21.

Sullivan, P. (2002). Course and outcome of anorexia nervosa and bulimia nervosa. In C.G. Fairburn & K.O. Brownell (Eds.), *Eating disorders and obesity: A comprehensive handbook* (2nd ed., pp. 226–230). New York: Guilford.

Sysko, R. (2008). Eating disorders. In J. Hunsley & E.J. Mash (Eds.), *A guide to assessments that work* (pp. 515–534). New York: Oxford.

Treasure, J., & Schmidt, U. (2008). Motivational interviewing in eating disorders. In H. Arkowitz, H.A. Westra, W.R. Miller & S. Rollnick (Eds.), *Motivational interviewing in the treatment of psychological problems* (pp. 194–224). New York: Guilford.

Vitousek, K., Watson, S., & Wilson, G.T. (1998). Enhancing motivation for change in treatment-resistant eating disorders. *Clinical Psychology Review, 18*, 391–420.

CHAPTER 4

The Clinical Assessment of a Patient With Borderline Personality Disorder

Andrew J. Lewis

This case presents some of the challenges encountered in the assessment of a patient with a complex personality disorder. Such cases often come to the attention of a clinical psychologist through a circuitous referral pathway, with the patient and sometimes even other health professionals unaware of the personality issues underlying the more manifest and sometime urgent problems. It is not uncommon that, by the time the patient arrives for a comprehensive clinical assessment, they already have a long complex and frustrating experience of the health system that can be an impediment to both the assessment and treatment process.

In the present case, for instance, the patient repeatedly presented with eating disordered symptoms to a hospital Accident and Emergency department, which was often accompanied by self-harming and suicidal behaviour. She was subsequently referred to a private psychiatrist for management, who quickly discovered that the patient presented with complex family issues, was often crisis-driven, and was impossible to contain within a busy private practice. Essentially, the referral by the private psychiatrist was motivated by a request to assess the patient's suitability for a hospital-based, outpatient psychological therapy within an adult mental health team.

In order to assess the patient's suitability for an intervention of this kind, it was necessary to consider carefully the management of several risk factors. These included her own risk of suicide and the ongoing health risks associated with her self-harming and disordered eating. The risks to her family members also needed to be considered, which arose from the significant degree of dysfunction and crisis generated within their lives as a result of the patient's presenting condition.

Having assessed whether it would be possible to put in place an adequate crisis management plan, the assessment needed to focus on the underlying therapeutic capacities and motivation for treatment. From the outset, since the treatment evidence suggests that patient's presenting with complex personality disorders will require a long-term intervention, it is critical to focus the assessment on such capacities and motivation. Alongside this goal stands the question of whether the patient and her family could establish the necessary stability in their lives in order to commit to and, in turn, benefit from such an intervention. Accordingly, the assessment was principally focused on both developmental and personality factors, as well as their possible interaction and predictors of her engagement with a long-term treatment process. This focus aimed to establish the degree and key domains of personality dysfunction, the developmental history and possible causal factors in prior interpersonal dynamics that predisposed the patient towards such dysfunction. The other focus was the possible interpersonal strengths that may be able to sustain her through what promised to be a turbulent therapeutic relationship.

Another important aspect of this assessment was to rule out any complications in the presentation resulting from the patient's cognitive capacities. Both the extensive history of self-harm and her educational performance suggested a comprehensive cognitive assessment was indicated before making treatment recommendations. Cognitive assessment was particularly indicated given the patient's history of drug overdose, which was often accompanied by loss of consciousness.

The Case of Sharon

CLINICAL PSYCHOLOGY ASSESSMENT[1]
PRIVATE AND CONFIDENTIAL

CASE FILE NUMBER: 196846

NAME:	Sharon
ADDRESS:	40 Tipperary Way, West Avalon, Arcadia
AGE:	40
DOB:	January 11, 1962
REFERRED BY:	Dr H.C. Earwicker, Consultant Psychiatrist
CLINICIAN:	Dr Shem Penman, Clinical Psychologist, Holzweg Hospital
DATES SEEN:	Jan 12, 2002, (Initial Interview); Jan 18 (Assessment Interview followed by administration of MCMI-III); January 26 (Administration of WAIS-IV); February 5; (Feedback and treatment planning).

Presenting Problems

Sharon is a 40-year-old mother of four children who was refereed by her consultant psychiatrist for assessment of her suitability for psychological therapy. She presented with a history of self-harm, including self-lacerations. Currently, her self-harming consists of approximately weekly self-lacerations to the wrist, lower arm and torso. Since a young adult in her 20s she has been bulimic on a monthly basis, which had increased to a weekly basis at the time of referral. Sharon presented with chronic suicidal ideation but without a history of suicidal behaviour. She also presented with a complex history of relationship instability including a marriage breakdown in 1998. In the context of interpersonal stressors she displays difficulty controlling her emotional states with oscillations between anger, sadness and what she describes as a 'numbing' state of mind being the most dominant emotions. Over the course of the assessment she continued to display suicidal ideation in each session, but upon assessment it was clear that this did not progress onto any form of suicidal behaviour or concrete plan for suicide. Sharon also displayed lowered mood, poor sleep and anxiety symptoms.

History of Presenting Problem and Previous Treatment

The current symptoms of suicidal ideation commenced when Sharon was 27 years of age following her involvement in a motor vehicle accident where a passenger and close female friend were killed. Initially Sharon coped well with the birth of her children with her former husband Barry when she was 24, but self-harming and disordered eating commenced when she separated from her first husband at the age of 35. At this time she did access psychological treatment in an outpatient setting with a male psychiatrist. She describes attending around 10 sessions of what appears to have been a supportive mode of therapy, but was unable to sustain treatment as a result of what she described as her therapist's lack of compassion and interest in her. Since that time Sharon has had frequent admissions to psychiatric inpatient units and hospital Accident and Emergency (A&E) departments over a four-year period. Typically, she presents in a state of agitation with suicidal ideation and after having lacerated her wrist or arm. In the last 12 months she has presented to her local A&E seven times in a state of distress and agitation. Such presentations appear to be precipitated by intense and emotive arguments with her husband and she often requests admission to an eating disorders unit.

Family History

Sharon was one of three children and has two brothers, each two years apart. Her family of origin was characterised by parental alcoholism and domestic violence and frequent separations from her parents, who worked as seasonal fruit pickers. Sharon frequently stayed with a succession of 'Aunties', who were apparently unrelated, while her parents travelled in search of work. Her relationship with her elder siblings was characterised by violence. One incident she recalls from early childhood when she was approximately 5 years of age was her elder brother breaking her arm by hitting her with a chair.

She married for the first time when she was 19 years old and moved out of home at that time. Her first marriage was a violent relationship in which her husband Barry would physically assault her approximately monthly, typically following his alcoholic binges. The relationship ended when she was 35 when she left to stay in a refuge. She has not had any further contact and remains fearful that Barry will try to locate her and the children. Sharon has two daughters with Barry, Jenny (now 16) and Cindy (now 14), who also have no contact with their biological father. Sharon remarried to David (58) four years ago and now has two children to him: Jasmine (3) and Tim (2). David suffers from bipolar disorder, which is well managed by a private psychiatrist. Sharon currently resides with David and her four children.

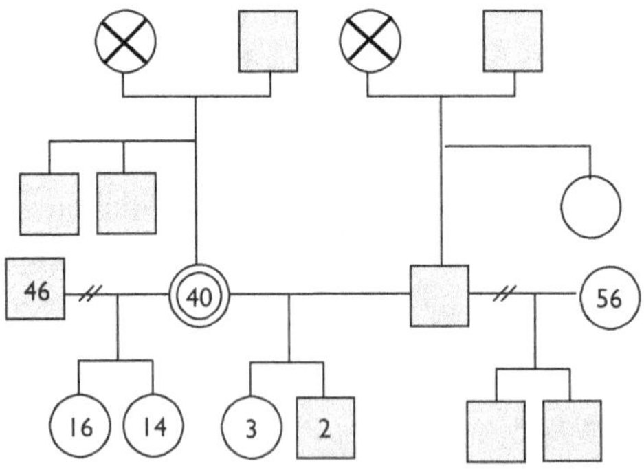

Figure 4.1
Family genogram.

Family Relationship Functioning

The current parental relationship is highly enmeshed given that both David and Sharon present with high needs and their family circumstances are often overwhelming. There are high levels of co-dependency, marked by frequent verbally aggressive exchanges. There are limited supports from family of origin due to conflictual relations with parents and unresolved matters from the past. There are also conflictual and ambivalent relations between children and parents, with notable parenting difficulties due to lack of consistency and some suspected traumatisation of the children due to their mother's psychiatric condition.

Medical History

Significant medical complications include asthma and abdominal ulcers that may be sequelae of bulimia. Sharon also presents with medical issues related to her self-harming. No other medical complications were reported.

Developmental History

Developmental history is unclear and not well documented due to Sharon being a poor historian. Sharon was unable to recall developmental milestones but, in response to these questions, she commented that she remembers struggling to write and spell in school. Family of origin appears to include significant neglect as an infant and in early childhood as evidenced by three factors. First, the event reported above concerning her brother's violence; second, her impression that her parents 'weren't around much'; and third, her parents chronic alcoholism. Sharon also reports frequent distress and disorientation as a child when being left in the care of strangers or in the care of her elder brother as her parents pursued work opportunities or were substance-affected. Sharon's brother reportedly suffered from an intellectual disability and assaulted her continually throughout her childhood. Sharon's parents appeared powerless to protect her, were unaware of the brother's aggression, or blamed her for provoking her brother. When questioned, Sharon did not recall commencing school, or her experiences of formal education. She appears to have attended numerous schools and could not recall a favourite teacher or friend from that period of time. During adolescence, there is some evidence of poor peer relations including conflictual peer relationships, but again, details of enduring or significant relationships outside her family were not forthcoming.

Educational History

Sharon's family moved across several states and consequently Sharon attended numerous primary and secondary schools. Sharon finished school in Year 9 when she was 15 years of age. She reported difficulty and disinterest in learning but refused to provide further details. She does not recall participating in sports or interests outside of school hours.

Mental State Examination

Appearance, attitude, activity. Sharon presented neatly dressed and well groomed. She was hesitant in her interactions but mostly willing to cooperate with the interview and assessment process. She became somewhat agitated and distressed during the discussion of difficult events in her development and current circumstances.

Mood and affect. Sharon displayed sad affect appropriate to the personal losses she described and became more labile in response to discussion of traumatic events from past. When asked about her mood, the patient became sullen and nonresponsive. Eventually she commented that she felt 'just fine really'.

Speech. Sharon demonstrated some pressure of speech during the discussion of traumatic memories but otherwise spoke in a normal manner.

Thought process. Sharon's thought process was mostly normal with some brief instances of a loosening of associations during the discussion of distressing events, which appears to be consistent with some avoidance of traumatic material. There were no instances of thought blocking, illogical thought or significant tangentiality.

Thought content. The content of Sharon's discussion was mostly focused on the presenting issues and showed some suicidal ideation in response to current and past traumatic circumstances and in relation to her prevailing lowered mood. She also discussed feelings of emptiness and what appeared to be dissociative episodes where she felt 'disconnected' and 'outside of herself'.

Perception. Although no disturbances of perception were noted that might indicate psychotic phenomena the patient did display a fixed gaze and become nonresponsive to questions for brief moments in what appeared to be mild dissociation when discussing past traumas.

Cognition.

- Orientation: oriented to time, place and person.
- Attention and concentration: able to attend and concentrate throughout the interview.
- Memory: details of past events were very minimal and Sharon frequently commented that she could not recall information since it was long ago. She had no trouble recalling information from the recent past.

Given the history of learning problems and the possible exposure to overdose formal cognitive assessment was indicated and is described in detail below.

Insight and judgment. Sharon showed some insight into her current circumstances insofar as they are linked to a history of maltreatment and poor coping with life stressors as an adult.

Psychological Testing

Observations during cognitive testing suggested that Sharon may have been quite uncomfortable about the testing procedure. She participated with considerable hesitation. She reported that she was 'not sure why all this was necessary'. During written tasks, she was sometimes reluctant to commit to an answer and frequently expressed a wish to 'finish it off quickly'. During the structured interview task Sharon was somewhat more relaxed and forthcoming. She appeared to welcome the opportunity to discuss topics related to her upbringing.

Tests Administered

- The Millon™ Clinical Multiaxial Inventory-III (MCMI-III)
- Adult Attachment Interview (AAI)
- Wechsler Adult Intelligence Scale, 4th Edition (WAIS-IV)

Test Results and Interpretation

MCMI-III

Sharon was administered the MCMI-III, which is a self-report questionnaire consisting of 175 items administered in order to elicit clinical syndromes and personality traits. This was conducted to assess personality functioning and results indicated that her profile was valid and suitable for interpretation. No critical items requiring immediate or crisis interventions were identified. Sharon scored in the clinical range for borderline personality pathology. In the clinical personality patterns she scored in the clinical range for avoidant, dependent and depressive personality. She also scored in the clinical range for dysthymia and anxiety with elevated levels of posttraumatic stress.

WAIS-IV

Sharon was administered the Wechsler Adult Intelligence Scale — Fourth Edition (WAIS-IV), which is an individually administered test of a person's intellectual ability and cognitive strengths and weaknesses. As Sharon was only administered seven subtests from the WAIS-IV due to time constraints and compliance issues, it is not possible to determine a full-scale IQ score. Instead, as there was no significant difference between her verbal and nonverbal components, the General Ability Index (GAI) was calculated as an appropriate measure of Sharon's general level of cognitive functioning. Sharon's GAI score placed her in the average range and ranks her at the 32nd percentile when compared to other adults of the same age, indicating that she performs better than 32% of individuals of a similar age.

No significant difference was found between Sharon's scores on the Verbal Comprehension (VCI) and Perceptual Reasoning (PRI) Indexes, with both index scores placing her in the average range for her age and ranking her at the 37th percentile for VCI and the 30th percentile for PRI. The VCI is a measure of acquired knowledge, verbal reasoning and comprehension of verbal information. Sharon demonstrated sound understanding of words and her general vocabulary skills were a particular strength for her. She also performed in the average range for her age on the comprehension subtest, indicating good social judgment, practical knowledge and common sense. Sharon scored in the average range on PRI, reflecting sound skills in novel, nonverbal problem-solving and visuo-spatial construction. Her PRI score was prorated based on two of the three core subtests for this index and must be interpreted with caution, Sharon tended to work methodically through the visually based problems presented to her. She was slow to complete many of the items but used a systematic trial-and-error approach.

In contrast, Sharon scored in the borderline to low average range on the Working Memory Index (WMI), ranking her at the 1st percentile when compared to same aged peers. This score is significantly lower than her VCI or PRI scores, a discrepancy that is considerable and clinically significant (occurring in less than 2.5% of the general population). Further examination of Sharon's performance on the WMI revealed an average immediate memory span, but a specific difficulty with working memory. Working memory is the ability to hold information in mind for a brief period of time while mentally manipulating it. While Sharon was able to repeat up to six digits accurately, indicating intact immediate memory skills, she was only able to accurately report a series of two numbers in reverse sequence compared to how they were read to her, revealing a significant weakness in working memory capacity. Poor working memory functioning is often associated with learning difficulties at school and is consistent with Sharon's low educational attainment.

AAI

The Adult Attachment Interview (AAI) was developed by Mary Main and colleagues and is a narrative-based structured interview that typically takes 60–90 minutes. Participants describe the circumstances of their family background and are then asked to provide five adjectives that describe their relationship to each parent and specific memories related to each adjective. The interview also examines direct care-giving experiences and invites the participant to reflect on why their parents behaved as they did during the participant's childhood. Of particular clinical relevance are sections of the interview that examine significant losses and traumas in the participant's life.

Sharon provided mostly negative adjectives for both parents including 'angry' and 'uninterested' for both parents. Her description of episodic memories was long and sometimes confused, becoming progressively more resentful and angered as new memories came to mind. She appeared to be confused and at times incoherent when asked to reflect on her childhood experiences and relationship with her parents.

The AAI classifies adult attachment in terms of a person's state of mind about attachment as expressed in discursive qualities, each of which reflects the overall coherence of the individual's narratives. While the specific content of memories is important, it is thought that the quality of attachment is indicated by the overall coherency of the discourse and the presence of well-defined characteristics of secure versus insecure discursive strategies. Sharon's interview showed many of the qualities of preoccupied attachment in which the participant appears to be mentally preoccupied by their past relationship with their parents. She was at times verbose and digressed readily. In particular, she showed growing anger that sometimes evoked the caregiver as if they were present.

When discussing the traumatic events surrounding her relationship with her brother, Sharon displayed features of being unresolved/disorganised with respect to trauma. This included breaking off in silence for an extended period, confusing details such as times, places and what occurred and describing small apparently incidental aspects such as what she was wearing in great detail. This suggests that these experiences continue to evoke complex and contradictory emotions, as well as evoking dissociative defences and confusion of past and present. Sharon's AAI was coded as primarily Unresolved/Disorganised with respect to trauma with a subclassification of Preoccupied Attachment.

Formulation

Sharon is a 40-year-old woman who presents with a long history of borderline personality disorder against a background of trauma, neglect and separation in her family of origin. Sharon has dissociative episodes and feelings of emptiness consistent with an impoverished sense of self and limited self-efficacy. It is suggested that Sharon's experiences in childhood were traumatic and remain unresolved. These have impeded her capacity to both mentalise and effectively process emotional arousal. Her scores on the MCMI in terms of the seemingly contradictory personality patterns of avoidant, dependent and depressive features is consistent with these problems of emotional regulation. Her parents' unavailability and inconsistent care-giving precipitated a significant disturbance in her attachment system that has been pervasive within most interpersonal relationships. At times she is unable to differentiate her internal state from reality and, with this, she shows a tendency to attribute her own complex and conflicting emotional states to others. Sharon also has difficulty integrating conflicting ideas. These difficulties lead to her experiencing confusion, distress and overwhelming emotions and manifest in her impulsive self-harming and suicidal ideation. Her suicidal ideation is likely to be linked to unresolved complex post-traumatic symptoms complicated by these personality factors. Self-harm and suicidal ideation have become her only coping mechanisms, despite their injurious nature. She appears to repeat experiences of extreme emotional overreaction based on the misinterpretation of social and interpersonal cues. Impulsivity is again based in difficulties in emotional regulation that are not understood by her family or carers, both personal and professional. This leads to continual and perpetuating experiences of invalidation when seeking assistance, which perpetuate her condition and decrease her engagement in effective treatments. Sharon's presentation cannot be accounted for by a cognitive impairment, although working memory deficits may well have impacted on some of her educational difficulties. Provisional diagnosis would be borderline personality disorder (BPD) as the primary condition requiring treatment. Differential diagnoses would include posttraumatic stress disorder and major depression. Although Sharon presented with disordered eating, such symptoms can be better understood within the context of poor emotional regulation and self-harm characteristic of BPD.

Diagnosis

Axis I	296.35	Major depressive disorder (recurrent, in partial remission)
Axis II	301.83	Borderline personality disorder (Principal Diagnosis)
Axis III		Asthma, stomach ulcers
Axis IV		History of trauma, poor family supports and lack of general social supports, difficulties using medical and psychiatric system effectively
Axis V	GAF	40 (current)

Treatment Plan

Crisis Plan

On account of the high degree of suicidality and the history of frequent suicide attempts, a comprehensive crisis plan has been developed in consultation and agreement with family members and other professionals involved. A written version has been distributed. The crisis plan in the event that Sharon experiences suicidal thoughts reaching a distressing intensity includes:

- seeking support and clearly communicating her distress to her husband David, or if he is unavailable contacting her friend and neighbour Betty

- use of diversionary and self-soothing strategies as demonstrated and practised in sessions; assistance in the use of these techniques by husband or friend
- phone contact with case manager during business hours
- phone call to Crisis Assessment Team outside business hours
- in the event of self-harm or suicide attempt presentation to Inpatient unit, Accident and Emergency Section of Holzweg Hospital and referral to Psychiatric Inpatient unit.

General Ongoing Treatment Plan

Multi-modal treatment is required from an experienced treatment team. This would include:

- protective and family support
- psychiatric management and liaison with crisis psychiatric services
- psychological treatment using mentalisation-based therapy (MBT) on a twice-weekly basis. This is to be reviewed in six months but is likely to require at least several years of treatment before significant progress is likely.
- repeating MCMI-III on a six-monthly basis as a measure of treatment progress and ultimately as outcome and follow-up measures.

Individual Psychological Therapy

As discussed, it is suggested that Sharon's past and current difficulties stem from an inability to understand herself and others in terms of mental states and to regulate her emotional states within close relationships. As such, a treatment focused on these abilities and derived from an understanding of disorganised attachment systems, such as MBT is indicated.

Currently, Sharon continues to show evidence of behavioural disturbances associated with impulsivity. As such, it is suggested that an intensive outpatient MBT is suitable. This requires a 50-minute individual therapy session twice per week for a period of at least 18 months. This can be supplemented with attendance at a group therapy, which will be conducted by different therapists.

In general, Sharon's treatment goal will be for her to develop the ability to understand her own and other internal states and, with this, increase the security of her interpersonal relationships.

More specifically this will entail:

- being able to identify and appropriately express her emotions, in multiple contexts
- being able to recognise, understand and counteract her usual pattern of attachment related deactivation of her ability to mentalise
- decreasing any behavioural tendencies used to regulate and make sense of confusing and distressing emotions.

Dr Shem Penman, Clinical Psychologist, Holzweg Hospital, February 20, 2002

Commentary on Assessment

Aims and Techniques Used in Assessment

Assessment of all patients by clinical psychologists ought to routinely consider the presence of personality dysfunction and disorder as a component of the clinical picture. In many cases it can be ruled out and the assessment can proceed with a focus on symptom-based clinical syndromes. Clinical psychologists are also fortunate that their training and expertise in the use of complex psychometric instruments enables them to assess a patient's personality using a number of measures such as the Minnesota Multiphasic Personality Inventory (MMPI 2), MCMI-III or the Inventory of Interpersonal Problems. However, the use of such measures is only ever a supplement to a high-quality, engaging and thorough clinical interview process. In most instances, this process will require several face-to-face meetings and, ideally, information derived from other sources such as the referrer, other health professionals or family members. It is particularly important to be mindful that the diagnosis of a personality disorder always refers to a longstanding and pervasive pattern of personal and interpersonal functioning, so this requires multiple and ideally overlapping sources of information and confirmation from multiple sources to be sure of the diagnosis.

The assessment of a patient presenting with BPD entails further complications. A number of studies have demonstrated that mental health clinicians tend to emphasise different diagnostic features, depending on the service setting they work within (Commons Treloar & Lewis, 2008a, 2008b; Treloar & Lewis, 2009). Patients who present with self-harming behaviour to an emergency department are more likely to be diagnosed with BPD, while clinicians working in outpatient settings are more likely to emphasise the identity, cognitive and affective dimensions in their diagnostic decisions. Such findings suggest that clinicians need to focus more directly on consistent diagnostic criteria in order to minimise the impact of the service setting on diagnostic decision-making.

These findings may well reflect a broader issue in the assessment of BPD patients whose self-harming and suicidality can evoke negative and harsh service responses. Issues such as splitting among services or professionals and boundary violations are well-known difficulties when treating such patients, but it is equally likely that these will be challenges within an assessment as well. Clarity of communication between professionals; clear and well-documented treatment planning; clarification of goals, expectations and procedures between clinician and patient help to reduce the risk that such factors will interfere with the assessment.

Choice of Measures

In this assessment, as in many others, a strategic and parsimonious choice of measures was crucial. The patient already had previous negative experiences with mental health professionals and was unlikely to tolerate extensive psychological testing. It was necessary to introduce each test in a careful manner, well prior to undertaking the testing and to be very clear about the reason it was indicated and how it would assist the assessment and treatment process. It was also necessary to be clear and also diplomatic about the feedback from each measure.

Personality Assessment

Given that the referral itself and the initial meeting raised issues concerning personality disorder, it was necessary to both assess this within the clinical interview but also to confirm or critically examine such information through the use of alternative assessment methods. In this case, a common approach was adopted, that is, the use of a self-report measure. The MCMI-III was chosen for this purpose. The MCMI is one of a suite of self-report measures developed by Theodore Millon (Strack, 2008). The measure has been used extensively in research and in a variety of clinical and forensic settings. The MCMI-III assesses Axis I, clinical syndromes and Axis II, personality disorders as defined in the *Diagnostic and Statistical Manual of Mental Disorders*, 4th Edition. With 175 items it is a convenient and time-efficient tool to aid in diagnosis and to suggest further areas for exploration within the assessment process. At a more complex level, the measure is informed by Millon's theory of personality (Millon, 1997). The measure is psychometrically very robust with internal consistency generally exceeding .80 for 20 of the 26 scales (Groth-Marnat, 2009) and the test–retest reliability of the scales averaging .91 (Groth-Marnat, 2009). Another advantage of this measure is that it provides clinical norms that are adjusted according to the setting in which the patient is assessed. These data can be analysed in terms of elevations into the clinical range (75 and above) and the clinical significance of interventions determined in terms of reduction of psychopathology into the normative range (65 and below). These features make the MCMI a useful tool by which to set a baseline measurement of clinical and personality function and to readminister periodically to assist in treatment monitoring. In the present case, where a long-term therapy could be anticipated, this aspect of the MCMI makes it a clear choice.

Adult Attachment Interview (AAI)

The AAI is a structured interview designed to assess attachment state of mind. It consists of 20 questions and a series of prompts and follow-up questions (Hesse, 1999). Generally, it requires around 60 minutes to complete but in some cases this can be considerably longer. It can be scored using several different coding systems, each of which requires specialised training that can be obtained from the developers of the measure. The AAI is one of the key measures used in attachment research and a recently published book elaborates the variety of clinical applications of this measure (Steele, Steele, & Jacobvitz, 2008). There is a vast literature using the AAI to examine developmental and clinical issues that can be drawn on. In the present case, the AAI was not formally scored but used in a qualitative manner to explore the patient's attachment history and to orient the patient to attachment themes that were clearly a feature of her presentation.

WAIS-IV

Given the concerns raised by the patient's current functioning, her poor capacity to engage in employment, her developmental history including a number of possibly injurious events and a history of substance abuse, including overdose, cognitive testing was clearly indicated. Despite the clear indication, it was also a concern as to how Sharon would tolerate such a structured and potentially confronting form of testing. A number of modifications were therefore introduced and the testing was completed with the minimum formality required.

It should be noted that the Comprehension subtest was administered as a substitute for the core subtest of Information. Sharon became distressed when asked to respond to general knowledge questions, due to her poor educational background, and refused to continue with the Information subtest. While the inclusion of Comprehension instead of Information (upon which Sharon would clearly have performed at a relatively low level) may have artificially elevated her VCI score, Sharon's overall profile is still considered valid. The information subtest shows a high correlation with level of education (Kaufman & Lichtenberger, 2006) and individuals with a positive attitude towards school, a strong educational history and an intellectual curiosity tend to score well on this subtest (Groth-Marnat, 2009). Given Sharon's self-reported disinterest in learning and that she left school in Year 9, her refusal to complete the Information subtest is not surprising and it is likely that her inability to complete this task reflects an impoverished educational background.

It should also be noted that Sharon's WMI score was based on substituting an optional task for the core subtest of Arithmetic, which Sharon was unwilling to complete, explaining she has always found maths a difficult subject at school and becoming visibly distressed at the prospect of undertaking such a task. As with the Information subtest, Sharon's refusal to complete this subtest necessitated the substitution of Letter–Number Sequencing for Arithmetic in order to calculate the WMI score. Substitution was selected in preference to prorating any of the index scores.

Choice of Treatment

Mentalisation-based treatment was chosen as a treatment approach on the basis of its strong evidence base for BPD, the clinician's familiarity with the approach and a view that the patient would benefit from the focus on mentalising ability and affect regulation, which are key features (Bateman & Fonagy, 2008). MBT has been extensively discussed and described in the clinical literature and training in this approach is available (Bateman & Fonagy, 2003, 2004; Fonagy & Bateman, 2006).

The treatment requires the development of a strong therapeutic relationship where the therapist is required to model a reflective focus on the patient's mental states. Alternative perspectives about others' mental states are explored, identifying cognitive and affective processes that lead to them. This stage involves much disclosure, as the therapist reveals their perspective on others' mental states, to demonstrate that people will often have different views about others' mental states. In doing this, it is important to focus on the here and now and how the current use of mentalising is influenced by Sharon's past, rather than focusing on the past itself. In this sense, MBT differs from a traditional psychodynamic therapy that can sometime be destablising for a patient such as this.

MBT has been shown to be efficacious in the treatment of BPD. In one randomised control trial and two subsequent follow-up studies (at 18 months and at 5 years), Bateman and Fonagy found that participants receiving MBT with partial hospitalisation demonstrated statistically and clinically significant improvements on measures examining suicidal behaviour, depressive symptoms and interpersonal functioning.

Endnote

1 This case assessment is fictional and is to be used for the purposes of demonstration only. Any resemblance to persons known is entirely coincidental.

References

Bateman, A. W., & Fonagy, P. (2003). The development of an attachment-based treatment program for borderline personality disorder. *Bulletin of the Menninger Clinic, 67*(3), 187–211.

Bateman, A.W., & Fonagy, P. (2004). Mentalization-based treatment of BPD. *Journal of Personality Disorders, 18*(1), 36–51.

Bateman, A.W., & Fonagy, P. (2008). 8-year follow-up of patients treated for borderline personality disorder: Mentalization-based treatment versus treatment as usual. *American Journal of Psychiatry, 165*(5), 631–638.

Commons Treloar, A., & Lewis, A. (2008a). Professional attitudes towards deliberate self-harm in patients with borderline personality disorder. *Australian and New Zealand Journal of Psychiatry, 42*(7), 578–584.

Commons Treloar, A., & Lewis, A. (2008b). Targeted clinical education for staff attitudes towards deliberate self-harm in borderline personality disorder: randomized controlled trial. *Australian and New Zealand Journal of Psychiatry, 42*(11), 981–988.

Fonagy, P., & Bateman, A.W. (2006). Mechanisms of change in mentalization-based treatment of BPD. *Journal of Clinical Psychology, 62*(4), 411–430.

Groth-Marnat, G. (2009). *Handbook of psychological assessment.* Hoboken, NJ: Wiley.

Hesse, E. (1999). The adult attachment interview: Historical and current perspectives. In J. Cassidy & P. Shaver (Eds.) *Handbook of attachment: Theory, research, and clinical applications* (pp. 395–433). New York: Guilford.

Kaufman, A.S., & Lichtenberger, E.O. (2006). *Assessing adolescent and adult intelligence* (3rd ed.). Boston: Allyn & Bacon.

Millon, T. (1997). *The Millon inventories: Clinical and personality assessment.* New York: Guilford Press, New York.

Steele, H., Steele, M., & Jacobvitz, D. (2008). *Clinical applications of the adult attachment interview.* New York: Guilford Press.

Strack, S. (2008). *Essentials of Millon inventories assessment.* New York: Wiley.

Treloar, C., & Lewis, A. (2009). Diagnosing borderline personality disorder: Examination of how clinical indicators are used by professionals in the health setting. *Clinical Psychologist, 13*(1), 21–27.

PART II

CHILD ASSESSMENTS

CHAPTER 5 | A Case of Childhood Depression

Cherine Habib

This chapter will describe the assessment of a case involving a depressed 9-year-old boy, known here as Donald, who was referred to the author at the Child and Adolescent Mental Health Service (CAMHS) by his teacher. Donald had become uncharacteristically aggressive with his peers at school and complained that he had no friends. Furthermore, Donald's grades had declined since he commenced at the school at the beginning of 2004. The teacher was concerned that Donald was not adjusting well, and may have had a learning disorder that was manifesting itself with a more complex curriculum. Donald had moved with his mother and siblings following his parents' separation a year previously. Donald's mother was agreeable to the assessment and reported that she was 'at the end of her tether'.

Depression is a disorder that involves maladaptive changes in mood, cognition and behaviour, as well as associated somatic and psychomotor functioning. A child is likely to be suffering from depression if he or she shows pronounced, persistent and troubling changes in function. According to current diagnostic criteria (American Psychiatric Association, 2000) such changes pertain to a sad or unhappy mood or loss of interest or pleasure in their usual range of activities and pursuits for a period of two weeks. Developmentally, the DSM-IV-TR criterion also recognises that the disturbed mood in children can be one of irritability and restlessness, not just depressive or apathetic in nature. In addition, the child must present with at least four symptoms from an array that includes the following: feelings of worthlessness or guilt with suicidal ideation; poor concentration and difficulty with completing work; and changes in weight, appetite, activity level, or sleep. A clinically depressed child may hold a negative and distorted self-concept in terms of their self-worth and body image, withdraw from friends and family, experience sensory pain and discomfort (headaches, stomach pains) and complain about bodily functioning (Hammen & Rudolph, 2003).

Depression can occur and reoccur from infancy to old age (APA, 2000; Lancaster, 2003). It affects many of our young, with a lifetime prevalence reported to be between 20–24% (Australian National Health and Medical Research Council [NHMRC], 1997; Lewinsohn, Clarke, Seeley, & Rohde, 1994). In the United States, a number of epidemiological studies have reported that up to 2.5% of children and up to 8.3% of adolescents suffer from depression (Birmaher, Ryan, Williamson, Brent, Kaufman, Dahl et al., 1996; Costello, Mustillo, Erkanli et al, 2003; Lewinsohn, Rohde, & Seeley, 1998). In Australia, 4.1% or 65,000 of 12- to 17-year-olds were diagnosed with a depressive disorder in 1998 (Australian Institute of Health and Welfare, 2003). Similarly, Sawyer et al. (2001) reported that 3% or 95,000 (a population estimate) of 6- to 17-year-olds in Australia will suffer from depression during any one year.

Epidemiologically, the usual onset of a major depressive disorder is between the ages of 13 and 15 (Lewinsohn, Clarke, et al., 1994; Lewinsohn, Hops, Roberts, Seeley, & Andrews, 1993). While clinical depression is less commonly diagnosed in young children (Sims, Nottelmann, Koretz, & Pearson, 2006), some evidence suggests the occurrence of depression is rising and the age of onset is declining (Collishaw, Maughan, Goodman, & Pickles, 2004; Frombonne, 1998; Stark, Sander, Yancy, Bronick, & Hoke, 2000), while other evidence suggests it is not, although it had been underdiagnosed for many years (Costello, Erkanli, & Angold, 2006). While gender differences in the prevalence of depression emerge prominently at adolescence, largely related to puberty (Angold & Costello, 2006; Patton & Viner, 2007), depression is equally common among primary school-aged children (Angold & Costello, 2006; Speier, Sherak, Hirsch, & Cantwell,

1995). However, girls tend to present more with negative self-concept and affect than boys (Rudolph, Hammen, & Daley, 2006).

In middle-childhood (ages 5 to 12) the phenomenology of depression is usually characterised by outward negativity and resistance to the expectations of others as the child struggles internally with misery, hopelessness and self-blame. Unfortunately, depression at this age can be missed or dismissed by parents and even by health professionals. Childhood depression may also be judged as a passing phase of negativity, irritability, of reckless or restless behaviour, about annoying physical and social complaints. It may also be perceived as emotional neediness yet disagreeableness, the latter perhaps reflecting an unrecognised underlying strong ambivalence towards others, particularly parents, siblings and significant people. There may be anxiety in parents and others that if attention is given to these moods and related behaviours that it may make the child worse. It can be distressing to think that a child can become clinically depressed. There may be a tendency — in both the adults and the child — to ignore or even deny these difficulties as a way of coping or not comprehending that a child could become seriously troubled with sadness or be so unhappy. There may be differences of opinion regarding the meaning of the child's functioning by parents, teachers, siblings and others. Ultimately, if not assessed and treated, depression can have a detrimental impact on the child and his or her family and, at worst, perhaps tragic but rare consequences through self-harming behaviour or suicide.

There is no single overriding conceptualisation of the experience and clinical manifestations of depression in children. Instead there are several models or explanations that help account for the emergence and maintenance of the disorder and reflect interactive contributions from within the child and his psychosocial environment. In this way, we can arrive at a more fully informed integrative psychological assessment of the child. Among the explanations are cognitive–behavioural theory (CBT), interpersonal and psychodynamic theory, attachment theory and family systems theory.

CBT accounts for the child's depressive behaviour with reference to a combination of two explanatory concepts: (a) a poverty of reinforcers from others and the environment generally, and this may be due to insufficient availability of reinforcers or the child's ability to obtain reinforcers; and (b) learnt maladaptive negative thought patterns and perceptions about self, others and/or the future, and may include attributions about experience with an external locus of control, a sense of helplessness and hopelessness. There are interpersonal theories of childhood depression, which stress the child's experience of depression being related to problem rumination, poor problem-solving and ineffectual emotional regulation, particularly within the context of peer interaction. Family theories emphasise the interactional context in which the depression occurs, placing the meaning of depression within the family's functioning and history. In this model, depression may be a response to draw attention away from a more vulnerable person or relationship within the family that can threaten the family's overall coping and development. Psychodynamic theories of depression highlight the child's inner conflicts in relation to coping with a significant relationship loss or disturbance. The conflict usually takes the form of a dynamic between overt sadness yet unconscious anger about the loss. Attachment theory suggests that early relationship disruptions may leave a child vulnerable to developing depression to subsequent disruptions or rejections. Temperament and genetic vulnerability can also interplay within a stressful developmental and social context to cause a child to become depressed.

Consequently, an understanding of the nature of the child's experience of depression is best understood from a contextual and multitheoretical or integrative perspective. Such a perspective is the basis for a comprehensive integrative psychological assessment, and involves an evaluation of the child's individual difficulties, coping and capacities, as well as the familial and social context in which the presenting depression manifests. This will then ultimately determine appropriate interventions.

The Case of Donald Perry

CLINICAL PSYCHOLOGY ASSESSMENT[1]
PRIVATE AND CONFIDENTIAL

NAME:	Donald Perry
AGE:	9
ADDRESS:	123 Aye Street, Beetown
REFERRED:	Ms Mary Tulcum, teacher at Beetown Primary School
DATE OF REFERRAL:	September 2004.
DATES SEEN:	September 9, 2004, September 16, 2004, September 23, 2004, October 7, 2004, and October 17, 2004

Referral and Presenting Problem

Donald is a 9-year-old boy in Grade 4 at Beetown Primary School. His teacher, Ms Mary Tulcum, referred him for assessment. Ms Tulcum reported that Donald had become aggressive with his peers at school, complaining of not having any friends and was disruptive in class. Furthermore, Donald's grades had declined since he commenced at the school at the beginning of 2004. The teacher was concerned that Donald was not adjusting well to his new school, and may have had a learning disorder that was manifesting itself in reaction to increasing academic demands. Donald's mother, Sarah Perry, was agreeable to the assessment and reported that she was 'at the end of her tether' with Donald.

History of the Presenting Problem

Donald commenced at Beetown Primary School in Grade 4 in January 2004. After a relatively settled period, Ms Perry stated that Donald started having difficulties with making new friends. He also described difficulties concentrating in class, with his mind wandering to thoughts of his old friends and school. His first-term school report indicated that he had not completed a number of assignments, produced poor quality work and he was struggling generally. By the end of the second term, Donald had punched a peer at school over some teasing about a new haircut. Ms Tulcum reported poor academic progress, and Ms Perry was surprised as Donald had always been a good student in previous years. Two further aggressive outbursts at school were reported, as well as minimal work completion. By the time of the referral, Donald had no friends at school, was not performing, had become irritable at times with his teacher and had stopped playing all sports.

At home, Ms Perry stated that Donald was increasingly neglecting his chores and this had become a source of conflict between them and a burden on her. Ms Perry also described how Donald had become more easily frustrated and irritable with his two younger siblings and sometimes fought with them; in the past few months he had spent much of his time at home in his room. She indicated that she had been too busy looking after the two younger children (both girls) on her own to notice, but thought that he had not had much fun this year and was not the usually active and happy Donald he was prior to his parents' separation in 2003. Ms Perry stated that Donald had not lost any weight, but he seemed not to have grown much this year and his appetite had certainly diminished. She was unsure of his sleep, but described him as usually tired in the morning and most of the time, she stated that he increasingly complained of non-specific 'pain in his body', without an apparent illness.

Ms Perry indicated that her marriage had ended acrimoniously in November 2003 and continues to be unresolved over contact arrangements for the children. Ms Perry was unsure how Donald felt about the separation as he had refused to speak to her about it, but she recognised he was 'unsettled'. On the other hand, she believed he would gradually 'get over it' and did not want to press him on the issue. She indicated that she relied on Donald to support her in her care of her daughters since the separation.

Ms Perry agreed to contact being made with Mr John Perry, Donald's father, for the purpose of the assessment. The children have fortnightly contact with Mr Perry across a weekend. Mr Perry believed his son had been angry and sad about the separation and that his 'heart and mind' were not right for the new school. He believed Donald was happier at the previous school and had argued with his ex-wife about returning Donald to live with him so he can return to the old school and friends. He believed if this occurred Donald would be better off.

Developmental History

The developmental history was gathered from both parents at a single interview. Donald is the eldest child of three siblings and the first to his parents. He was a planned and wanted child. The pregnancy and birth were unremarkable, with Donald born at an average weight and in good health. Mother and father reported coping relatively well with the transition to parenthood. They had the support of both sides of the family and this time was said to be joyous.

As a baby, Donald was described as a 'cuddly … smiley … but demanding' baby who had some difficulties establishing regular sleep and feeding routines (breastfed till 9 months of age). Ms Perry, an accountant, provided the primary care during her year of maternity leave. She experienced breastfeeding as demanding, and irregular sleep as draining. Ms Perry struggled with being away from work, where she saw herself as a competent and well-regarded professional, whereas parenting Donald was stressful and isolating. Mr Perry worked full-time as a social worker in a public hospital and cared for Donald in the evenings.

Motor, language and toileting milestones were reached within average limits. Donald experienced no major separations from his attachment figures, and was often cared for by maternal and paternal grandparents. These times of separation were usually fraught with initial separation anxieties, which eventually settled. Donald encountered the usual childhood illnesses.

When Donald was aged 3 and then at 5, he was joined by his two sisters, Tara and Dana, respectively. Donald's adjustment to Tara and Dana seemed appropriate, although he was a little anxious about starting kindergarten and then school, milestones that coincided with each of his sister's entrance into the family. He required extra attention from his parents and grandparents, to which he responded well.

At primary school, he generally adapted positively to social and academic challenges and became an above average student who was well liked by peers and teachers. When he was six years old, Tara became ill with severe asthma and was admitted to hospital on several occasions. Over a seven-month period, Ms Perry had stayed with her at the hospital on many occasions. Donald visited and missed his sister but also began to resent his mother's absence. Mr Perry reduced his work hours and became the primary parent during these times, with support from extended family. Both parents denied any major impact on Donald at this time, but noted that he became more vigilant of their whereabouts. Both parents acknowledged that a level of conflict and tension over parenting responsibilities began emerging at this time, that is, during 2001. From this period till just before the separation at the end of 2003, Donald was said to take on a different and more helpful attitude towards his sisters, even at times 'being like one of us … a daddy or mummy substitute'.

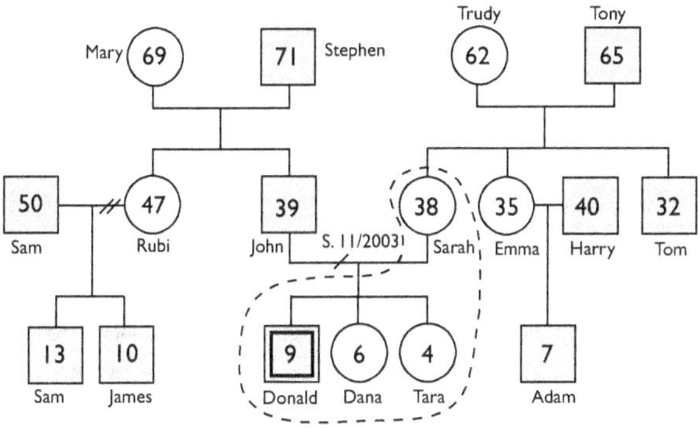

Figure 5.1

The Perry family genogram across three generations.

Family History

Maternal Family of Origin

Ms Perry is a 38-year-old accountant who currently works for a medium-size company. She is the eldest of three siblings (see Figure 5.1). Both her parents — Trudy and Tony — are retired; her father was a maths high school teacher and her mother a general nurse. Ms Perry's younger sister, Emma, works in administration, is married to Harry and they have a 7-year-old boy called Adam. Her brother, Tom, is the youngest, unemployed and living at home. Ms Perry maintains regular contact with her family and described herself as a strong and assertive woman.

Ms Perry described a happy and close-knit family life during her childhood. She was close to her sister, but reports an ambivalent relationship with her brother, whom she described as 'the baby' in the family and 'always been mummy's boy'. Ms Perry had been close to her parents but felt her mother drifted away emotionally about 10 years ago when Tony had a car accident and Trudy became very involved in his welfare. This time coincided with Ms Perry's marriage and pregnancy with Donald.

Tom is said to suffer with what appears as chronic depression and anxiety following a motor vehicle accident 10 years ago in which he sustained the loss of a limb and the death of his best friend. Subsequently, Tom moved back with his parents and has been cared for by his parents ever since. He has received some professional treatment with short-term improvement. No other family psychiatric history was reported.

Ms Perry recalled her adolescence and school life as 'fairly normal' and healthy. Ms Perry was an above average student and appeared to have a positive social history. She had several romantic relationships prior to meeting her husband at the age of 25. She married him at 27. She described a satisfying and supportive relationship. While the first two children had been planned and wanted, Dana was an accident and Ms Perry felt her husband would have preferred a termination. She felt they struggled to parent her as she was a more demanding and sensitive child compared to Tara and Donald. The couple separated in November 2003 and the children reside with their mother. Contact arrangements are usually fortnightly during weekends, but have been erratic. Conflict revolves around Mr Perry wanting Donald to live with him and feeling unable to cope with having all three children during weekend visits, especially with Dana's emotional needs and Tara's physical needs (around her asthma).

Paternal Family of Origin

Mr Perry is a 39-year-old social worker, who currently works in a public hospital. He is the younger of two children to his parents, Stephen and Mary, aged 71 and 69 respectively. A sister, Rubi, is a 49-year-old partner in a large law firm, divorced with two boys aged 13 (Sam Jnr) and 10 (James) who live interstate with their father, Sam (see Figure 5.1).

Stephen is a retired bus driver and described as a caring but absent father. Mary has always been at home and was described as 'needy' and 'snobby', and very proud of Rubi's successful career. Mr Perry had always felt closer to his father, while his sister was said to be closer to their mother. Mr Perry has minimal contact with his sister due to her work commitments and described an indifferent relationship with no shared interests or values over the years as siblings. Mr Perry's self-description was marked by some self-doubt and a little disappointment. There is neither history of mental illness in the family nor any significant medical problems.

Mr Perry struggled socially at school, as he did not fit in with the male-only culture of sports and competitive values, which paralleled his relationship with his sister. While a bright and successful student who was liked by his teachers, he had few friends. Mr Perry had a more positive social experience at university where there was more choice of friends and more contact with females. He had several romantic relationships with women that seemed to end in 'being left behind'.

Mr Perry enjoys his work despite the stressors. He reports drinking a bottle of wine each evening when he is not caring for his children. He has received a couple of fines for driving while intoxicated. He has no significant medical history.

Mr Perry admits to struggling with his daughters' care and ambivalently regrets having three children. He believes he and his wife need counselling but has not been able to convince her to get help.

Mental Status Examination

Overall Donald's mental state did not alter significantly during the individual assessment. On examination he was cooperative and his test performance appeared to be a reliable index of his functioning. He engendered warmth and some rapport developed, despite him being a sad, withdrawn and at times irritable child. His irritability was more evident when challenged cognitively, during the Thematic Apperception Test (TAT) administration and when reflecting on his family. There was neither motor retardation nor unusual behaviours. Speech was impoverished yet well communicated. He was oriented to person, place and time. Donald denied suicidal ideation but guilt and self-blame were prominent thought content, in addition to some confusion and despair about the future of his family, to which he also attributed self-blame. No obsessions, specific fears, delusions, or formal thought disorder were observed or elicited. Neither were there any illusions or hallucinations. Some insight was noted but he tended to mitigate his sadness and anger with self-blame and displacement.

Psychological Testing

Tests Administered

- Parents: ASEBA Child Behaviour Checklist (CBCL)
- Teacher: Student Behaviour Survey (SBS)
- Donald:
    - Wechsler Intelligence Scale for Children—IV (WISC-IV)
    - Wechsler Individual Achievement Test (WIAT)
    - Neale Analysis of Reading Ability
    - Personality Inventory for Youth (PIY)
    - Thematic Apperception Test (TAT)
    - Free drawings

Test Results and Interpretation

Prior to Donald's individual sessions, each parent completed the CBCL, and his teacher the SBS. Mother's CBCL showed elevations on the following subscales: Aggressive Behaviour, Social Problems and Attention Problems. Father's CBCL indicated a similar profile as well as clinical elevations on the Withdrawn subscale. In summary, the parents' responses focus on externalising behaviour, although Donald's father is also suggesting his son has become less emotionally accessible. The teacher's SBS profile indicated that Donald's academic resources were a concern with poor achievement levels, low participation in the classroom and diminished social skills. The teacher perceived adequate involvement from the parents. The major areas of psychological maladjustment identified by Donald's teacher centred on mood-related difficulties (self-critical, anhedonic, emotionally labile, preoccupied/strange) and social disruptiveness (argumentative, impulsive, angers peers by insensitive behaviour).

Donald was seen individually on two occasions. Cognitive testing on the WISC-IV estimated Donald's general intellectual ability to be within the average range (50th percentile). There were no major discrepancies between the major scales, but there was evidence of reduced processing speed and auditory attention span. Educational testing revealed no major deficits in reading and spelling, but some mild delay in arithmetic skills.

On the PYI, Donald's self-reported ratings included a number of subscale elevations. He was experiencing significant Psychological Discomfort (depression), Family Dysfunction (parent–child conflict, parental maladjustment and marital discord) and Cognitive Impairment (poor achievement & memory, learning problems). The Delinquency scale showed marginally high elevations (with noncompliance, antisocial behaviour and dyscontrol).

Finally, Donald's drawings and TAT responses exhibited themes of family disintegration, confusion of roles, feelings of guilt, loneliness, hopelessness and helplessness, as well as anger with authority figures for perceived injustices.

Formulation

Donald is a 9-year-old in Grade 4, living with his separated mother and two younger sisters. His teacher referred him with concerns about a possible learning disorder contributing to diminishing academic achievement, an aggressive manner and provoked angry outbursts towards peers, and increasing isolation from peers. At home, he was withdrawing from contact with family, easily frustrated with his sisters, failing to put on weight with reduced appetite, morning tiredness, nonspecific somatic pain, and not completing his usual chores. In essence, Donald presented with a major depression characterised by a 12-month history of sustained lowered and irritable mood, poor concentration with underachievement, loss of interest in usual activities and loss of peer relationships, as well as sleep, appetite and somatic disturbance. While usually well liked at school, Donald was becoming increasingly socially isolated at school and home due to his disruptive behaviour, which was secondary to his depression. His diminished academic performance also appears secondary to the depression. His developmental history indicates some anxiety and possibly insecurity in response to separations from attachment figures, which may predispose him to internalising psychopathology such as depression and a tendency to attribute causes of interpersonal problems to himself. An uncle with a history of anxiety and depression hints at the presence of genetic vulnerability to mood disorders.

Twelve months ago, his parents separated acrimoniously, and continue to fight over contact arrangements. This is a likely precipitant to Donald's difficulties. Donald appears to hold the belief that he is to blame for the separation. He feels overly responsible yet frustrated by his inability to attend to his other needs and extrafamilial demands. This usually leads to displacing his guilt and anger to siblings and peers, as his feelings are not processed with him within the family. His mother is conflicted in her parenting, drawn to her daughters' needs but less connected with Donald's, yet relies on Donald to help her with managing the younger children. Her family of origin experiences suggest emotional vulnerabilities related to unresolved resentment towards the relationship between her mother and brother, which appears to undermine her sensitivity to her son. For Donald, a closer relationship with his father comes at the cost of the father's ambivalent parental investment with his sisters and ongoing conflict with mother. Donald's father has reported a history consistent with perceived inadequacy as a man and a parent, which may be related to unexamined conflict with his mother and older sister, as well as an underinvolved relationship with his own father. This family of origin history has contributed to significant difficulties for the parents in coping with the task of successfully incorporating all three children. Protective factors include the family's willingness to seek help, the absence of comorbid disorders, Donald's positive premorbid peer and academic history, and his willingness to engage despite his distress. In addition, a responsive school environment, and accessible grandparents (despite fraught relationships with the parents) are all positive resources for Donald and his family.

Diagnosis

Axis I:	Major depression, moderate, single episode
Axis II:	Nil.
	Psychological defences include displacement and overidentification.
	Likely internal and global attribution style to negative events
	Possible insecure attachment status under stress.
Axis III:	Nil
Axis IV:	Parental separation and ongoing conflict with parental disharmony.
	Siblings with notable medical and emotional needs.
	New school environment.
Axis V:	GAF = 55

Treatment Plan

Treatment will need to attend to Donald's depression, his parents' ongoing conflict and parental responsibilities, as well as reconnecting him with his social network and attending to his academic difficulties at school. Accordingly, the following concurrent treatment plan is recommended:

- Integrated psychoeducation, interpersonal and play therapy for Donald
- Parent therapy
- School-based support and interventions
- Family sessions
- Medication: medication would be considered if the above psychological approaches fail to produce desirable change, particularly from the point of view of Donald's mood disturbance and related symptoms.

Dr Cherine Habib, Clinical Psychologist, CAMHS
October 24, 2004

Commentary on the Assessment

Aims and Techniques Used in the Assessment

Donald's case illustrates that depression in childhood manifests itself in developmentally appropriate features and that an assessment must take this into account for an accurate diagnosis. In addition, depression, as an internalising disorder, may be overlooked by behaviour that is directed externally towards others and objects and by educational difficulties. Features such as negativistic and angry behaviour with aggressive outbursts, poor academic achievement, and failure to gain weight or size and somatic complaints were all features in Donald's childhood presentation. Furthermore, at Donald's age, and unlike depression in adolescence and adulthood, his insights into his own experience of depression (that is, with respect to his sensations, emotions, thoughts and behaviour) are only beginning to emerge and be communicated directly. Consequently, the clinical assessment required an examination of his (and any child's) experience through multiple means, including the parents' report of history, direct clinical observation, significant others' reports (e.g., teachers and other professionals), the impact on his functioning and the incorporation of validated psychological tests and other useful assessment tools.

The assessment also highlights that the process of differential diagnosis and examining comorbidity are always a necessary part of a comprehensive integrative psychological evaluation. Donald's teacher thought he had a learning difficulty and remarked on his angry behaviour, while his mother emphasised Donald's behavioural disturbance. It was important to rule out the presence of a specific learning disorder or a disruptive behaviour disorder. In the end, it was a comprehensive evaluation that led to the opinion that Donald's educational and behavioural symptoms spoke of his coping with overwhelming unhappiness, rather than being a result of primary learning or antisocial disorders.

Donald's depression was best understood from the interplay between individual and contextual influences and resources. Donald's individual maladaptive contributions included his possible genetic vulnerability to a mood disorder, somewhat insecure attachment to his mother in particular, and his maladaptive cognitive attribution style. Donald's adaptive characteristics included his positive adaptation to school, including his academic achievement and peer sociability prior to the separation, as well as his estimated intellectual ability and capacity to engage and respond to others. Unfortunately, one of the most distressing disruptions a child can experience — a marital separation — is likely to be experienced severely in a child like Donald; that is, an internally focused child with a probable insecure attachment status under stress and enough intelligence to be too negatively thoughtful about his experience. With all this, combined with parents who are distracted by their own troubles and vulnerable to emotional disconnectedness with their children, the scene is primed for a depressive disorder. On the other hand, the parents do realise a problem exists that requires their attention and help from others, and the wider social environment (i.e., school and grandparents) appear available and responsive. Thus, it is probable that the severity of the depression has been mitigated by such protective factors.

Finally, on the question of assessment process, it is recommended that the characteristics of the child be considered when deciding on the sequence of the assessment method. For example, with children of Donald's age and presentation (possible existence of a learning disorder and reported withdrawn demeanour), it is best that the assessment process commence with more structured activities such as cognitive tests, or structured interviews than with potentially distressing or defence-producing unstructured methods such as projective tests, which may have a counterproductive impact on subsequent activities in the assessment.

Choice of Measures

One of the hallmarks of psychological assessment is the gathering of data from different sources and using multiple techniques and tools to arrive at a diagnosis and formulation (Groth-Marnat, 2009). Each informant's perspective — and it is important to remember that perceptions are just that, not facts — provides data to be understood and integrated. In cases involving children, this assessment principle is particularly relevant, as children are limited by their developmental capacities and highly dependent on the network of adults and environments in which they function (Smith & Handler, 2007). In Donald's case, the teacher's, mother's, father's and Donald's perceptions provided relevant information arising from their knowledge and experience and, in turn, provided a piece of the puzzle for the assessment. Relying on only one informant, using one method would have precluded an accurate and full assessment.

A variety of psychometric tools are available to the psychologist in assessing depression in a child (see Sattler & Hoge, 2005; and Semrud-Clikeman, Fine, & Butcher, 2007). There are a number of structured and semistructured clinical interviews, clinical rating scales (for children, parents and teachers) and projective methods, as well as general nonstructured clinical interviews that include both verbal and nonverbal behaviour of the informants. Not all methods have the same degree of reliability and validity or ease of use in terms of their length and administration, in terms of having complementary informant forms and the level of training required for their use. In addition, the methods are not all appropriate for all ages, nor are all clinicians experts in all methods. Accordingly, the choice becomes delineated by a number of variables in the case at hand.

The choice of methods used with Donald relied upon using a combination of widely used and validated instruments that were appropriate for his age and assessment needs (e.g., an ASEBA scale such as the Child Behaviour Checklist, the Student Behaviour Survey, the Wechsler Intelligence Scale for Children–IV, the Wechsler Individual Achievement Test, the Neale Analysis of Reading Ability, and the Personality Inventory for Youth). In addition, a nonstructured clinical interview process was conducted in routine phases within a hospital-based CAMHS (including a family session and parent session) to gather as much historical and other contextual information as required about Donald's presentation. A number of projective methods (such as his free drawings, story-telling and free play) provided some insight into Donald's mental state during the two individual sessions.

A potentially useful tool to assess attachment status in middle-childhood is the Manchester Child Attachment Story Task (MCAST) by Green, Stanley, Smith and Goldwyn (2000). It is a validated semi-structured standardised test, which uses relationship-oriented story tasks with children aged 4½–8½ years of age. Unfortunately, Donald was technically too old for the MCAST, and formal licensed training limited its administration and interpretation.

Choice of Treatment

Most treatment plans concerning childhood disorders inevitably require a coordinated integrative approach based on a combination of factors: the diagnostic formulation arising from the assessment, the scientific evidence base for technical interventions (including efficacy, effectiveness and pragmatic wisdom from case studies), the individual characteristics of the clients involved (such as their goals, motivations, preferences, resources), and the clinical experience, training and judgment of the clinical psychologist. This approach is in keeping with local and international standards of evidence-based practice (American Psychological Association, 2005; Australian Psychological Society, 2010; National Institute of Health and Clinical Excellence [NICE] of the United Kingdom) and practice-based evidence (Charman & Barkham, 2005). In the case presented in this chapter, treatment involved five elements that have been guided by the assessment process and findings, as well as these factors. Let us discuss these treatments in brief detail.

Integrated psychoeducation and interpersonal therapy with play techniques for Donald. Most of the evidence base for the efficacy and effectiveness of psychological treatment for depression points towards the most researched therapies — such as psychoeducation, cognitive–behavioural and interpersonal therapies (Brown et al., 2008; Carr, 2006; Fonagy, Target, Cottrell, Phillips, & Kurtz, 2005) — and largely in relation to adapting adult approaches to adolescents. The proposed intervention arises from what is available in the limited evidence-based literature for children, as well as the author's experience and training. Such an approach aims to educate Donald about the nature of his distress, what has contributed to his depression and assist him in relieving or at least managing his symptoms. The therapy would utilise his strengths (intellect, motivation, personality) and his natural childhood inclination to play to examine maladaptive perceptions of himself and others and enhance his emotional and interpersonal coping. Initially, given his likely defensive verbal reluctance, play may offer a less confronting, less demanding and more engaging mode of therapeutic interaction. The individual treatment will also assist him in distancing himself from the unresolved tension between his parents while working through and validating his conflicting emotions and thoughts arising from the separation. The therapeutic relationship with the psychologist will form a foundation of trust and relational experience, through which play and verbal discussion can occur. In conjunction with the other interventions, this will hopefully alleviate feelings of guilt, sadness and grief, making him more available for (or less frustrated by and avoidant of) age-appropriate pursuits, such as learning, socialising, sibling interaction and sporting activity.

Parent therapy. Apart from feedback and discussion about the formulation, the main aim of this treatment component is to support and intervene with the parents in relation to their conflict over their responsibilities towards each other and the children, and their adjustment to the separation. Helping them see the roots of vulnerability from their transition into parenthood and their families of origin may provide needed perspective to reunite them on the task of dealing with their responsibilities in more adaptive ways. This would then be complemented by a pragmatic focus, with specific communication and parenting strategies as suggested by the research evidence (Fonagy et al., 2005). The need for concurrent or subsequent individual therapy for either parent would be considered when indicated.

School-based interventions. The aim here would be to dispel concerns regarding the question of a learning disorder and to suggest practical ways in which the school could support Donald. Ideally, this intervention would provide:

1. feedback to the teacher about testing results
2. a plan to diminish social isolation:
   - Create a buddy dyad for support and social integration, which could arise out of the class intervention, so as to prevent potential stigma and generalise learning to all students.
   - If other children in Donald's class have shown signs of behavioural or emotional difficulties, it might be desirable that the class receive educational input on emotional wellness and how students & teachers can support each other (e.g., use of KidsMatter material). This is preferably facilitated by the school psychologist, or by the CAMHS clinician as an alternative.
3. recalibration of expectations regarding work output to reduce level of stress and create experiences of mastery
4. a set of tangible rewards for desirable behaviour, such as seeking help from teacher, schoolwork production, and class participation
5. liaison with the sports teacher to devise an approach to entice Donald to return to his usual sporting activities; for example, using a buddy system or graduated expectations of involvement and re-mastery.

Family sessions. It may be helpful to schedule some family sessions after some progress has been made, at least within the parent therapy. There is some evidence for the helpfulness of family therapy for depression in children (Carr, 2009). There is also a good theoretical basis given that depression in children usually arises in association with stressful social systems where there is limited access to supportive relationships (Shortt & Spence, 2006). Family-based therapy thus aims to reduce stress and increase support for young people within their families. In Donald's family, sessions with family members may assist communication and validation of feelings, delineation of responsibilities and more cohesion between members. Family sessions would also enable the inclusion of Donald's siblings into treatment and provide opportunities for intervening with the family as a whole, as well as evaluating progress of family functioning. Donald's depression is, in part, a response to the family's difficulties in adapting to various family life cycle transition points, more recently the separation, but also in relation to moving from a couple to becoming a family and coping with children's needs. Moreover, family sessions can illustrate to all members the resources they have as a family to cope with their problems.

Medication. Medication would be considered if the above psychological approaches fail to produce desirable change, particularly from the point of view of Donald's mood disturbance and related symptoms. There is no substantial scientific evidence for the first-line use of antidepressant medication for primary school-aged children with mild to moderate depression (Brown et al., 2008).

Endnote

1 This case assessment is fictional and is to be used for the purposes of demonstration only. Any resemblance to persons known is entirely coincidental.

References

American Psychiatric Association. (2000). *Diagnostic and statistical manual of mental disorders* (Revised 4th ed.). Washington, DC: Author.

American Psychological Association. (2005). *Policy statement on evidence-based practice in psychology. 2005 presidential task force on evidence-based practice.* Washington, DC: Author.

Angold, A., & Costello, E.J. (2006). Puberty and depression. *Child and Adolescent Psychiatric Clinics of North America, 15,* 919–937.

Australian Institute of Health and Welfare. (2003). *Australia's young people: Their health and wellbeing 2003* (AIHW Cat. No. PHE 50). Canberra, Australia: Author.

Australian Psychological Society. (2010). *Evidence-based psychological interventions in the treatment of mental disorders: A literature review* (3rd ed.) Melbourne, Australia: Author.

Birmaher, B., Ryan, N.D., Williamson, D.E., Brent, D.A., Kaufman, J., Dahl, R.E., Perel, J., & Nelson, B. (1996). Childhood and adolescent depression: Part I. A review of the past ten years. *Journal of the Academy of Child and Adolescent Psychiatry, 35,* 1427–1439.

Brown, R.T., Antonuccio, D.O., DuPaul, C.J., Fristad, M.A., King, C.A., Leslie, L.K. et al. (2008). *Childhood mental health disorders: Evidence base and contextual factors for psychosocial, psychopharmacological, and combined interventions.* Washington, DC: American Psychological Association.

Carr, A. (2006). *The handbook of child and adolescent clinical psychology: A contextual approach* (2nd ed.). London: Routledge.

Carr, A. (2009). The effectiveness of family therapy and systemic interventions for child focused problems. *Journal of Family Therapy, 41*, 3–45.

Charman, D. & Barkham, M. (2005). Psychological treatments: Evidence-based practice and practice-based evidence. *InPsych, 27*, 8–13.

Collishaw, S., Maughan, B., Goodman, R., & Pickles, A. (2004). Time trends in adolescent mental health. *Journal of Child Psychology and Psychiatry, 45*(8), 1350–1362.

Costello, E.J., Mustillo, S., Erkanli, A., Keeler, G., & Angold, A. (2003). Prevalence and development of psychiatric disorders in childhood and adolescence. *Archives of General Psychiatry, 60*(8), 837–844.

Costello, E.J., Erkanli, A., & Angold, A. (2006). Is there an epidemic of child or adolescent depression? *Journal of Child Psychology and Psychiatry, 47*, 1263–1271.

Fonagy, P., Target, M., Cottrell, D., Phillips, J., & Kurtz, Z. (2005). *What works for whom? A critical review of treatments for children and adolescents.* New York: Guilford.

Frombonne, E. (1998). Increased rates of psychosocial disorders in youth. *European Archives of Psychiatry and Clinical Neuroscience, 248*, 14–21.

Green, J., Stanley, C., Smith, V., & Goldwyn, R. (2000). A new method of evaluating attachment representations in young school-age children: The Manchester child attachment story task. *Attachment & Human Development, 2*(1), 48–70.

Groth-Marnat, G. (2009). *Handbook of psychological assessment* (5th ed.). New York: John Wiley & Sons.

Hammen, C., & Rudolph, K.D. (2003). Childhood mood disorders. In E. Mash and R. Barkley (Eds.), *Child Psychopathology* (2nd ed., pp. 233–278). New York: Guilford Press.

Kidsmatter. (2009). *Australian primary schools mental health initiative.* Retrieved December 8, 2009, from http://www.kidsmatter. edu.au/primary

Lancaster, S. (Ed.). (2003). *Psychologists working with depression across the lifecycle.* Brisbane, Australia: Australian Academic Press.

Lewinsohn, P.M., Clarke, G.N., Seeley, J.R., & Rohde, P. (1994). Major depression in community adolescents: Age at onset, episode duration, and time to recurrence. *Journal of the American Academy of Child and Adolescent Psychiatry, 33*, 809–818.

Lewinsohn, P.M., Hops, H., Roberts, R.E., Seeley, J.R., & Andrews, J.A. (1993). Adolescent psychopathology: I. Prevalence and incidence of depression and other DSM-III-R disorders in high school students. *Journal of Abnormal Psychology, 102*, 133–144.

Lewinsohn, P.M., Rohde, P., & Seeley, J.R. (1998). Major depressive disorder in older adolescents: Prevalence, risk factors and clinical implications. *Clinical Psychology Review, 18*, 765–794.

National Health and Medical Research Council. (1997). *Depression in young people: Clinical practice guidelines.* Canberra, Australia: Commonwealth Department of Health and Family Services.

National Institute of Health and Clinical Excellence (NICE) Guidelines. (2009). Retrieved on December 10, 2009, from http://www.nice.org.uk/

Patton, G.C., & Viner, R. (2007). Pubertal transitions in health. *The Lancet*, 369, 1130–1139.

Rudolph, K., Hammen, C., & Daley, S. (2006). Adolescent mood disorders. In D.A. Wolfe & E.J. Mash (Eds.), *Behavioral and emotional disorders in adolescence: Nature, assessment, and treatment* (pp. 300–342). New York: Guilford.

Rudolph, K., Hammen, C., & Daley, S. (2006). Adolescent mood disorders. In D.A. Wolfe & E.J. Mash (Eds.), *Behavioral and emotional disorders in adolescence: Nature, assessment, and treatment* (pp. 300–342). New York: Guilford Press.

Sattler, J.M., & Hoge, R.D. (2005). *Assessment of children: Behavioral, social, and clinical foundations* (5th ed.). San Diego, CA: Jerome M. Sattler.

Sawyer, M.G., Arney, P.A., Baghurst, J.J., Clark, B.W., Graetz, R.J., Kosky, B., et al. (2001). The mental health of young people in Australia: Key findings from the child and adolescent component of the national survey of mental health and well-being. *Australian and New Zealand Journal of Psychiatry, 35*, 806–814.

Semrud-Clikeman, M., Fine, J.G., & Butcher, B. (2007). The assessment of depression in children and adolescents. In S.R. Smith & L. Handler (Eds.), *The clinical assessment of children and adolescents: A practitioner's handbook* (pp.485–503). Mahwah, NJ: Lawrence Erlbaum Associates.

Shortt, A., & Spence, S. (2006). Risk and protective factors for depression in youth. *Behaviour Change, 23*, 1–30.

Sims, B.E., Nottelmann, E.D., Koretz, D., & Pearson, J. (2006). Prevention of depression in children and adolescents. *American Journal of Preventative Medicine, 31*(6, Suppl. 1), 99–103.

Smith, S.R., & Handler, L. (Eds.). (2007). *The clinical assessment of children and adolescents: A practitioner's handbook.* Mahwah, NJ: Lawrence Erlbaum Associates.

Stark, K.D., Sander, J.B., Yancy, M.G., Bronick, M.D., & Hoke, J.A. (2000). Treatment of depression in childhood and adolescence: Cognitive behavioural procedures for the individual and family. In P.C. Kendall (Ed.), *Child and adolescent therapy: Cognitive–behavioral procedures* (2nd ed., pp. 173–234). New York: Guilford Press.

Speier, P.L., Sherak, D.L., Hirsch, S., & Cantwell, D.P. (1995). Depression in children and adolescents. In E.E. Beckham & W.R. Leber (Eds.), *Handbook of depression* (2nd ed., pp. 467–566). New York: Guilford Press.

CHAPTER 6

The Clinical Assessment of a Child Presenting With Tics, Obsessive Behaviours and Problems With Attention

Jane A. McGillivray

This case highlights the difficulties associated with determining which of several possible diagnoses fits the clinical presentation (differential diagnosis) and whether there is a simultaneous co-occurrence of more than one independent clinical diagnosis (psychiatric comorbidity).

Differential diagnosis is complicated, in particular, by the somewhat artificial subdivision of syndromes and the high prevalence of overlapping diagnostic criteria evident across different disorders. In addition, the source and nature of the referral can introduce bias and the phenomenon of diagnostic overshadowing can limit consideration of alternate more appropriate diagnoses. In general, diagnostic practice should adhere to the law of parsimony; that is, 'plurality should not be postulated without necessity' (attributed to William of Ockham, 1285–1349). The potential for artifactual comorbidity is widely acknowledged and suggests caution in any determination of multiple diagnoses. However, it is also the case that more than one diagnosis may be required to accurately describe the set of difficulties evident in a particular clinical presentation.

This case also demonstrates the importance of a comprehensive assessment in which information across a variety of domains is derived from multiple sources and across different settings. Although the assessment process commenced with a referral, the limited information derived from this source was supplemented and challenged by information gained from a direct assessment of the child, informant report from both a parent and teacher, information from a previous assessment and an observation in a naturalistic setting. The use of multiple sources enables confirmation of findings and the development of an integrated picture of the child to inform a diagnosis. A diagnostic assessment of a child requires a developmental history, the determination of their age at symptom onset and a close examination of the consistency and pervasiveness of symptoms across lifetime and settings. It is important to examine the forms and quality of presenting symptoms and to determine whether they present the full range of symptoms consistent with a particular diagnosis, whether they are limited to those plausibly encompassed by the diagnostic criteria for a particular disorder, or whether they extend beyond these and thus justify a comorbid diagnosis.

The importance of accuracy in the assessment and diagnostic process is underscored. A missed or an incorrect diagnosis can result in the child being denied treatment or receiving treatment that is inappropriate to their condition. Overdiagnosis can also result in less than optimal treatment. Such inaccuracies, in turn, can impact negatively on the child's development and functioning, as well as reduce the quality of life experienced by the child and their family.

The Case of Jacob

CLINICAL PSYCHOLOGY ASSESSMENT[1]
PRIVATE AND CONFIDENTIAL

CASE FILE NUMBER: 133447

NAME: Jacob

ADDRESS:	32 Umpire Street, Warendale North, Victoria
AGE:	10
DOB:	January 1, 1999
REFERRED BY:	Dr M. Seagee, GP
CLINICIAN:	Dr Susan Nasus, Clinical Psychologist, Head First Clinic
DATES SEEN:	June 15, 2009 (initial interview with mother); June 17 (assessment interview 1 with Jacob); June 24 (assessment interview 2 with Jacob); June 30 (observation of Jacob at school and interview of teacher); July 14 (feedback, treatment planning and report to referring general practitioner).

Presenting Problems

Jacob is a 10-year-old boy who was referred by a local general practitioner (GP) for a diagnostic assessment. In his referral letter, Dr Seagee explained that Jacob's family were new to his practice. During a routine health check, his mother had expressed her concerns about Jacob. She reported that he had a number of tics and, in her estimation, they appeared to be getting more pronounced. He also displayed obsessive behaviours and problems with attention and organisation. Dr Seagee's referral letter specifically queried attention deficit hyperactive disorder (ADHD), obsessive–compulsive disorder and perhaps also Tourette's disorder as possible diagnoses. A previous teacher had also suggested to his mother that Jacob may have ADHD.

Source of Information

During initial telephone contact with the family, Jacob's mother requested an initial session without Jacob being present. She explained that he was quite sensitive to discussions about his behaviour and she wanted an opportunity to talk freely about his tics, as well as the results from a previous educational assessment. Her request was granted.

The information obtained in this report was derived from an extended interview with his mother, which included administration of the Yale Global Tic Severity Scale (YGTSS; Leckman et al., 1989) and the Autism Spectrum Quotient–Children's Version (AQ-Child; Auyeung et al., 2008); the results of an assessment with the Wechsler Intelligence Scale for Children — Fourth Edition (WISC-IV; Wechsler, 2003) conducted in October 2008 by a school psychologist in Tasmania; two interviews with Jacob; and a school visit that included observation of him in the school setting and an interview with his teacher. The information obtained from these sources is amalgamated in the various sections of this report.

Family Structure and History

Jacob is the eldest of two children (see genogram, Figure 6.1). His sister, Becky, is 6 years old and is completing her first year at the same school as Jacob. Becky is an easygoing child who has settled into school easily and has no tics, obsessive characteristics or other behavioural problems. The family moved to Melbourne from Tasmania approximately 6 months ago.

Jacob's mother, Diane, is a registered nurse who works two shifts per week in the emergency department at the local hospital. Her father is deceased and her mother and two sisters live in Tasmania, where her sisters are both married with five children between them. Diane described her family as close and supportive. Diane's family were unremarkable for tics, obsessive–compulsive symptoms and any neurologic or other psychiatric problems.

Jacob's father Ron is a computer science graduate who works in information technology. Ron's parents are both deceased and he has two brothers. The elder brother is described as 'a bit of a loner' who has never married. The

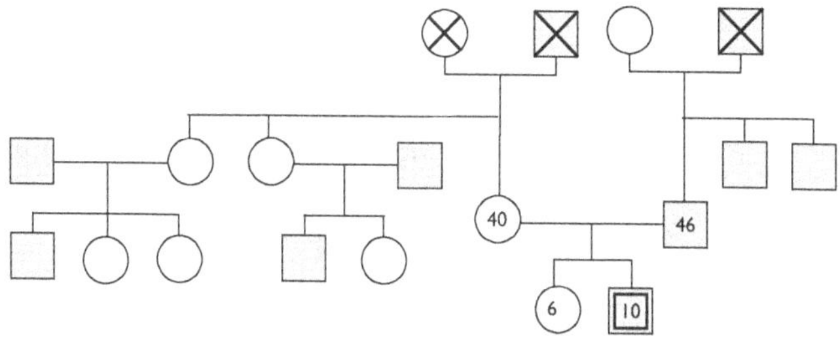

Figure 6.1

Family genogram.

younger brother has an intellectual disability in the moderate range and receives full-time care in a community residential unit. Diane did not know very much about this brother-in-law, but was able to recall that he was nonverbal and made a high pitched noise, particularly when he was agitated. Both Ron's siblings live in the outer eastern suburbs of Melbourne, although Diane reported that they rarely have contact with each other. She described Ron as a very hard worker who does not have much time for socialising. She did not think that he had any particular obsessions or tics, although on further prompting, she disclosed that he often cleared his throat several times in succession, particularly in the evenings when he was watching television.

Medical History

Jacob has mild eczema, but no other medical conditions. His mother reported that there had been an initial query about the possibility that his tics were a form of epilepsy, but this had been discounted by a paediatrician on the basis of the variability of his movements. Jacob had occasionally used an antihistamine cream for his eczema, but was currently using only moisturiser to relieve the itch. He had no other history of medication use.

Developmental History

According to his mother, Jacob was the product of a normal gestation and delivery. He was a colicky baby who was difficult to settle. Diane breastfed him for three months, but then switched to formula because his weight gain was below that expected and she thought that he may not be getting enough milk. She reported that she had felt overwhelmed with parenting her first child and that at times she wondered whether she lacked the 'maternal instinct' that other mothers seemed to have. Looking back, and with the experience of her second child, Becky, she now thinks that Jacob really was a very difficult baby. When asked to describe life with Jacob as a toddler, Diane recalled that he would get very upset at any change in his environment or activities and she was forced to stick to a fairly tight routine to avoid tantrums. He had not been especially interested in the birth of his sister, although he often started yelling when she was crying. He commonly overreacted and sometimes displayed emotion inappropriate to a particular situation, such as giggling when another child was hurt or upset. He was a very fussy eater and refused to try many foods, preferring to stick to a few favourite foods, such as fish fingers and bananas. He also appeared to have a decreased need for sleep, being both difficult to settle and frequently waking during the night. This contributed significantly to the household stress at that time.

Jacob's key developmental milestones, including language development, were within the normal range. He was using single words communicatively at 18 months old and spontaneous phrases before he was 3 years old. He displayed curiosity about household appliances and how they worked at a young age. The only odd communicative behaviour that his mother could recall was his refusal to wave goodbye. Also, he rarely smiled and photos of him during his early years show a serious-looking child. Diane reported that he developed adaptive behaviours, including toilet training, at the appropriate age. His cognitive abilities were well developed and he commenced school with advanced literacy and numeracy skills. According to his mother, he seemed to have learnt these on his own through his interest in learning all he could about his football team.

Behavioural Characteristics

During the assessment interview and school observation, Jacob was observed to have several tics. These consisted of bilateral nasal contraction as well as occasional lip pursing, throat clearing and teeth clicking. He also exhibited stereotypic hand gestures with frequent touching of the opposite hand. During the school observation, it was particularly noted that his hand gestures increased in frequency during tasks with time limitations.

Jacob's mother reported that she first noticed that he exhibited grunts and sniffing when he was seven years of age. Prior to this time, he had some abnormal tongue movements as well as blinking and staring. The grunting and sniffing have increased in frequency and severity and now occur several times each day. The clicking of teeth has only been evident during the past six months. During the assessment interview, it was established that Jacob was aware of his tics. He described them as occurring abruptly when he was engaging in normal activities. Frequently they were preceded by a sensation of vague discomfort (premonitory sensation[2]) and sometimes he was able to suppress them temporarily. He expressed concern that they were getting worse and that he was being teased by the other children at school.

Jacob's mother also reported that he exhibited some ritualistic behaviours. Most particularly, he turns his plate around several times during meal time and often sniffs his food prior to eating. He has remained fussy about his food. Although his repertoire had increased over time, he was still reluctant to vary his diet or to try new foods. He also puts his socks on in a very specific manner, involving a ritual of laying them out and smoothing them before he puts them on. He does not like 'fancy socks' — that is, anything other than his regular black or grey socks. In the interview, Jacob also acknowledged his ritualistic behaviour. He stated that he realised it was 'stupid' and that it made his mother cross. Although he tried to control it, this was only ever partially successful. He reported that he did not think about these behaviours beyond their occurrence and he was not aware of performing the activities to reduce anxiety. When asked how he would feel if he was prevented from completing the rituals, he responded, 'That would be weird, just not quite right ... and then for sure, I would do it next time.'

Language Skills

Although Jacob's language development was within the normal range and he was able to read before his peers, speech and language peculiarities were evident. During the assessment interview, it was noted that he did not readily modulate his voice to reflect rhythm or tone, particularly when he was directly answering a question. In addition, he was unusually talkative and displayed a formal style of conversation and sometimes used phrases that were overly complex. In contrast, he would sometimes respond with a simple 'Yes' to a question that would usually solicit a more detailed response.

Much of his conversation was peppered with facts and figures, mostly about football, even when it was not relevant to the topic at hand. In addition, he used odd expressions such as 'It will end up with a face to the tribunal'. He showed evidence of being quite literal in his interpretations. When asked the meaning of 'a stitch in time saves nine' Jacob responded 'the big dipper, 240 games between 75 and 91, and not forgetting Crawford'. It was subsequently established that he was referring to a former Hawthorn football player — Robert Dipierdomenico — who played in the number 9 jersey between 1975 and 1991, and more recently Shane Crawford who was also number 9.

Social Skills

Jacob was described by his mother as a child who seemed most comfortable with his own company. As a toddler, he was known for his building skills. At playgroup, the other mothers often commented to Diane that he was on his way to a career in engineering or building. Each session he would head for the Lego and other blocks and would spend the entire time constructing towers or bridges. He showed no interest in the games the other children played and became quite upset when others attempted to assist him with his building projects. Although he was happy to commence school, he did not readily engage with other children and was rarely included in parties and sleepovers. According to his mother, he had not seemed particularly bothered by this apparent exclusion when he was younger. She described that he was now more interested in playing with his peers, but that he was struggling in his efforts to form friendships at his new school. Apparently, the other children teased him about his tics. Diane also thought that perhaps he was trying too hard and this was off-putting to the other children. Jacob has increasingly shown signs of wanting to be accepted by his peers and had been hurt and frustrated by his lack of social success.

Jacob's current teacher described him as socially awkward and somewhat arrogant. She gave an example of how he often breaks into the conversation of others or tries to dominate with inappropriate content, but then may just walk away. In addition, the other children are upset when he points out their mistakes or blurts out something personal about them. She explained 'it's like he doesn't have any filters'.

During the school visit, Jacob was observed in a classroom activity involving some instruction from the teacher, followed by some project work. Jacob appeared to be not listening to the teacher. However, when she told the class that they were to work with their group and come up with some strategies for using fewer resources at school, he impulsively shouted out several strategies. He did not appear to be aware that this was inappropriate, despite the obvious displeasure evident on the face of his teacher, and he looked confused when the other children laughed. He was also observed pushing in on other children who were waiting in an orderly manner to collect materials. Having obtained the materials, he then set about working on his project independently and did not interact with his group. The other children at his table chattered and helped each other, but essentially ignored him. At lunch time, he grabbed a football and raced to the oval, where he was observed kicking it around the oval. Although there were other boys kicking footballs, he did not appear to playing with any of them.

At the assessment interview, Jacob greeted the psychologist with a handshake and said 'A very good morning to you'. He then proceeded to tell her that she shouldn't keep people waiting (the psychologist was delayed by a telephone call for no more than five minutes).

During the second interview, Jacob was asked about his relationship with other children. At first, he stated that his troubles may be the result of being new. He also thought that his tics made him stand out as different, and that he didn't really know what he needed to do to get other children to play with him.

Emotional Characteristics

Although both recognised that Jacob is sometimes hurt by the rejection and teasing he receives from some of his peers, neither Jacob's mother nor his teacher thought that he was depressed. Providing that he was permitted to pursue the things he liked to do, his teacher believed that he was 'quite happy'. His mother wondered if his self-esteem may be a bit low, due perhaps to the apparent discrepancy between his intelligence and his actual level of achievement, and also from the teasing he sometimes received from his peers.

Both informants also emphasised that Jacob did not like surprises and did not respond well to change in routine or inconsistencies. According to his teacher, Jacob becomes quite distressed when things do not work out the way he expected them to. On these and other stressful occasions, his tics increased in frequency. His teacher described a recent situation where the class had decided to vary the rules of a game they were playing. Jacob became extremely agitated, had shouted out that it was wrong and had then totally withdrawn from the activity. At this time, his tics were very pronounced.

His teacher also noted that his tics were particularly evident when he was under pressure to perform, such as when she set a time limit on an activity. She further reported that Jacob asked lots of questions about what was happening and apparently needed constant reassurance.

When asked during the assessment interview 'How do you/would you feel when ...?' Jacob appeared to be limited in his ability to fully describe his emotions. For example, when asked 'How would you feel if you were invited to watch a secret training session and then meet the Hawthorn football players?' he responded 'It would be OK to meet them, although a secret is a secret'. In response to a question about how he felt when he was teased by other children, he said 'They have no idea'. When prompted, 'But how do you feel?' he said, 'It's not a smiley feeling'.

Motor Skills

Although Jacob was observed kicking a football on the oval at school, he did not appear very proficient at the activity. According to his teacher, his ball catching and other perceptual motor skills were unusually poor for his age. His mother confirmed that he is not at all coordinated and has never been good at physical activities or sport. She also stated that he had never been particularly active and preferred more sedentary activities.

Special Interests

Jacob's mother described his interest in Australian Rules football as an obsession. She said that he had a phenomenal memory for facts around his beloved Hawthorn team and would watch video replays of the games all day if she allowed him. He could describe the tactics used in the various games and could recite the play statistics for every player. During the assessment interview, the extent of this special interest was evident when he was asked about his favourite activities. He continued to talk about football when it was clear that his audience had little interest in the topic and he persevered, even after he had been told that it was important that he focused on some other things for the remainder of the session.

Jacob is also very interested in computer games. He appears most relaxed when he is playing these games and can remain focused in his play for hours on end. Diane reported that he becomes quite angry when he is told that he has to switch it off.

Learning and Cognition

According to his teacher, Jacob's achievements in maths and reading are at least consistent with his peers and sometimes more advanced. She commented, however, that his performance varied with his interest level in the task at hand. For example, he is very skilled at completing puzzles and he is expert at calculating averages when they relate to 'footy scores'. It is well acknowledged by all who know him that Jacob has an extraordinary memory for facts about football. In contrast, however, his teacher reported that he often raised his hand in class and then claimed that he had forgotten his answer to the question — or even had forgotten the question. His mother also reported that he sometimes struggles with retaining simple information and particularly remembering the successive steps involved in completing a task.

According to his teacher, Jacob has difficulties with planning and organisation, especially relating to projects, completing his homework and other activities that require prioritising work within a time frame. She also referred to his difficulties in maintaining his attention to tasks in the classroom. Upon further questioning, she explained that his attention to detail was actually very good. However, he sometimes becomes distracted by irrelevant detail to the extent of missing the point of the activity. She explained that he appeared to have difficulty determining what to look for when confronted with a multifaceted problem and that she had come to understand that he does better when he is given specific instruction on what he should look for. Although brilliant at learning and reciting facts, he seems to have difficulties integrating these into any kind of conclusion or analysis. His ability to recite facts verbatim appears to have previously set him ahead of other children. However, the increasing expectation for analysis of information and consideration of different perspectives that is associated with his current educational level was resulting in a lower level of achievement in some areas than would be expected. During his assessment interview, when Jacob was asked about family activities and other events, he reported some irrelevant detail and did not portray a coherent overall story.

According to his mother, Jacob was impulsive and had problems in response inhibition when he was younger. He seemed to respond without thinking of the context and without reference to experience. She believes that he is now more able to think things out before deciding what to say or do, although he was still inclined to be impulsive when he was under stress or having to wait his turn.

Jacob was described by his teacher as a 'bit of a perfectionist' who is inclined to focus on accuracy rather than speed. She reported that he tended to get upset when he is corrected, appearing to regard any suggestion as a criticism. She further reported that Jacob has a 'one-track mind' and has difficulty shifting his attention from one task to another. For example, if the school bell rings before he has completed an activity, unlike the other children who commence packing up, Jacob continues working and gets very frustrated when he is told to cease. He also gets angry if he is redirected or required to switch activities, particularly if this is from a preferred activity, such as working on the computer. According to his teacher, he has an inability to modify his methods or plans on the basis of outcomes and he is reluctant to follow advice. He does not seem to learn from his mistakes, even when there are clear indications of a need for a change because his chosen strategy is not working. He does not readily examine options or different solutions and appears to lack self-monitoring and self-reflection, suggesting deficits in his use of internal dialogue. She noted, however, that this was in contrast to his tendency to talk to himself as he attempted to follow a plan. This kind of talking out loud was the source of additional teasing from his peers.

Intellectual Assessment

In October 2008, when Jacob was 9 years and 9 months old, he was assessed by a school psychologist with the Wechsler Intelligence Scale for Children — Fourth Edition (WISC-IV; Wechsler, 2003). Jacob's mother was not sure exactly why the assessment was undertaken, but she thought that it was to determine whether some difficulties he was experiencing in his school work were due to some kind of learning disability. Although she had a formal copy of the scaled scores for the 15 subtests administered and his composite scores, the remainder of the report had been lost in the move to Melbourne. She

WISC-IV Subtest and Index Scores

Jacob ....

Age at assessment: 9 yrs 9 months

Subtest	Aged scaled score
Block design	12
Similarities	11
Digit span	7
Picture concepts	12
Coding	6
Vocabulary	12
Letter-number sequence	6
Matrix reasoning	13
Comprehension	8
Symbol search	7
(Supplementary subtests):	
Picture completion	10
Cancellation	8
Information	13
Arithmetic	9
Word reasoning	10
Index Scores	
Full Scale IQ	96
Verbal comprehension	100
Perceptual reasoning	115
Working memory	80
Processing speed	83

Figure 6.2

Previous assessment using the WISC-IV.

recalled being told that his ability was uneven, but that he did not have a problem with intelligence and did not have a specific learning disability. My attempts to obtain a full copy of the report from the psychologist who was employed by Jacob's school in Tasmania had been unsuccessful.

Although some caution is needed in the interpretation of scores obtained by another psychologist and in the absence of a complete report, Jacob's general cognitive ability appears to be within the average range of intellectual functioning, as measured by the full scale IQ (FSIQ). His overall thinking and reasoning abilities exceed those of approximately 39% of children his age (FSIQ = 96; 95% confidence interval = 90–102).

Jacob's verbal reasoning abilities as measured by the Verbal Comprehension Index were in the average range and above those of approximately 50% of his peers (VCI = 100; 95% confidence interval = 92–108). The Verbal Comprehension Index is designed to measure verbal reasoning and concept formation. Jacob's performance on the comprehension subtest was less strong (Scaled Score = 8) than his performance on the other subtests (Similarities and Vocabulary) and his general knowledge was well developed (Information Scaled Score = 13). The comprehension test involves response to questions requiring an understanding of social situations, reflecting common sense, social judgment, behaviour and conventional standards.

Jacob's nonverbal reasoning abilities as measured by the Perceptual Reasoning Index were in the high average range and above those of approximately 84% of his peers (PRI = 115; 95% confidence interval = 106–122). The Perceptual Reasoning Index is designed to measure nonverbal concept formation, visual perception and organisation, simultaneous processing, visual-motor coordination, learning and the ability to separate figure and ground in visual stimuli. Jacob's performances on the subtests that contributed to the PRI were all in the high average range. His best performance was achieved on the nonverbal Matrix Reasoning subtest (Scaled Score = 13), with good scores also achieved on the Block Design and Picture Concepts subtests (Scaled Score = 12 respectively). The Matrix Reasoning subtest required Jacob to look at an incomplete matrix and select the missing portion from five response options. This subtest measures visual information processing and abstract reasoning skills. The Block Design subtest assesses ability to mentally organise visual information.

In contrast, Jacob's working memory abilities as measured by the Working Memory Index are in the Low Average/ Borderline range and above those of 9% of his peers (WMI = 80; 95% confidence interval = 74–90). These tests particularly measure abilities to sustain attention and concentration. His scores in the Letter–Number Sequencing subtest (scaled score = 6) and Digit Span (scaled score = 7) are among his lowest. Jacob's apparent difficulty when asked to repeat strings of numbers backward suggests a relative weakness in mental control, which makes the processing of complex information more time consuming and possibly results in more frequent errors. It is possible that the difficulties with schoolwork that prompted the WISC-IV assessment may be related to this weakness. Jacob performed significantly better on the Arithmetic subtest (scaled score = 9) than on the Letter–Number Sequencing subtest (scaled score = 6). Both of these tasks require attention, concentration and mental control, but the Arithmetic subtest also requires specific abilities in numerical operations and mathematics reasoning.

Jacob's speed of processing abilities as measured by the Processing Speed Index were also in the low average range and above those of approximately only 27% of his peers (PSI = 83; 95% confidence interval = 76–95). His performance on the Coding and the Symbol Search subtests were among his lowest (scaled scores = 6 and 7 respectively). Processing speed is an indication of the rapidity with which he can mentally process simple or routine information without making errors. Performance on this task may be influenced by visual discrimination and visual–motor coordination. Jacob appears to have relative deficits in his ability to process visual material quickly. Because learning often involves a combination of routine information processing (such as reading) and complex information processing (such as reasoning), a relative weakness in the speed of processing routine information may make the task of comprehending novel information more time-consuming and difficult for Jacob. Thus, this relative weakness in simple visual scanning and tracking may result in him having less time and capacity for the complex task of comprehending new material. Again his assessment with the WISC-IV may have been prompted by academic difficulties arising from this weakness in processing speed.

Jacob's index scores show an uneven profile. Most particularly, the discrepancy between his perceptual reasoning with both his working memory and processing speed indicate clinical significance, occurring in less than 1% and 2% of the general population respectively.

Tests Administered

Informant Report (completed by Jacob's mother)

- Yale Global Tic Severity Scale (YGTSS; Leckman, Riddle, Hardin, Ort, Swartz, Stevenson, & Cohen, 1989).
- Autism Spectrum Quotient (AQ-child version); Auyeung, Baron-Cohen, Wheelwright, & Allison (2008).

Test Results and Interpretation

Yale Global Tic Severity Scale (YGTSS; Leckman et al., 1989). The YGTSS is a semistructured clinical interview designed to measure current tic severity. This scale consists of a detailed symptom checklist of current and previous tics and derives a separate severity rating for motor tics (total 0 to 25) and vocal tics (total 0 to 25). Ratings on a scale from 0 to 5 are made along five dimensions (number, frequency, intensity, complexity and interference). Summation of these scores (i.e., 0 to 50) provides a Total Tic Severity score. The YGTSS also contains a separate ranking of impairment (Tic Impairment Score) on a scale from 0 = *None* to 50 = *Severe*, on the basis of the impact of the tics on areas such as self-esteem, social acceptance and interference with school and family life. The YGTSS has demonstrated high internal consistency and convergent and divergent validity (Leckman et al., 1989) and is a reliable and valid instrument for the assessment of tics in children (Storch et al., 2005, 2007).

The symptom checklist provided a clinical picture of Jacob's tics across time and type. Jacob obtained a score of 15 on Motor Tic Severity and 14 on Vocal Tic Severity, with a total Tic Severity Score of 29 out of a possible 50. His level of impairment was rated as 30, and he thus received a Total Yale Global Tic Severity Score of 59 out of 100. This score confirms that he has moderate to severe symptoms that are currently more severe than at any time previously.

The Autism Spectrum Quotient–Children's Version (AQ-Child) (Auyeung et al., 2008). The AQ-Child is a 50-item parent-report questionnaire developed to detect and quantify autistic traits in children at 4–11 years of age. The scale consists of a series of descriptive statements designed to assess five areas associated with autism spectrum disorders: social skills, attention switching, attention to detail, communication and imagination, each represented by ten items. On a 4-point Likert scale, parents rate the extent to which they agree or disagree with the statements about their child, with the following answer categories: 0 representing *Definitely agree*, 1 *Slightly agree*, 2 *Slightly disagree* and 3 *definitely disagree*. Items are worded to produce an approximately equal agree/disagree response in order to avoid a response bias, with reverse scoring as necessary. Higher scores correspond to more 'autistic-like' behaviour. Total AQ scores are represented by the sum of the item scores (minimum = 0; maximum = 150), with higher scores corresponding to more 'autistic-like' behaviour. According to Auyeung et al., the AQ-Child has good test–retest reliability, high internal consistency and a cut-off score of 76 yields high sensitivity and specificity (95% respectively). Jacob received a total AQ of 129 out of a possible 150, indicating high levels of autistic behaviour.

Formulation

Jacob is a 10-year-old boy who presents with a range of tics, attention problems, circumscribed interests and ritualistic behaviours. Although not identified in his referral, Jacob displayed a constellation of characteristics indicative of an Autism Spectrum Disorder and satisfied DSM-IV-TR (American Psychiatric Association [APA], 2000) inclusion criteria for the diagnosis of Asperger's disorder: (1) qualitative impairment in social interaction; (2) restricted, repetitive patterns of behaviour, activities and interests; (3) clinically significant impairment in social, occupational, or other important areas of functioning; (4) preserved language development; and (5) no delay in cognitive development, self-help skills, or adaptive behaviour (with the exception of social interaction). As is typical of children with an autism spectrum disorder, the retrospective account from his mother suggests that Jacob displayed evidence of indicative features throughout his early development.

Jacob's score on the AQ-Child (Auyeung et al., 2008) indicates a high level of autistic traits and he demonstrates a range of specific behaviours typical of individuals with Asperger's disorder. For example, although there was no delay in his language development, his speech and use of language appears qualitatively different to the norm. Difficulties are evident in his pragmatic use of language, and his speech is aprosodic in character, with odd intonation and inflections. He has a special interest in football and his well-developed knowledge is inclined to dominate his conversation. He is quite literal and he shows inflexibility, difficulties coping with change and a preference for routines and rituals. Jacob also has longstanding difficulties with social skills and impoverished peer relationships, which are impacting negatively on his adjustment.

Although of average to above-average intelligence, Jacob's intellectual and learning profile is uneven and shows some similarities to that of other children with Asperger's disorder (see, e.g., p. 96 of the *WISC-IV Technical and Interpretative Manual*; Wechsler, 2003). Most particularly, Jacob's perceptual reasoning ability was high, with strengths in activities involving visual information processing and the analysis and synthesis of abstract stimuli. He also showed good factual and lexical (word) knowledge, with average or greater scores on subtests that measure vocabulary, general knowledge and verbal problem-solving. These strengths were contrasted by relatively poor performance on working memory and processing speed indices. He displays some difficulty with attention span, planning and organisation and his achievements at school are often lower than would be expected on the basis of his apparent strengths.

Jacob also meets the DSM-IV-TR (APA, 2000) diagnostic criteria for Tourette's disorder: (1) both multiple motor and one or more phonic tics present at some stage, although not necessarily concurrently; (2) tics occur many times a day, nearly every day, or intermittently throughout a period of one year; (3) the anatomical location, number, frequency, type, complexity or severity of the tics must change over time; onset before the age of 21 years (5) involuntary movements and noises cannot be explained by other medical conditions. Jacob has multiple tics, which have changed across time. He is aware of his tics and reports premonitory sensation prior to their occurrence. According to the YGTSS (Leckman et al., 1989) his symptoms are moderate to severe and cause him significant impairment.

Although he has difficulties with attention, Jacob's attention inconsistencies can be viewed as part of his Asperger's disorder. The overlap in symptoms between Asperger's disorder and ADHD is recognised. However, Asperger's disorder remains an exclusionary criterion for ADHD in the current DSM. Jacob's obsessive tendencies and his ritualistic and stereotypic behaviours are also subsumed by his Asperger's disorder. Specifically, the characteristic pattern of the thoughts and behaviours that occur in obsessive–compulsive disorder are absent. These additional diagnoses are thus not warranted.

The predisposing factors in Jacob's presentation are largely neurodevelopmental. Asperger's disorder is a condition that is most likely derived from an underlying genetic vulnerability and is more common in boys. Tourette's syndrome is also highly genetically heritable. Jacob's family history suggests a possible line of inheritance via the paternal line; that is, one of his paternal uncles has an intellectual disability with some autistic characteristics, and the other appears to be socially isolated. Furthermore, Jacob's father is not highly social and has indications of some tic behaviours. The direct precipitant to his current presentation appears to be the family's recent move from Tasmania and Jacob commencing at a new school. Difficulties with managing change and dealing with stress is a central characteristic of Asperger's disorder. There is also an indication that tics occur more often in association with stress. Perpetuating factors are for the most part those associated with Asperger's disorder such as obsessive tendencies, ritualistic and stereotypic behaviours, social difficulties and deficits in attention, planning and organisation. Despite some intellectual strengths, these characteristics are likely to impede Jacob's integration and academic achievements at school. In addition, as a result of the family's move to Melbourne, Jacob's mother has less support from her extended family. This loss may contribute to enhanced family stress. Jacob has a number of strengths that are protective, including his average to above average intelligence, his willingness to attend and engage with a therapist, and his mother's concern for his wellbeing.

DSM-IV-TR Diagnosis

Axis I	299.80	Asperger's disorder (Major diagnosis)
	307.23	Tourette's disorder
Axis II	V71.09	No diagnosis
Axis III	Eczema	
Axis IV	None	
Axis V	GAF	60 (current)

Treatment Plan

It is important that Jacob's diagnosis and its implications are communicated sensitively to his family and that verbal and written information about Asperger's disorder and Tourette's disorder be made available to his parents and other relevant family and friends. It is recommended that his parents, and most particularly his mother, receive supportive counselling and encouragement to attend an autism spectrum disorder parent support group.

With his parent's permission, it is also important that Jacob's school receive a report detailing the results of this assessment, as well as ongoing consultation to assist his teachers to understand his behaviours and his learning needs. It is possible that a greater understanding of his information-processing style and learning characteristic will minimise anxiety and lead to enhanced opportunities for Jacob to excel at school. Support from a special education teacher who can devise specialised strategies to assist Jacob to learn is also indicated. Such a program would emphasise his cognitive strengths and assist him, for example, to focus on critical variables and shift his attention when required. It is important that his academic ability is emphasised and promoted, so that his self-esteem is enhanced.

Participation in sport is important to self-esteem and acceptance in the school environment. This presents as a particular challenge for Jacob. It is recommended that consideration be given to the involvement of Jacob in a support role in school sports. Most particularly, his memory for football rules, figures and facts may, in time, make him a good umpire.

It is further recommended that an intervention with Jacob's peers be considered in the future, in order to enhance their understanding of individual differences and most particularly Jacob's difficulties within the social domain. Because Jacob is aware of the reactions of his peers, a reduction in the negative feedback that he receives may reduce his anxiety and assist him to respond more appropriately.

It is also recommended that Jacob attend individual therapy. The focus of these sessions will include:

- Social skills training, involving the use of role-play techniques and social stories (Gray, 2000) to address Jacob's expressed desire to learn how to interact better with his peers. A social story describes a situation, skill, or concept in terms of relevant social cues, perspectives, and common responses (Gray & Garand, 1993). More effective responses are encouraged through improved understanding of events, expectations, and the feelings of others. This could be supplemented by computer-based social-cognitive remediation programs, such as that developed by Bernard-Opitz, Sriram and Nakhoda-Sapuan (2001).
- Cognitive–behaviour therapy (CBT) to assist him to cope with stressful situations including teasing, as well as disruption and change (Sofronoff & Attwood, 2003). CBT will also be used to support his implementation of social skills and his adapted learning strategies.
- Behavioural therapy (habit reversal, competing response practice & self-monitoring) to assist Jacob to control his tics (e.g., Carr, 1995; Peterson & Azrin, 1993).

- Relaxation techniques to relieve the stress that may aggravate tics, as well as to control the tics (Peterson & Azrin, 1992).
- Cognitive and behaviour therapy to assist Jacob to control his ritualistic behaviours.
- Supportive counselling to assist Jacob to understand and cope with his Asperger's disorder and Tourette's disorder and the challenges that may arise from them. This will include a focus on building his self-esteem.

The option of a trial of medication to assist in alleviating Jacob's tics requires further consideration through referral by his general practitioner to a specialist child psychiatrist. Any decision to prescribe medication needs to be balanced by consideration of the risk of side effects, together with the possibility that Jacob's tics may decline with age (Scahill et al., 2001). It is my recommendation that Jacob commence an intensive behavioural therapy program to assist him to control his tics and that a decision regarding medication is deferred until a six-month review.

Dr Susan Nasus, Clinical Psychologist, Head First Clinic, July 14, 2009.

Commentary

Principal Diagnosis

Asperger's disorder is one of the subgroups of a larger diagnostic category variously called either pervasive developmental disorders or autistic spectrum disorders. It is characterised by poor social interactions and restrictive, repetitive patterns of behaviour, interests and activities, in the absence of delay or deviance in language acquisition and the absence of significant delays in cognitive development during the first three years of life (DSM-IV-TR; APA, 2000). Jacob clearly met these criteria. Although there was symptom overlap with autistic disorder, and

Asperger's disorder is not to be diagnosed if criteria are met for autistic disorder (APA, 2000, p.74), a diagnosis of Asperger's disorder was made due to Jacob's advanced language development in his early years.

Jacob had little interest in establishing friendships when he was younger and although now interested, he appears to lack the understanding and skill required for developing and maintaining reciprocal social interactions (Criterion A). He has difficulties with 'conventional rules of conversation, failure to appreciate nonverbal cues and limited capacity for self-monitoring' (APA, 2000, p. 81). His preoccupation with football satisfies Criterion B — 'preoccupations about a circumscribed topic or interest, about which the individual can amass a great deal of facts and information' (APA, 2000, p. 80) and he appears to lack awareness that others may not share his interest. His plate turning and behaviour with his socks also satisfies the criteria of 'an apparently inflexible adherence to specific, nonfunctional routines and rituals' (APA, 2000, p. 84). The social deficits and restricted patterns of interests, activities and behaviours impact considerably on his social adaptation (Criterion C).

Jacob developed advanced language skills at an early age, was curious about the environment and acquired age-appropriate learning skills and adaptive behaviour (Criteria D & E). Despite these apparent developmentally appropriate characteristics, a range of oddities in language and cognition are noted. According to the DSM-IV-TR (APA, 2000), subsequent language may be unusual in terms of its verbosity and the individuals preoccupation with certain topics. In addition, and although not emphasised in the DSM, a range of subtle and unusual qualities have been noted (Gillberg & Gillberg,1989), such as odd prosody and peculiar voice characteristics, formal pedantic language and idiosyncratic use of words, and difficulties with the pragmatic use of language. Although Jacob's vocabulary was good, he displayed a range of these qualitative differences in his use of language.

Similarly, although his intelligence appeared to be at least average, several characteristics of his learning profile were similar to those reported in people with Asperger's disorder (Wechsler, 2003). It has been noted, for example, that individuals with Asperger's disorder commonly have information-processing difficulties and weaknesses that relate to executive function, such as planning and organisation. In addition, they may show a weak central coherence, with good attention to detail, but less ability to see the big picture; with good capacity to learn facts, yet difficulty integrating these into any kind of conclusion or analysis.

Jacob satisfies the diagnostic criteria for Asperger's disorder and most of his behaviours can be subsumed by this diagnosis. Although the need for caution in the use of multiple diagnoses is recognised, it remains important to consider the possibility that additional independent clinical diagnoses may be required to accurately describe his particular set of difficulties.

Differential Diagnosis and Comorbidity

This case raises a number of issues relating to differential diagnosis and comorbidity. The diagnosis of an autism spectrum disorder is a complex process because these disorders involve impairment in several areas of development that present differently across age and in different children. Asperger's disorder is particularly difficult as children with this disorder can function well in many aspects of life and their strange behaviours may simply be attributed to individual differences and 'quirkiness'. In addition to being missed for any diagnosis, it is also the case that the characteristics of Asperger's disorder are sometimes attributed to other disorders, both on and off the autism spectrum, due to the high prevalence of overlapping diagnostic criteria and superficial similarities. Furthermore, difficulties with a differential diagnosis are compounded by the fact that some other disorders (not on the autism spectrum) can co-exist with Asperger's disorder. To warrant a comorbid diagnosis, however, it is essential that the individual presents with the full package of criteria for both disorders and not only some of the symptoms.

Attention Deficit Hyperactivity Disorder (ADHD)

In Jacobs's case, problems with attention span and organisation were emphasised in the referral from his GP, and a previous teacher had suggested the possibility of ADHD. However, there are several reasons why Jacob was not given a comorbid diagnosis of ADHD. First, as recognised in the DSM-IV-TR under Associated Features and Disorders (APA, 2000, p. 81), individuals with Asperger's disorder commonly show symptoms of overactivity and inattention, with some individuals possibly receiving a diagnosis of ADHD prior to one of Asperger's disorder. There is high symptom overlap, with several characteristics common to both disorders such as poor turn-taking, a tendency to interrupt and other impulse inhibition deficits; difficulties with planning and organisation; inflexibility; as well as a tendency to talk excessively and to monopolise the conversation. Although it is clinically recognised that many children with Asperger's disorder do show ADHD symptoms that are not subsumed by Asperger's disorder, dual diagnosis is currently not permitted in the current DSM-IV-TR (APA, 2000).

In the absence of this restriction, it is possible that Jacob may have satisfied the criteria for the predominantly inattentive subtype of ADHD now included in the DSM-IV-TR (APA, 2000, p.87). Notwithstanding this subtype, many clinicians continue to regard the defining characteristic of ADHD as hyperactivity. The DSM criteria for autism spectrum disorders do not refer to elevated activity level at all and certainly Jacob does not show this characteristic. In addition, the attention difficulties in ADHD most commonly relate to an underfocus resulting from an external distraction; whereas in autism spectrum disorder they tend to relate to an overfocus resulting from internal distraction — that is, Jacob displays more of an overfocus on things that he is interested in and underfocus on everything else. He is distracted by his thinking about a particular interest rather than, for example, another child talking or a bell ringing.

Jacob is clearly able to concentrate on the things that he finds interesting and he shows good attention in many domains. For example, he is able to notice details and he can remember and arrange facts of interest in a systematic manner. It may well be his tendency to focus on details, in fact, that leads to his inattention to the requirements of the bigger picture. As described by his teacher, he has a one-track mind when he is problem-solving and this sometimes results in him not achieving the set task. Whether the problems with attention that are so common in Asperger's disorder differ qualitatively from those in ADHD remains a moot point given the current DSM restrictions on a dual diagnosis (ADHD diagnostic Criterion E; APA, 2000, p. 93).

Obsessive–Compulsive Disorder (OCD)

Many individuals with Asperger's disorder show characteristics such as rituals and rigid thinking that appear common with those of OCD.

Although a comorbid diagnosis is possible, OCD is often incorrectly diagnosed in an individual with Asperger's disorder. This can either occur as a result of a differential diagnosis when the correct diagnosis is Asperger's disorder, or it can be given as a comorbid diagnosis when the apparent symptoms are actually more appropriately subsumed within the diagnosis of Asperger's disorder. It is important to note that the behavioural characteristics of Asperger's disorder usually differ from those in OCD and most people with OCD do not have difficulty, for example, in their social interactions or pragmatic use of language.

Jacob's ritualistic behaviour, preference for routines and obsessive interest in football initially prompted consideration of OCD as a comorbid diagnosis. However, there are several reasons why Jacob was not given this comorbid diagnosis. Foremost, Jacob's preoccupation with football (or circumscribed interest), is a defining characteristic of Asperger's disorder. Although 'obsessive' in the common use of the word, this special interest does not meet the criteria of obsessions in OCD, that is, obsessions are recurrent thoughts, ideas or impulses that are experienced as intrusive (APA, 2000, p. 457).

Similarly, Jacob displays some ritualistic behaviour, such as the routine he follows when he is putting on his socks. In OCD, compulsions are defined as repetitive behaviour that a person feels driven to perform in order to reduce or prevent anxiety (APA, 2000, p. 457), or more specifically to counteract the anxiety produced by the obsessions. Jacob's routines do not appear to arise directly from obsessions, are not specifically performed to reduce the anxiety arising from the obsessions and are more appropriately defined as ritualistic behaviours. Although tics, and more specifically Tourette's disorder, can co-occur with OCD (APA, 2000, p. 461) Jacob's tic behaviours are less complex than a compulsion and do not appear to be aimed at neutralising an obsession.

According to the DSM-IV-TR, the obsessions or compulsions are 'time-consuming (i.e., they take more than 1 hour per day) or cause marked distress or significant impairment (Criterion C; APA, 2000, p. 456)'. They are experienced as senseless, bizarre and intrusive. These are not characteristic of Jacob's circumscribed interests and ritualistic behaviours. When Jacob focuses on the amassed information he has about football, for example, he is not getting anxious but rather cataloguing and listing in his mind something that he is interested in and mostly finds pleasurable. It is not a problem for him — the problem is that he is not aware that others are not so interested.

Tourette's Disorder

Individuals with Asperger's disorder commonly display a range of compulsive stereotyped behaviours and vocalisations. Whether these are best described as tics or stereotypies, and whether the circumstances warrant a second diagnosis, presents a considerable clinical challenge.

It is usual to employ hierarchical decision-making in the diagnostic process when features that are part of the definition of one disorder are observed in another disorder. In Asperger's disorder, for example, stereoptyped motor mannerisms are included as a diagnostic feature and thus an additional diagnosis of stereotypic movement disorder would not be indicated. However, the determination of whether an individual with an autism spectrum disorder has a tic disorder, or more specifically satisfies the diagnostic criteria for Tourette's disorder, is more complex.

Tics are defined in the DSM-IV-TR as 'sudden, rapid, recurrent, non-rhythmic stereotyped motor movement and vocalization' (APA, 2000, p. 114). Although it is difficult to differentiate tics from stereotypic motor behaviours (Baron-Cohen, Scahill, Izaguirre, Hornsey, & Robertson, 1999) the later tend to be more repetitive and rhythmic, more complicated and more sustained in duration. They do not have the ever-changing, waxing and waning nature of tics and can remain constant for years (Gilbert, 2006). In addition, tics are commonly preceded by a premonitory urge (Leckman, Walker, & Cohen, 1993), while stereotypies are more associated with engrossment in another activity or self-stimulation. Finally, tics are usually suppressible for brief periods, and although children can be distracted from a stereotypy, they rarely consciously attempt to control them (Muthugovindan & Singer, 2009).

Tourette's disorder may be diagnosed when a person exhibits both multiple motor and one or more vocal tics (although these do not need to be concurrent) over the period of a year, with no more than three consecutive tic-free months (APA, 2000, p. 114). In this latest edition of the DSM, the requirement for marked distress or impairment has been removed. Although prevalence figures are confused by the difficulties in differentiating tics from stereotyped motor behaviours in people with autism spectrum disorders, comorbidity appears particularly prevalent in individuals with high-functioning forms of autism including Asperger's disorder (Ringman & Jankovic, 2000).

Jacob was observed to display several tics. He described a premonitory urge and believed that he was able to delay the tics on some occasions. His pattern of multiple motor and vocal tics satisfies the criteria for an additional diagnosis of Tourette's disorder.

Assessment Techniques

There is no specific diagnostic test for Asperger's disorder. The importance of a comprehensive clinical assessment undertaken by an experienced practitioner, and supplemented with supporting information derived from multiple sources and settings, is demonstrated in this case. The opportunity to consult with Jacob's teacher, as well as to conduct a direct observation of him in the school setting, confirmed and further informed the diagnostic process. Although an important component of the overall picture, caution is needed when considering referral and other informant information. In this case, the referring general practitioner and a previous teacher had made suggestions regarding possible diagnoses. The potential for bias and the possibility of a particular diagnosis overshadowing other possibilities is a particular risk with disorders that have overlapping symptoms.

It is crucial that the assessment includes a thorough retrospective review of the child's development, as well as the collection of information regarding potential familial patterns. The diagnosis of Asperger's disorder, for example, requires consideration of language and cognitive characteristics prior to the first three years of life (APA, 2000, p. 84), at which time parents may not have been alerted to the existence or extent of any difficulties. The increased understanding of the role of genetics in both autism spectrum disorders and tic disorders is also diagnostically relevant. Jacob has a paternal uncle who has characteristics that indicate that he may be on the autism spectrum (Ghaziuddin, 2005). In addition, Jacob's father has indications of a tic disorder. The heritable nature of Tourette's disorder and chronic tics has been well documented (Pauls, 2003).

Although a cognitive assessment is not essential to the diagnosis of Asperger's disorder, information about overall ability, as well as relative strengths and learning characteristics can assist in the process of confirming the diagnosis, as well as informing treatment recommendations. In Jacob's case, although not ideal, it was decided to draw on the findings of a previous cognitive assessment, supplemented with information derived from his teacher and mother. This decision was based on the fact that the WISC-IV had been administered relatively recently and his intellectual performance was not the presenting issue.

It is common for children with high-functioning autism to score in the normal or above normal range on the WISC-IV Perceptual Reasoning and Verbal Comprehension Indexes, but below normal on the Working Memory and Processing Speed Indexes (Mayes & Calhoun, 2008). Jacob's index scores were consistent with those of other individuals with High Functioning Autism (HFA). In addition, comparison of Jacob's test scores with the mean performance of children with Asperger's disorder presented in the technical manual of the WISC-IV (Wechsler, 2003, p. 96) show commonalities in the pattern of index and subtest scores. Although it is interesting to closely examine particular subtest scores, the absence of evidence to support the diagnostic utility of this practice has been well argued (Bray, Kehle, & Hintze, 1998; Watkins, 2003) on the basis that the subtests do not have validity over and above the composite or the cognitive domains represented by the index scores.

The use of scales, such as the Autism Quotient-Child (Auyeung et al., 2008) and the Yale Global Tic Severity Scale (YGTSS; Leckman et al., 1989), can complement the diagnostic process, although it is important to emphasise that the information obtained from such scales is not sufficient to make a definitive diagnosis. The detail provided from administration of these scales can also be used as a baseline when designing and evaluating individually tailored interventions.

Choice of Treatments

Autism

Children with Asperger's syndrome are often misunderstood. For example, their behaviours may be taken as a sign of arrogance or disobedience, and the discrepancy between their ability in some areas and their poor outcomes in others may be attributed to a lack of effort. It is also possible that aspects of the educational environment, such as the absence of routine or the requirement to work in groups may actually impede learning in a child with this disorder. In Jacob's case, the provision of consultancy to his school to promote understanding of the characteristics of Asperger's disorder and how these may impact on his participation and style of learning is imperative to maximise his school achievements and his wellbeing (Hinton, Sofronoff, & Sheffield, 2008).

Children with Asperger's disorder usually have problems in social interactions with their peers. They generally want to be accepted by others and are hurt by their lack of social success. The negative feedback they receive in social interactions is likely to confound their ability to respond appropriately, thus further inhibiting their social skills. Training in social skills training and the use of social stories (Gray, 2000) were chosen to assist Jacob to learn how to interact better with his peers. A social story describes a situation, skill or concept in terms of relevant social cues, perspectives and common responses (Gray & Garand, 1993). As the individual gains improved understanding of events and expectations, their response becomes more effective. There are numerous papers evaluating the use of social story interventions for children with autism spectrum disorders (e.g., Sansosti, Powell-Smith, & Kincaid, 2004).

There are now numerous publications describing and evaluating the use of cognitive and behavioural interventions for assisting individuals with Asperger's disorder to manage their emotions and enhance their wellbeing. A recent article by Sofronoff and Beaumont (2009) is a useful resource for consideration of the challenges of working with young people diagnosed with Asperger's disorder.

Tourette's Disorder

The focus of treatment of Tourette's disorder is on educating the patient, their family and surrounding community (such as friends, school); on identifying the characteristics of symptoms and assisting the individual manage these with behavioural and cognitive strategies. There is widespread empirical support for behavioural techniques in the treatment of tics. For example, in a review of published treatment outcome research on pharmacological and behavioural treatments, Peterson and Azrin (1993) report a 90% reduction in tics with habit reversal training. Although behavioural treatment can be time-consuming, it has the advantage that the skills learnt can be generalised and used on an ongoing basis.

Given that his tics become worse when he is stressed, it is recommended that Jacob learn relaxation, adaptive thinking and other cognitive self-management techniques to relieve the stress that may aggravate his tics. In addition to prevention, relaxation techniques have merit as a component of treatment (Peterson & Azrin, 1992).

The severity of his tics and their negative impact on Jacob's wellbeing may justify a trial of pharmacological treatment. According to Peterson and Azrin (1993), however, in addition to the superior outcomes from behavioural methods, the possibility of side effects and the fact that continuous use is required is a limitation of drug treatment. This is of particular significance given indications that prevalence is highest at 7–10 years (Scahill et al., 2001), with tics steadily declining for many individuals as they pass through adolescence (Leckman et al., 1998.

As emphasised in the introduction, it is critical that the assessment and diagnostic process be comprehensive and that the clinician is well informed regarding the range of possible disorders and issues of differential diagnosis. Without an accurate diagnosis there is no foundation for treatment recommendations that can maximise the development and overall wellbeing of the child.

Endnotes

1 This case assessment is fictional and is to be used for the purposes of demonstration only. Any resemblance to persons known is entirely coincidental.

2 An awareness of an urge, immediately preceding the onset of the tic, which is described as a build-up of tension to the point where the individual elects to engage in the tic in order to relieve the sensation.

References

American Psychiatric Association. (2000). *Diagnostic and statistical manual of mental disorders*, Fourth Edition, Text Revision (DSM-IV-TR), Arlington, VA: Author.

Auyeung, B., Baron-Cohen, S., Wheelwright, S., & Allison, C. (2008). The Autism Spectrum Quotient: Children's Version (AQ-Child), *Journal of Autism and Developmental Disorders*, 38 (7), 1230–1240.

Baron-Cohen, S., Scahill, J., Izaguirre, J., Hornsey, H., & Robertson, M.M. (1999).The prevalence of Gilles de la Tourette syndrome in children and adolescents with autism: A large scale study. *Psychological Medicine, 29*, 1151–1159.

Bernard-Opitz, V., Sriram, N., & Nakhoda-Sapuan, S. (2001). Enhancing social problem-solving in children with autism and normal children through computer-assisted instruction. *Journal of Autism and Developmental Disorders, 31*(4), 377–384

Bray, M.A., Kehle, T.J., & Hintze, J.M. (1998). Profile analysis with the Wechsler scales: Why does it persist? *School Psychology International, 19*, 209–220.

Carr, J.E. (1995). Competing responses for the treatment of Tourette syndrome and tic disorders. *Behaviour Research and Therapy, 33*(4), 455–456.

Ghaziuddin, M. (2005). A family history study of Asperger syndrome. *Journal of Autism and Developmental Disorders, 35*(2), 177–82.

Gillberg, C., & Gillberg, I.C. (1989). Asperger syndrome — some epidemiological considerations: A research note. *Journal of Child Psychology and Psychiatry, 30*, 631–638.

Gilbert, D. (2006). Treatment of children and adolescents with tics and Tourette syndrome. *Journal of Child Neurology*, 21(8), 690–700.

Gray, C.A. (2000). *The new social stories: Illustrated edition.* Arlington, TX: Future Horizons Inc.

Gray, C.A., & Garand, J.D. (1993). Social stories: Improving responses of students with autism with accurate social information. *Focus on Autistic Behavior, 8*(1), 1–10.

Hinton, S., Sofronoff, K., & Sheffield, J. (2008). Training teachers to manage students with Asperger syndrome in an inclusive classroom setting. *The Australian Educational and Developmental Psychologist*, 25, 34–47.

Leckman, J.F., Riddle, M.A., Hardin, M.T., Ort, S.I., Swartz, KL, Stevenson, J. et al. (1989). The Yale Global Tic Severity Scale: Initial testing of a clinician-rated scale of tic severity. *Journal of the American Academy of Child Adolescent Psychiatry, 28*(4), 566–573.

Leckman, J.F., Walker, D.E., & Cohen, D.J. (1993). Premonitory urges in Tourette syndrome. *American Journal of Psychiatry, 150*, 98–102.

Mayes, S.D., & Calhoun, S.L. (2008).WISC-IV and WIAT-II profiles in children with high-functioning Autism. *Journal of Autism and Developmental Disorders, 38*(3), 428–439.

Muthugovindan, D., & Singer, H. (2009). Motor stereotypy disorders. *Current Opinion in Neurology*, 22(2), 131–136.

Pauls, D.L. (2003). An update on the genetics of Gilles de la Tourette syndrome. *Journal of Psychosomatic Research, 55*, 7–12.

Peterson, A.L., & Azrin, N.H. (1992). An evaluation of behavioral treatments for Tourette syndrome. *Behaviour Research and Therapy, 30*(2), 167–174.

Peterson, A.L., & Azrin, N.H. (1993). Behavioral and pharmacological treatment for Tourette syndrome: A review. *Applied and Preventive Psychology, 2*(4), 231–242.

Ringman, J., & Jankovic, J. (2000). Occurrence of tics in Asperger's syndrome and autistic disorder. *Journal of Child Neurology, 15*(6), 394–400.

Sansosti, F.J., Powell-Smith, K.A., & Kincaid, D. (2004). *A research synthesis of social story interventions for children with autism spectrum disorders.* Focus on Autism and Other Developmental Disorders, 19, 194–204.

Scahill, L., Tanner, C., & Dure, L. (2001). The epidemiology of tics and Tourette syndrome in children and adolescents. *Advances in Neurology, 85*, 261–271.

Sofronoff, K., & Attwood, T. (2003). A cognitive behaviour therapy intervention for anxiety in children with Asperger syndrome. *Good Autism Practice*, 6, 1–8.

Sofronoff, K., & Beaumont, R. (2009). The challenges of working with young people diagnosed with Asperger syndrome. In D. McKay & E. Storch (Eds.), *Treating complex and refractory cases: Cognitive–behavior therapy for children.* New York: Springer Publishing.

Storch, E.A., Murphy, T.K., Geffken, G.R., Sajid, M, Allen, P., Roberti, J.W. et al. (2005). Reliability and validity of the Yale Global Tic Severity Scale. *Psychological Assessment, 17*(4), 486–491.

Storch, E.A., Murphy, T.K., Fernandez, M., Krishnan, M., Geffken, G.R., Kellgren, A. et al. (2007). Factor-analytic study of the Yale Global Tic Severity Scale. *Psychiatry Research*, 149(1), 231–237.

Watkins, M.W. (2003). IQ subtest analysis: Clinical acumen or clinical illusion? *Scientific Review of Mental Health Practice, 2*, 1–41.

Wechsler, D. (2003). *Wechsler Intelligence Scale for Children*–Fourth Edition (WISC-IV). San Antonio, TX: The Psychological Corporation.

William of Ockham (1285–1349). *Encyclopedia Brittanica*. Retrieved from http://www.britannica.com/EBchecked/topic/424706/Ockhams-razor

CHAPTER 7

The Assessment and Treatment of a Child With an Attachment Disorder

Nicole Phelps and Andrew J. Lewis

Attachment theory was formulated in the aftermath of World War II when the impact on children of geographic dislocation, loss of caregivers and war-related trauma was a major and very obvious health issue. It was founded as a clinical model for psychological health and vulnerability for psychopathology. Following a necessary period of scientific testing and validation of the theory, the clinical implications and applications of attachment theory continue to be actively investigated (Belsky & Nezworski, 1988; Bowlby, 1977, 2005; Steele & Steele, 2008).

The aim of this chapter is to demonstrate a number of the challenges faced by clinicians when assessing children who present with clear adversities in their early family environments. The second aim is to demonstrate some of the assessment techniques and instruments a clinician might use in order to determine the extent to which a child's early developmental experience might be an aetiological factor in that child's presenting psychopathology. The final aim is to discuss how a clinician assessing disorders of attachment can encounter challenges in terms of the utility of available diagnostic categories, well-validated and clinically applicable assessment instruments and access to structured interventions with a strong evidence base.

Since individual differences in a child's attachment pattern are derived, to a significant degree, from the nature of the interaction between the primary caregivers and the child, the clinical assessment of attachment takes on added complexity (De Wolff & van IJzendoorn, 1997). The clinician must assess the child, the primary caregiver and the interaction between the two. Maintaining the appropriate balance between these three factors can be very challenging and the main downfall of assessments in this area is due to the overemphasis on any one of these domains at the expense of the others. Often one finds a neglect of assessment of the parent's mental health within child-focused services or a neglect of the assessment of the infant or child in adult-focused services. Assessment in mental health services and the associated professions is typically focused on an individual and this framework assumes that psychopathology is an intrapersonal rather than an interpersonal phenomena. While in many cases this is a reasonable assumption, the assessment of children ought to routinely consider the interpersonal dynamics of the family environment. Furthermore, the concept of attachment is itself dynamic and transactional and therefore requires an assessment framework that gives equal weight to the child and their primary caregiver.

Not infrequently, children whose primary presenting problem is best conceptualised in terms of a dysfunction in their attachment behavioural system have been previously misdiagnosed with ADHD, conduct disorder or in some cases autism spectrum disorder (Guttmann-Steinmetz & Crowell, 2006; Rutter et al., 1999). This is not to say that features of these disorders are not present, particularly in terms of deficits in socioemotional functioning and regulatory capacity. However, a neglect of careful assessment of the child's development history, especially the unfolding relationship with the primary caregiver and failure to consider the child's behaviour within the context of the family environment, can result in a focus on the child's problematic behaviour without an adequate transactional framework to address its causal factors.

In the toddler–preschool period, attachment problems can sometimes manifest as behavioural problems and these can be the immediate reason for referral. Misdiagnosis of such behaviour leads to interventions that do not adequately address the child's attachment system and may do harm through identifying only pathology in the child. It is important also to consider the possibility of the comorbidity of attachment and another DSM disorders (Pinto, Turton, Hughes, White, & Gillberg, 2006). These complexities in the assessment of a child's attachment system show the importance of careful assessment over a number of sessions and involving examination of social behaviour in a number of settings, contexts and relationships.

Another feature of this case is the challenge that often arises in assessing such children when it is apparent that a significant contributing factor in the disruption to the attachment relationship is derived from the parent's psychological disorder. Since the clinician is assessing a dynamic and transactional relationship pattern between parent and child, intervention is going to have limited impact on the child unless the parent's own mental health is adequately addressed. This suggests that a comprehensive assessment for the parent is also indicated and the treatment plan needs to address the full family system in order to maximise the chance of success. Detection and treatment of parental mental illness can sometimes provide an efficient and effective resolution of the child's presenting problem.

Disorders of Attachment

The assessment of the child's attachment behaviour and the parent–child relationship ought to be a routine feature of child assessment. However, the diagnosis of disorders in attachment is somewhat controversial. A clinician can often discern anomalies in the child's manifest attachment behaviours or in the manner in which they represent their relationships with primary caregivers. Equally, it is common that the explicit reason for referral will entail problems in the child's social relations that become apparent in a school setting with teachers or peers which, upon investigation, can be linked to features of the home environment. However, when the clinician consults the current DSM-IV seeking a diagnostic indication of these relatively common presenting problems, there are few options. In current nosology only the most extreme dysfunction of attachment is recognised as a clinical disorder under the nomenclature of reactive attachment disorder (RAD; Boris & Zeanah, 1999).

The main diagnostic criteria in the DSM-IV for RAD refers to 'markedly disturbed and developmentally inappropriate social relatedness in most contexts; symptoms begin before age 5 years and are associated with grossly pathological care' (p. 130) that cannot be attributed to a pervasive developmental disorder (APA, 2000). These criteria distinguish between two subtypes of RAD: inhibited and disinhibited types. The inhibited type is defined as the persistent failure of the child to initiate and respond to social interactions with other children, who are persistently withdrawn, fearful and hypervigilant and can be reluctant to seek or receive comfort or affection (Boris & Zeanah, 1999). The disinhibited type is defined as displaying indiscriminate sociability or a lack of selectivity in the choice of attachment figure. Such children will hug, kiss and sit in the lap of strangers without being invited to do so, or may wander off with strangers without displaying separation distress. In our clinical research on attachment disorder we encountered examples of such disinhibition in a child who seems to lack a sense of personal boundaries, alternatively snuggling with the assessor and then clamouring over him to obtain toys. Another attachment-disordered child frequently loomed into the face of the assessor, holding his own face only centimetres from the assessor in a wide-eyed stare. Assessment of children under the age of 3 can also benefit from the use of the *Diagnostic Classification of Mental Health and Developmental Disorders of Infancy and Early Childhood, Revised Edition*, which includes expanded criteria for Deprivation/Maltreatment Disorder of Infancy (Zero to Three, 2005).

Children who meet the diagnostic criteria for RAD have been unable to make a selective attachment to an attachment figure suggesting that, in many cases, the disorder is better understood as one of nonattachment (Boris & Zeanah, 1999). RAD requires the clinician to substantiate that the disordered social behaviour is preceded and indeed caused by 'pathogenic care'. Thus RAD is one of the few DSM disorders that specifies a specific causal criteria. This is most probably because the most extreme features of the disorder have been found to diminish following provision of adequate care-giving provided the child has not experienced more than two years of pathogenic care and depending on the type and intensity of maltreatment or deprivation (Rutter, Kreppner, & O'Connor, 2001). Notwithstanding the fact that this is a difficult area in which to undertake research and conclusions are at best tentative, the very term 'reactive' is meant to suggest that the disorder is largely environmental.

In a series of papers, Charles Zeanah asserted that current DSM diagnostic criteria for clinical disorders of attachment are both too narrow and of limited clinical utility. Certainly, there is a subset of children who manifest these features of RAD, but the contribution of attachment theory and research has much more to offer to clinical diagnosis and intervention. The current DSM criteria for RAD are based on research on maltreated and institutionalised children and these criteria have their historical origin in Bowlby's landmark WHO report, as well as the work of Spitz and Tizard (Boris & Zeanah, 1999; Bowlby, 1951; Spitz, 1945). Boris and Zeanah offer a diagnostic model that expands attachment disorders to include what they call 'secure base distortions', where the child can reliably discriminate their attachment figure but the child does not use the attachment figure as a secure base. They also suggest that a category of 'disrupted attachment' to indicate the symptomatic response to abrupt separation or loss of a caregiver to whom the child has developed an attachment.

Notably, lack of attachment to a specific attachment figure has never been reported in the absence of serious neglect (Action, 2005). However, in addition to RAD, there is also considerable clinical interest in disorganised attachment in which a discriminated attachment relationship can be identified but its behavioural manifestation and cognitive representation is subject to disturbance and distortion (Green & Goldwyn, 2002; Lewis & Tooley, 2009). Disorganised attachment is much more prevalent than RAD and more likely to be associated with maltreatment than neglect. Disorganisation is not a disorder but a risk factor likely to interact with other features to produce psychopathology. However, the atypical parental behaviour shown to be associated with disorganised attachment is not of a sufficient magnitude to fulfil the RAD criteria for 'pathogenic care' (Madigan et al., 2006). While disorganised attachment can be discerned in both infancy and early childhood using a number of quite specialised research measures, there is currently no accepted clinical definition of disorganised attachment in young children (O'Connor & Byrne, 2007).

Assessing a Child's Attachment Status in a Clinical Setting

Assessment of a child's attachment status and investigation of the possibility of an attachment disorder should commence with a clinical interview taking a detailed history and elaborating the type and context of the child's attachment behaviour across different stages of development (Boris, Fueyo, & Zeanah, 1997). Some suggestions to guide a clinician in taking a developmental history with an emphasis on attachment are offered in an appendix to this chapter. The second aspect of the assessment is the careful observation of attachment behaviour within the context of the clinical interview. These observations can be focused on comparing the child's behaviour with familiar caregivers to the child's behaviour with strangers and noting the degree of inappropriate social approach within the clinical setting. Third, the clinician can engage a child of the appropriate age in an assessment of the child's cognitions or representations of attachment figures through the use of family drawing or structured play tasks. Both parental report and direct observation of the quality of the child–caregiver interaction is required and the evaluation of such interactions can be aided if these are video recorded. Evaluation of these observations and reports can be guided by an appraisal of the developmentally appropriate forms of attachment behaviour and cognition displayed by the child and the parental responsiveness, motivation and sensitivity to attachment-related cues. From preschool age onwards, the child's interactions and competence with peers can be evaluated as another aspect of the child's interpersonal social and emotional ability. As the age of the child decreases, the assessment becomes based more on attachment behaviours and less of the child's representation of attachment relationships.

The Case of Lee and Elaine

CLINICAL PSYCHOLOGY ASSESSMENT[1]
PRIVATE AND CONFIDENTIAL

CASE FILE NUMBER:	461968
NAME:	Lee and Elaine
ADDRESS:	40 Bowlby Way, Lewontin South, Darwin
AGE:	7 & 41
DOB:	Lee: January 16, 2001 Elaine: June 7, 1968
REFERRED BY:	Ms Martha Ainsworth, Family Services Worker, Holy Heart Services.
CLINICIAN:	Dr Theo Loveless, Clinical Psychologist, Wallace Hospital.
DATES SEEN:	January 12, (Initial Interview); January 18 (Assessment Interview followed by administration of MCAST); January 26; February 5; (Feedback and Treatment Planning).

Referral and Presenting Problems

Lee is a 7-year-old girl who presented accompanied by her mother Elaine. Elaine reported that over the past three years that she had noticed that Lee had been excessively affectionate and clingy with strangers and would often have tantrums that appeared to be without triggers. At times when she was under some stress or pressure to perform, Lee appeared to go into a 'world of her own' and gazed into the distance. Elaine also reported that Lee throws objects in the house, makes angry faces, grunts when she does not wish to do something and cries in an inconsolable manner when she has a minor accident (e.g., scratches self). To cope with these behaviours,

Elaine has reported responding by pushing or shaking Lee, raising her voice, or alternatively withdrawing and refusing to provide any comfort. Lee becomes extremely agitated and distressed on these occasions. Elaine also commented that Lee's challenging behaviour tends to occur in the family home much more than in the school setting. Elaine described her own feelings of frustration with Lee and at times feeling so overwhelmed with her own problems that she felt unconnected and unavailable to her daughter. Elaine recounted a history of severe postnatal depression (PND) requiring inpatient hospital admission following Lee's birth. Her relationship with Lee's father broke down when Lee was 12 months of age. Elaine also doubts her parenting abilities and worries that when Lee grows up she will have 'all the same problems as me'. Lee and Elaine were referred by her family services worker due to concerns regarding the parent-child relationship.

History of Presenting Problem and Previous Treatment

Elaine had previously presented to her GP for assistance with PND and was referred to a mother–baby inpatient unit for a two-week stay when Lee was three months of age. Treatment included short-term supportive therapy and prescription of citaloprim (40 mg). Upon discharge she was monitored by her GP and remains on the same medication regime. Her concerns about Lee's behaviour were raised with the GP when Lee was three years old, following an escalation of these behaviours with the birth of Lee's sister, Maisy. The teacher in Lee's private kindergarten suggested a consultation with an educational psychologist, who indicated Lee might have a behavioural disorder or autism and suggested consulting with a medical practitioner. Once Elaine had discussed the concerns with her family GP she was referred to a paediatrician. The paediatrician suggested the behaviour may have been a reaction to sibling rivalry and parental separation and suggested no intervention.

Family History

Elaine's family of origin appears to include a conflictual relationship between her parents and frequent dislocation due to instability in her father's employment as a member of the military services. Elaine met her first boyfriend when she was 16 and moved in with him within a year. She reports having numerous relationships that 'never went anywhere' until she meet Barry when aged 30. Elaine and Barry met at a nightclub and she moved in with him after a period of a few months. They married within a year despite conflict in the relationship from the beginning. She fell pregnant when she was 33 years old. Elaine reported experiencing a number of stressors while she was pregnant with Lee. These included conflict with Barry as he was opposed to having children. When Elaine fell pregnant she withheld this information from Barry for as long as possible. Elaine separated from her husband around the time of Lee's birth, reunited and then separated again and then commenced divorce proceedings around the time of Lee's first birthday. Following a brief reunification some years later, Elaine fell pregnant to Barry again but Barry denied paternity of Maisy.

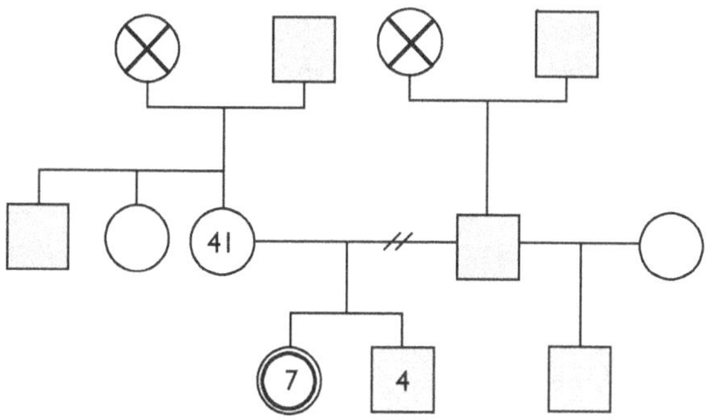

Figure 7.1
Family genogram.

Family Relationships

The parents' relationship had always been highly conflicted and this was exacerbated following the divorce. Elaine has very little support from family of origin due to conflicted relations with parents and unresolved matters from the past, including a poor relationship with her own mother. There are also consistent rivalries between the two children. The notable parenting difficulties are due to a lack of consistency and the impact on both children of their mother's poor psychological health.

Medical History

Significant medical complications include Lee being diagnosed with asthma, which commenced around the age of five and is well managed via the family GP. No other medical complications were reported for Elaine or Lee.

Developmental History

Elaine's pregnancy with Lee was a stressful time characterised by high conflict with her partner and her own doubts about how she was going to be able to care for Lee. She approached Lee's birth with fear and a sense of being out of control. Lee was a breech birth and Elaine required an emergency caesarean. In the initial days after Lee's birth Elaine reported feeling in a state of shock and having difficulties getting a full night's sleep. Her only memory of Lee was of nights interrupted by Lee's crying and her own state of feeling like a 'zombie' during the day. Her early bonding with Lee was poor and she reports feeling distanced and often having thoughts of wanting to escape or find someone 'better qualified' to look after Lee. Lee described feeling sad and empty for most of the day and crying for long periods of time in these first few months. Lee's breast feeding lasted for two weeks, after which Elaine switched her to bottle feeding since she felt that Lee wasn't 'getting enough from her'. After discussing these feelings with her GP, Elaine was referred to an inpatient mother–baby unit where she was diagnosed with major depressive disorder and had a two-week stay. Discharge treatment has been previously described. Elaine continued to struggle with depressive symptoms up until the current referral and describes her feelings towards Lee as not changing substantially. She coped by placing Lee in childcare for long periods and she would regularly leave Lee with her sister or other friends, sometimes for up to several weeks while she experienced depressive states or feelings of not coping.

Elaine found it difficult to provide details of Lee's development due to her depressed mood. She noted that Lee was a slow developing child and concerns had been raised about her difficulties playing with other children and her clingy behaviour with childcare staff.

Educational and Work History

Lee attends her local primary school, Haldane South Primary, and is reported to display considerable variance in her academic performance. While she shows capability in core areas of the curriculum and sometimes a strong interest, at other times she is easily distracted and will refuse to participate or produce work. Her teachers report that she is often in conflict with her peers and finds it difficult to maintain enduring friendships with her peers.

Elaine reported attendance at state high school and completion of Year 12. She has since completed professional training associated with her current work role as an administrative assistant. She has taken several months of maternity leave from this position following the birth of each child.

Mental State Examination of Elaine

Elaine presented well dressed and well groomed and wearing full make-up. She was distractible during the interview with anxious repetitive movements such as foot tapping. She was agitated and tense in her inactions and very willing to cooperate with the interview and assessment process. She was enthusiastic to receive assistance for Lee. Elaine displayed anxious affect, which was consistent throughout the interview. She became very distressed and angry when discussing her ex-husband and then became sullen. When asked about her mood, she commented that she felt 'pretty down generally'. Elaine's speech was pressured and her thought process was normal. There were no instances of thought blocking, illogical thought or significant tangentiality. Thought content was focused on the family and developmental history. There was no suicidal ideation. No disturbances of perception were noted that might indicate psychotic phenomena. Elaine was oriented to time, place and person and she displayed no lapses in attention and concentrated well throughout the interview. Some details of past events were obscured due to depressive disorder. Elaine had no trouble recalling information from the recent past and formal cognitive assessment was not indicated. Elaine showed some insight into her current circumstances and is genuinely concerned about the dynamics of her relationship with Lee.

Mental State Examination of Lee

Lee presented as well dressed and well groomed. She was initially inhibited but quickly became very familiar and sat on the lap of the assessors and stroked the arm and back of the assessor, despite her mother's disapproval. Lee was occasionally elevated in her affect and she commented that she felt 'fine, you know happy'. Lee's speech was simple and somewhat limited in elaboration. She also made grunting noises at times when she did not get her own way. Lee's thought process showed no abnormalities and her content was mostly related to play within the session. Although no disturbances of perception were noted that might indicate psychotic phenomena Lee did display a fixed gaze and at times stared into space in what appeared to be mild dissociation. Lee was otherwise well oriented to time, place and person. Some lapses in attention and concentration throughout the interview were noted. Lee avoided memory of details of past events but she had no trouble recalling information from the recent past. Formal cognitive assessment was not indicated. Lee shows limited insight into her current circumstances or the dynamics of her relationship with her mother, as one would expect of a child her age.

Psychological Testing

Tests Administered

- Parent self-report: The Millon™ Clinical Multiaxial Inventory-III (MCMI-III)
- Child standardised test: Manchester Child Attachment Story Task (MCAST)
- Parental report on child: Reactive Attachment Disorder Questionnaire (RADQ)
- Parental report on child: Child Behaviour Checklist 6–18 yrs (CBCL 6–18)

Test Results and Interpretation

Child attachment status. Lee was administered the Manchester Child Attachment Story Task (MCAST), which is a story stem measure of the child's representation of attachment. It includes four vignettes thought to activate the child's attachment system in relation to a particular attachment figure (Green, Stanley, Smith, & Goldwyn, 2000). The child is asked to choose a doll to represent them and another doll to represent their primary caregiver. The child is then asked to listen to the beginning of a story and then complete the story at the tester's request. The MCAST is videotaped in order for the vignettes to be coded. The method of coding draws on concepts from the coding system of the Strange Situations

Procedure and from the discourse analysis methods used in the Adult Attachment Interview (Green et al., 2000; Hesse, 1999). The coding takes into consideration the content and the structure of the child's narrative completion of the stories and direct observations of behaviour while responding to the narratives and play tasks. Coding of the child's play and behavioural response to each vignette are rated on a 9-point continuous scale, evaluating secure, avoidant and ambivalent attachment patterns. Disorganised attachment is rated as either a breakdown in the narrative coherence as a whole with no clearly discernable attachment strategy or episodes of dissociative or disoriented behaviour which interrupt the narrative coherence.

Lee's MCAST suggested a number of sequences that were coded as disorganised. For example, in the vignette where the 'Lee doll' had a bad dream she responded to the examiner's display of the doll's distress by saying loudly, 'Don't say that! It hurts my ears', and holding her hands over her ears and hiding her face on the table. After around 20 seconds in this posture, Lee commenced the story by bringing the mother doll into the Lee doll's room and saying sternly, 'Go back to bed! Or else it's more time out'. The mother doll then went back to bed after which the Lee doll woke up feeling very scared, hid in the cupboard and went to sleep there standing up. The mother doll then took Lee doll out of the cupboard and put her back to bed, without demonstrating warmth or comfort. In the morning, the Lee doll was too tired to get up and so stayed in bed. Lee then picked up the mother doll and threw her into the kitchen angrily. The quality of Lee's voice changed at this time, increasing in rate and lowering in pitch. After breakfast, the mother doll went back into Lee doll's bedroom, where the mother doll was seen to vigorously jump up and down beside Lee doll's bed and subsequently kicked Lee doll such that she fell out of bed and out of the doll house. The vignette suggested a conflicted representation of the parent–child relationship, with repeated aspects of fear-inducing exchanges without resolution within the narrative and play. The initial response to the vignette, which was also repeated several times in the midst of other vignettes, suggested what is called 'episodic disorganisation'; in this case a significant difficulty in processing emotional states of distress seems to cause her to break off her engagement with the task and adopt a defensive position.

Lee's overall attachment classification was rated as D1/A2 with a Disorganisation score of 7.5 (the D score is the average rating of the four vignettes on a 9-point scale where a score of 1 suggests *No evidence of disorganisation* and 9 suggests a *Very severe and intense disorganisation/disorientation*). Lee's overall classification on the MCAST was disorganised, with an alternative weakly avoidant strategy. The overall classification suggests the lack of a clearly organised strategy and minimal reduction in distress, known as 'assuagement' in this assessment procedure. The most organised narrative generally involved avoidance of the mother doll as an interpersonal strategy, with minimal reduction of distress.

The Reactive Attachment Disorder Questionnaire (RADQ) (Minnis, Rabe-Hesketh, & Wolkind, 2006) was also used to assist in the diagnosis of attachment disorders according to DSM-IV criteria. The RADQ is a 17-item parent report measure that identifies diagnostic features of RAD, distinguishing between the two RAD subtypes: inhibited and disinhibited. It is to be noted that this measure was developed and validated with children who had experienced significant maltreatment but does not have population norms or clinical cut-off scores. The majority of the items loading on the disinhibited subscale of the RADQ were endorsed by Elaine.

Parent's mental health. The MCMI-III inventory is a standardised, self-report measure, consisting of 175-items scored true or false. It assesses a wide range of information related to a client's personality, emotional adjustment and attitude towards taking tests (Groth-Marnat, 2009). Item scores produce 28 scales divided into the categories of Modifying Indices, Clinical Personality Patterns, Severe Personality Pathology, Clinical Syndromes and Severe Clinical Syndromes.

Elaine completed a valid MCMI-III profile with elevations in the clinical range on the Negativistic and Masochistic scales of the personality styles and a similar elevation on the Borderline Personality Pathology Scale. Such a personality profile suggests that her combination of negativistic and masochistic traits can be interpreted as features of the more severe borderline personality disturbance. People who score high on the borderline scale of the MCMI often have feelings of emptiness and oscillate between affectionate and even somewhat idealised views of others to aggressive and denigrating views over the course of their relationship. It is also common for such people to have intense fears of abandonment or separation within close relationships (including the therapeutic relationship), which are not typically based in reality. Within this context masochistic traits are best understood as feelings of being hurt, poorly treated or rejected as a result of feelings of being unworthy or undeserving. Negativistic traits can alternatively be described as passive–aggressive traits and high scores on this subscale often indicate a difficulty accepting the authority of others and a tendency to respond to other's needs and desires with overt or covert anger. They tend to see others as exploitative or corrupt. Interestingly, given her psychiatric history, there was a minor elevation in the Severe Clinical Syndrome scale on Major Depression but not on any other clinical scale.

Child behavioural adjustment. Elaine completed the Child Behaviour Check List: 6–18 (CBCL/6–18; Achenbach & Rescorla, 2001). The CBCL includes 112 items and measures internalising, externalising and total problems in children and adolescents. The Internalising scale encompasses the anxious/depressed, withdrawn/depressed and somatic complaints scales, while the Externalising scale includes rule breaking and aggressive behaviour. Lee's CBCL profile showed elevations in the clinical range for both internalising and externalising. Specifically, Lee was rated in the clinical range on Withdrawn/Depressed, Social problems, Thought problems and Attention problems.

Formulation

Elaine (41) and Lee (7) present with a complex and disrupted history of compromised caregiving on account of Elaine's postnatal depression and ongoing family conflict. Elaine's care of Lee has been disrupted regularly due to the impact of severe postnatal depression. In addition, their interaction is characterised by Elaine's sense of helplessness and Lee's distress and frustration. This has precipitated a significant disturbance in Lee's attachment system, apparent in both formal measurement and as observed clinically.

Elaine's scores on a personality inventory combining personality patterns of Negativistic and Masochistic, Borderline and Depressive features is consistent with problems of emotional regulation suggesting some personality traits consistent with cluster B personality features. While these may be perpetuating features of her relationship conflict with Lee, clinical assessment suggests that Elaine does not meet sufficient DSM criteria for a personality disorder diagnosis. Elaine meets diagnostic criteria for major depressive disorder, recurrent with postpartum onset (in partial remission) with some cluster B personality traits on Axis II. She has a range of psychosocial issues including poor family supports and lack of general social supports and difficulties using the medical and psychiatric system effectively.

Lee is a 7-year-old girl who presents with a 3-year history of persisting social and emotional disturbance against a background of compromised and disrupted caregiving. She displays indiscriminate affection to relative strangers and minimal separation distress. She does not consistently seek her mother's comfort when distressed. Her externalising behaviour is largely directed towards her mother and not generalised to other settings, whereas her social behaviour in other settings is problematic. Her current presentation is not consistent with a diagnosis of pervasive developmental disorder, ADHD or developmental delay.

Diagnosis

Axis I	313.89	Reactive attachment disorder (Disinhibited subtype)
Axis II		Nil
Axis III		Asthma
Axis IV		History of disruption in parental care due to maternal depression.
Axis V	GAF	60 (current)

Treatment Plan

It is recommended that Lee and Elaine receive an integrated treatment consisting of individual psychological therapy for Elaine and dyadic therapy for Elaine and Lee. The therapist will implement a structured therapy known as attachment-based therapy (ABT), which is a manualised, treatment conducted over 15 sessions (Lewis & Anderson, 2006).

ABT aims to modify caregiving behaviour by enhancing the caregiver's awareness of their representations of their child and the effect of these on their parenting. The first six sessions of ABT are focused on modifying the parent's internal working models of attachment. The therapist acts as a secure base for the primary caregiver to explore her own experiences of being parented and the impact of those experiences on her personality, relationships and parenting style. Throughout this process the individual treatment seeks to contain parental distress and encourage adaptive coping with the parenting role. The parent is encouraged to spend 'special time' playing exclusively with her child for at least 10 minutes per day. The aim of this task is to build the parent–child relationship and to provide additional material for the parent sessions.

After approximately six individual sessions, the intervention adds on a dyad therapy while the individual sessions continue. For the dyad sessions both parent and child attended for one session per week, over six weeks. These techniques draw upon mother–infant dyadic therapy as pioneered by a number of infant psychotherapies (Galbally et al., 2006). During these sessions, the child is asked to lead the play while the therapist observes, supports and provides feedback on the interaction. The therapist is also active in discussing positive and negative emotional responses of both parent and child as they emerge within the interaction. The therapist encourages the parent to think beyond the usual ways they account for their child's behaviour, such as attributing attachment-related behaviour to 'attention seeking', being 'needy' or and being 'naughty'. The parent is encouraged to ask their child about their motivations for certain behaviour — particularly those that the parent regards as problematic, rather than assuming the behaviour is problematic. The aim here is to build a more fluid and discursive relationship between parent and child where the child is continually encouraged to verbalise emotional and motivational states and for the parent to be highly receptive of such overtures.

Theo Loveless, PhD, Clinical Psychologist, Wallace Hospital
September 15, 2007

Commentary on the Assessment

Aims and Techniques Used in the Assessment

Although the preference for an attachment figure becomes a salient feature of a child's development between 7 and 9 months of age, the minimum age for being able to reliably assess attachment is 12 months of age. This requires the use of the Strange Situations Procedure, and a considerable amount of training and expertise (Ainsworth, Waters, & Wall, 1978). Clinicians often refer loosely to 'attachment' in infants younger than this age, but a clear distinction is necessary between the child's attachment behaviours — proximity-seeking and maintenance, separation and reunion responses and secure base behaviours — and the caregiver's sensitivity and responsiveness that may be indicative of their emotional bond with the child. A parental bond can be inferred from observed interaction and discussion with the parent. In addition, as used in this assessment, an instrument such as the Adult Attachment Interview can be used as a measure of a caregiver's 'attachment state of mind', that is, how they represent close relationships generally based on their appraisal of their past experience as a child. Attachment is a complex and dyadic phenomena which unfolds between parent and child so can be easily be misunderstood in a mental health context where the focus is typically on individual functioning.

The importance of developmental history-taking cannot be underestimated in the clinical assessment of children. In a clinical context one has no other choice but to engage the parent in a retrospective recall of developmental information about their child, despite the limitations in accuracy of memory and conscious or unconscious distortions. The limitation of this information needs to be acknowledged and weighed against other sources of information gathered in the assessment. Broadly speaking, one is looking for continuities, patterns of developmental processes that continue in a cohesive manner over time. This does not mean that a given developmental phenomena needs to be the same over time (Sroufe & Waters, 1977). In terms of psychopathology, one has to judge changes in pathological process unfolding over time as they depart from what one would expect within normal development. The other major benefit of a systematic and structured developmental history is that it places in context any major precipitating events to the current form of psychopathology.

One is interested in a child's functioning up until a major event and then how it changed afterwards and how the family structure itself may have changed.

Another important feature of the approach in this assessment is careful consideration of the mother's mental health status. As mentioned earlier, thorough assessment of the mental health of the primary caregiver is essential in any child assessment. Once attachment issues are suspected such investigation becomes even more important. There is strong evidence for links between maternal depression and disorganised attachment in infancy. A recent meta-analysis of six studies found an average increase in disorganised attachment from 17% to 28% to be consistently associated with a history of maternal depression when compared to unaffected mothers (Martins & Gaffan, 2000). In this case, the mother's history of depression complicated with personality disturbance needs to be one of the key factors to address within the recommended treatment.

Choice of Assessment Measures

The assessment of attachment in preschool age and school-age children (age 4 to 8 years) is achieved by measuring a child's representations or working model of attachment through cognitive and language-based assessments. The Manchester Child Attachment Story Task (MCAST) includes vignettes that are thought to activate the child's attachment system and attachment cognitions, which focus specifically on the child and a particular attachment figure, such as mother or father (Green et al., 2000). Unlike many other child attachment measures, the MCAST is particularly well adapted to the clinical situation (Green et al., 2000). The MCAST was complemented by the use of the RADQ which is the only measure of its kind, namely a parental report of RAD features compatible with DSM diagnosis. This measure was selected as a supplementary source of information regarding diagnostically relevant information on the child.

The mental health of the primary caregiver was assessed using the Millon Clinical Multiaxial Inventory-III (MCMI-III; Millon, Davis, & Millon, 1997). These scales are closely aligned to both Millon's theory of personality and the *Diagnostic and Statistical Manual of Mental Disorders, Fourth Edition* (DSM-IV) (Groth-Marnat, 2009).

The CBCL/6–18 was selected for use instead of the Eyberg Child Behavioural Inventory (Eyberg & Ross, 1978) and the Strengths and Difficulties Questionnaire (Goodman, 2001) because the CBCL is a widely used, standardised, cross-informant measure, incorporating a wide age range. In addition, the CBCL provides DSM-IV-orientated scales, and internalising and externalising scales.

Treatment Recommendations: Attachment-Based Therapy

Treatment options for children with attachment disorders are hampered by the limitations of current diagnostic criteria, as previously discussed. Treatments purporting to facilitate attachment relationships have mostly been evaluated in terms of their ability to improve the sensitivity of caregiving (Bakermans-Kranenburg, Van Ijzendoorn, & Juffer, 2003). Few studies have examined the extent to which there is an improvement in the quality of attachment relationship. Part of the impediment to the evaluation of attachment as an outcome of intervention is that there are limited reliable measures of attachment quality that cover a sufficiently extended developmental period (O'Connor & Zeanah, 2003). There are few structured interventions for the age group of 4- to 8-year-olds designed specifically to address attachment disorders or disorganisation. In general, interventions have focused on children under the age of 3 and are aimed at enhancing parental sensitivity, changing a caregiver's behaviour or changing caregiver's mental representations. A meta-analysis conducted in 2005 of 15 preventive interventions that used disorganised attachment as an outcome measure suggested that effective interventions that reduced disorganised attachment started after six months of age and focused directly on enhancing caregiver sensitivity (Bakermans-Kranenburg, Van Ijzendoorn, & Juffer, 2005). The common features of interventions that showed an impact on attachment disorganisation started at six months of age, focused on risk factors relating to infants, implemented behavioural techniques and were administered by trained professionals. All the interventions in Bakermans-Kranenburg's review were individualised and conducted in the participant's home. Intervention efforts focusing on changing caregiver's mental representations to promote secure attachment also showed promising results and were implemented by a trained and experienced therapist over a period of at least 20 sessions.

The current case presents a model of intervention that is currently being evaluated with promising results. Attachment-based therapy (ABT) is a manualised treatment developed by Lewis and Anderson (2007). The manual is currently unpublished but available to those who have trained in the intervention. ABT is designed to enhance a child's attachment security and produce associated improvements in social and behavioural functioning. The initial trial of the intervention recruited maltreated children and their families between the ages of 18 months and 5 years. This pilot study of nine participants produced promising results, including a reduction in internalising ($d = 1.24$) and externalising behaviour ($d = .80$), increased caregiver attachment security ($d = .36$), and decreases in fearful ($d = .82$) and hostile ($d = .23$) parenting reactions.

Endnote

1 This case assessment is fictional and is to be used for the purposes of demonstration only. Any resemblance to persons known is entirely coincidental.

References

Achenbach, T., & Rescorla, L. (2001). *Manual for the ASEBA school-age forms and profiles.* Burlington, VT: ASEBA.

Action, A. (2005). Practice parameter for the assessment and treatment of children and adolescents with reactive attachment disorder of infancy and early childhood. *Journal of the American Academy of Child and Adolescent Psychiatry, 44*(11), 1207.

Ainsworth, M., Waters, E., & Wall, S. (1978). *Patterns of attachment: A psychological study of the strange situation.* Hillsdale, NJ: Lawrence Erlbaum.

Bakermans-Kranenburg, M., Van Ijzendoorn, M., & Juffer, F. (2003). Less is more: Meta-analyses of sensitivity and attachment interventions in early childhood. *Psychological Bulletin, 129*(2), 195–215.

Bakermans-Kranenburg, M.J., Van Ijzendoorn, M.H., & Juffer, F. (2005). Disorganized infant attachment and preventive interventions: A review and meta-analysis. *Infant Mental Health Journal, 26*(3), 191–216.

Belsky, J., & Nezworski, T. (1988). *Clinical implications of attachment.* London: Lawrence Erlbaum Hillsdale.

Boris, N., Fueyo, M., & Zeanah, C. (1997). The clinical assessment of attachment in children under five. *Journal of the American Academy of Child & Adolescent Psychiatry, 36*(2), 291.

Boris, N.W., & Zeanah, C.H. (1999). Disturbances and disorders of attachment in infancy: An overview. *Infant Mental Health Journal, 20*(1), 1–9.

Bowlby, J. (1951). Maternal care and mental health. *Bulletin of the World Health Organization, 3*(3), 355–533.

Bowlby, J. (1977). The making and breaking of affectional bonds. I. Aetiology and psychopathology in the light of attachment theory. [An expanded version of the Fiftieth Maudsley Lecture, delivered before the Royal College of Psychiatrists, 19 November 1976]. *British Journal of Psychiatry, 130*, 201–210.

Bowlby, J. (2005). *A secure base: Clinical applications of attachment theory.* Philadelphia: Taylor & Francis.

De Wolff, M., & van Ijzendoorn, M. (1997). Sensitivity and attachment: A meta-analysis on parental antecedents of infant attachment. *Child Development, 68*(4), 571–591.

Eyberg, S., & Ross, A. (1978). Assessment of child behavior problems: The validation of a new inventory. *Journal of Clinical Child & Adolescent Psychology, 7*(2), 113–116.

Galbally, M., Lewis, A., Snellen, M., Paul, C., Szego, K., & Trauer, T. (2006). Mother–infant psychotherapy and perinatal psychiatry: Current clinical practice and future directions. *Australasian Psychiatry, 14*(4), 384–389.

Goodman, R. (2001). Psychometric properties of the strengths and difficulties questionnaire. Journal *of the American Academy of Child & Adolescent Psychiatry, 40*(11), 1337.

Green, J., & Goldwyn, R. (2002). Annotation: Attachment disorganisation and psychopathology: New findings in attachment research and their potential implications for developmental psychopathology in childhood. *Journal of Child Psychology and Psychiatry, 43*(7), 835–846.

Green, J., Stanley, C., Smith, V., & Goldwyn, R. (2000). A new method of evaluating attachment representations in young school-age children: The Manchester Child Attachment Story Task. *Attachment & Human Development, 2*(1), 48–70.

Groth-Marnat, G. (2009). *Handbook of psychological assessment.* New York: Wiley.

Guttmann-Steinmetz, S., & Crowell, J. (2006). Attachment and externalizing disorders: A developmental psychopathology perspective. *Journal of the American Academy of Child & Adolescent Psychiatry, 45*(4), 440.

Hesse, E. (1999). The adult attachment interview: Historical and current perspectives. In J. Cassidy & P. Shaver (Eds.), *Handbook of attachment: Theory, research, and clinical applications* (pp. 395–433). New York: Guilford.

Lewis, A., & Tooley, G. (2009). Disorganized attachment and reproductive strategies. *Behavioral and Brain Sciences, 32*(01), 35–36.

Lewis, A.J., & Anderson, G. (2006). *Attachment-based therapy treatment manual.* Unpublished manuscript.

Madigan, S., Bakermans-Kranenburg, M., Van Ijzendoorn, M., Moran, G., Pederson, D., & Benoit, D. (2006). Unresolved states of mind, anomalous parental behavior, and disorganized attachment: A review and meta-analysis of a transmission gap. *Attachment & Human Development, 8*(2), 89–111.

Martins, C., & Gaffan, E. (2000). Effects of early maternal depression on patterns of infant–mother attachment: A meta-analytic investigation. *The Journal of Child Psychology and Psychiatry and Allied Disciplines, 41*(06), 737–746.

Minnis, H., Rabe-Hesketh, S., & Wolkind, S. (2006). Development of a brief, clinically relevant, scale for measuring attachment disorders. *International Journal of Methods in Psychiatric Research, 11*(2), 90–98.

O'Connor, T., & Byrne, J. (2007). Attachment measures for research and practice. *Child and Adolescent Mental Health, 12*(4), 187–192.

Pinto, C., Turton, P., Hughes, P., White, S., & Gillberg, C. (2006). ADHD and infant disorganized attachment: A prospective study of children next-born after stillbirth. *Journal of Attention Disorders, 10*(1), 83–91.

Zero to Three. (2005). *Diagnostic classification of mental health and developmental disorders of infancy and early childhood.* Washington, DC: Author.

Rutter, M., Andersen-Wood, L., Beckett, C., Bredenkamp, D., Castle, J., Groothues, C., et al. (1999). Quasi-autistic patterns following severe early global privation. *The Journal of Child Psychology and Psychiatry and Allied Disciplines, 40*(04), 537–549.

Rutter, M., Kreppner, J., & O'Connor, T. (2001). Specificity and heterogeneity in children's responses to profound institutional privation. *The British Journal of Psychiatry, 179*(2), 97.

Spitz, R. (1945). Hospitalism: An Inquiry into the genesis of psychiatric conditions in early childhood. *Psychoanalytic Study of the Child, 1*, 53–74.

Sroufe, L.A., & Waters, E. (1977). Attachment as an organizational construct. *Child Development, 48*(4), 1184–1199.

Steele, H., & Steele, M. (2008). *Clinical applications of the adult attachment interview.* New York: The Guilford Press.

Appendix 7A

Suggestions for semi-structured interview questions to be used for assessing attachment history via the primary caregiver

Introduce the topic of a developmental history typically after having clarified presenting problem, previous treatment, the family structure and history.

I'd like to ask you about your child's background and development:

1. Can tell me about your pregnancy with your child?
   a. Any major complications? If so what?
   b. Any major psychosocial stressors?
   c. Any potential exposures during pregnancy — for example, medication, drugs, alcohol?
   d. Can you tell me about whether your child was a planned baby or not?
   e. What was your reaction to falling pregnant
2. I'm interested in your child's birth: were there any complications?
   a. Who was present?
   b. What was your experience of the birth
   c. How would you describe your child when s/he was first born?
3. Could you describe your child's behaviour and temperament over the first year of your life
   a. Who looked after your child? How much childcare? Who did this?
   b. What kind of a baby was your child — for example, happy baby, active, slow to warm up, 'colicy', unsettled, and so on?
4. Was your child breastfeed?
   a. How long for, why did that stop, do you recall how ____________ reacted to being weaned?
5. Where there any early problems — for example, how was sleeping, feeding, routine?
6. Early fears or anxieties, stranger anxiety, separation anxiety
7. Moving onto when _______________was around 12 months of age, can you recall how s/he reacted to being separated from you (or primary caregiver) — for example, was s/he clingy, fearful, untroubled by this.
8. Around 3 years, how was s/he around other children, ie social /play skills; interest in others; level of interpersonal aggression
   a. Where there any issues of conflict between you and _______________ — for example, toilet training, going to bed, sibling conflicts, being oppositional?
   b. If so, how did you manage that?
   c. Did you have any concerns about your child running off? Following instructions? Being distracted?

6\. How was your child when s/he went to school or kinder for the first time?
   a. How did you react to that?
   b. How did s/he get along with other children?
   c. How did s/he get along with teachers, favourite teachers?

PART III

SPECIALIST ASSESSMENTS

CHAPTER 8 | Forensic Risk Assessment of a Sexual Offender

James Vess

This case illustrates a variety of the issues involved in conducting risk assessments with sexual offenders in a forensic context. Such cases are typically referred for assessment by government agencies such as the Department of Corrections or the Parole Board, or by defence attorneys seeking an independent opinion to present in judicial hearings. The primary goal of such an assessment is to present specific and objective information to judicial decision-makers regarding the risk for specific types of reoffending. Such assessments can have an important influence in legal proceedings that will determine sentencing, release from prison, parole conditions, access to treatment or eligibility for the application of recent forms of special public protection legislation like extended supervision in the community or involuntary civil commitment.

In the present case, the offender has been sentenced to prison for repeated sexual offending against children. He is approaching the end of his prison term and is being considered for the imposition of an Extended Supervision Order. Extended supervision allows for the continued monitoring and supervision of an offender beyond the period of their original sentence if they are considered by the Court to present a sufficiently high risk of sexual reoffending if not placed under ongoing supervision once they are released to the community. It also allows the Court to impose restrictions on the offender, such as where he can live, how often he must report to a Parole Officer and when he can leave his home or travel to other states. Such legal decisions must attempt to balance the risk of future harm to the public with the individual human rights of the offender. If the risk of reoffending is underestimated and the offender is released with insufficient precautions in place, it may result in additional victims of sexual violence. If the risk of reoffending is overestimated and restrictions placed on an offender who would not have sexually reoffended, the freedom of the individual is unnecessarily curtailed (Vess, 2008, 2009a).

The field of risk assessment with violent and sexual offenders has undergone substantial development over the past 20 years. The main source of improvements in the accuracy and utility of risk assessment has been the development of actuarial risk measures that have been empirically validated with specific groups of offenders. Briefly, actuarial measures work by identifying risk factors that have demonstrated an association with violent or sexual reoffending. Such risk factors must be clearly defined and are usually based on unchanging, historical or 'static' variables such as the number and type of previous offences and the type of victim. These factors have been studied in large samples of offenders over increasingly long periods of time, so that there is now a substantial research base for placing an offender into a group that can be designated as higher or lower risk based on the number of such factors that are present. The strength of this actuarial approach is that offenders can be consistently and objectively assessed as belonging to a subgroup of offenders who have specific observed rates of reoffending over time.

There are limitations, however, to just knowing that an individual belongs to a group with a known rate of reoffending (at least known through official recidivism data such as arrests or convictions, which will probably underestimate the true rates of reoffending because of crimes that go undetected). Risk is always contingent on internal factors such as cognitions and mood states, and external conditions such as social influences and victim access. These are considered to be dynamic or changeable risk factors. As shown in the case that follows, there are now standardised measures for specific dynamic risk factors known to be associated with sexual reoffending. Any thorough and defensible risk assessment must take into consideration the influence of these dynamic risk factors.

Group information derived from static actuarial measures, even when modified through the consideration of standardised dynamic risk factors, does not tell us the likelihood of reoffending for the particular individual who is being assessed, nor will it tell us the specific factors and conditions that will serve to raise or lower his risk over time. For this we need an understanding of the factors that contributed to the individual's previous offending. We need to develop an aetiological, explanatory formulation of risk based on this individual's prior offending. This is where other clinical assessment measures that address such aspects as personality patterns and intellectual functioning can contribute to our understanding of the case and provide more individualised risk information. This is also perhaps the most challenging part of a thorough risk assessment, because it requires going beyond the skilled but essentially mechanical work of administering and combining standardised risk measures. Such an assessment requires the sophisticated integration of developmental, clinical and contextual information with empirically validated risk factors that provides not only an accurate understanding of the individual's risk, but also guides decision-makers and others in effectively managing that risk.

The format of the following report is drawn from similar reports provided to the courts and parole boards by psychologists working for government agencies and in private practice as consultants to attorneys. Different employers and different applications will sometimes involve using somewhat different report writing styles. However, all such reports should include the fundamental report writing elements of a clear statement of the referral issue, the sources of information reviewed and tests administered, the findings and a case formulation. Because these reports often must present the relevant criminal history and legal context for the risk assessment, they are sometimes longer than other types of assessment reports. We must also remember that the role of the assessor is to provide objective information about risk to the judicial decision-maker, not to take a position on the legal decision itself. The proper role of the risk assessment expert is to provide a nonpartisan professional opinion, not to advocate for a specific outcome favourable to one side or the other.

The following case of Mr Smith is a fictional characterisation drawn from various aspects of the author's forensic experience. Any resemblance to specific individuals is entirely coincidental.

The Case of David Smith

FORENSIC ASSESSMENT[1]
PRIVATE AND CONFIDENTIAL

CASE FILE NUMBER:	684619
NAME:	David Smith
AGE:	41
ADDRESS:	Soledad Prison, Nilhilville.

Identifying Information and Reason for Referral

Mr Smith is a 41-year-old Caucasian male who is currently serving the final portion of a 12-year prison sentence following his conviction for kidnapping, sexual violation and indecent assault upon a 15-year-old male. He was referred by his legal counsel in the matter of his upcoming hearing to consider an application by the Department of Corrections for an Extended Supervision Order. The specific purposes of the evaluation were to assess Mr Smith's risk for sexual reoffending, to identify treatment needs and special conditions that might reduce his risk of reoffending following his release to the community and, in light of conflicting information in prior reports regarding his intellectual functioning, to address whether this factor has a significant influence on his risk and responsivity to treatment.

The purposes of the assessment were explained to Mr Smith and his written consent to participate was obtained.

The limits of confidentially were explained and Mr Smith understood these. He was interviewed at Soledad Prison, were he is currently held. He was seen on April 20 and 21, 2006, for a total of 5.5 hours.

Sources of Information

The following sources of information were used in the preparation of this report:

- Psychiatric report to the District Court by Dr D. Greer, dated August 19, 1987
- Victoria Police Summary of Facts, dated June 1, 1990
- Presentence Report to the District Court by L. Hamilton, dated June 12, 1990
- Judge's sentencing notes of P. Power, dated 20 June 1990
- Wechsler Adult Intelligence Scale — Revised, administered by T. Rogers, dated March 5, 1991
- Sex Offender Treatment Program report by D. Fielding and P. Richter covering the period from March 12 to April 16, 1991
- Victoria Police Summary of Facts for offence of August 29, 1992 by A. Porter, undated
- Psychological Services Report to the High Court by B. Tengdahl, dated October 20, 1992
- Sentencing notes of Justice Eastwood, dated October 23, 1992
- Psychological Services Report to Community Corrections Service by D. Simpson, September 23, 1992
- Sex Offender Assessment and Treatment Outcome Report by I. Jarvis, dated June 1992
- Psychological Services Report to the Public Prison Services by M. Webster, dated July 23, 1996
- Psychological Services Report to the Victoria Parole Board by K. Groves, dated September 20, 2002

- Psychopathy Checklist Screening Version administered by S. Richardson, September 13, 2002
- Criminal and Traffic History, dated August 5, 2004

Measures Administered or Reviewed

- Psychopathy Checklist Screening Version (PCL: SV): A screening measure for psychopathy
- PCL-R (PCL-R): The full assessment measure for psychopathy
- Static-99: An actuarial measure of risk for sexual reoffending based on Static historical factors
- Stable-2007: A measure of risk for sexual reoffending based on changing dynamic risk factors
- Millon Clinical Multiaxial Inventory, 3rd Edition (MCMI-III): A measure of personality functioning

Presentation

Mr Smith initially appeared mildly apprehensive and moderately anxious, but remained courteous and cooperative throughout the interview. He was adequately groomed and dressed in prison-issue clothing. His speech was logical and coherent, with no indication of unusual thought content or cognitive impairment. His affect was appropriate to the topics discussed, although he struggled at times in attempting to describe the emotional aspects of his offences for both the victim and himself. He appears to have some cognitive understanding of the significance of his offences, but has trouble in accessing or expressing the associated emotional feelings. He seemed to exert a conscientious effort to respond to the questions posed to him in a thoughtful and candid manner, with a minimum of impression management to present himself in an overly positive fashion, as has been described in earlier assessment reports.

Background Information

Developmental and Criminal History

Offender Background

Mr Smith grew up in a suburb of a large industrial city, with his mother, father and younger sister. He reports being doted on and materialistically overindulged as a child by his mother and grandmother. His father became ill with a form of progressive dementia when Mr Smith was 8 years of age, with a corresponding reduction in parental discipline. Mr Smith appears to have resented the family's focus on his father's illness and reports indicate that he began to behave disrespectfully or even abusively toward his father. He became exceptionally self-focused and developed a sense of entitlement in relation to his passive, dependent and overindulgent mother and ineffectual father. Mr Smith developed the capacity to lie and manipulate his mother in order to get what he wanted. He is described as having poor impulse control, poor ability to delay gratification and deficits in social skills appropriate for his age, including a lack of empathy for others. His father died when Mr Smith was 16 years old. It has been reported that Mr Smith continues to experience feelings of guilt, shame and anger in relation to his behaviour with his father.

Mr Smith has described himself as a slow learner who preferred to stay home rather than attend school. He reports being severely teased by his peers regarding his small stature, eczema and chronic asthma. He also appears to have been ashamed of his father's condition. He seems not to have been well accepted by his peers, leading to a self-perception of social inadequacy and corresponding feelings of anxiety and rejection. He developed maladaptive strategies to attempt to align himself socially, such as telling exaggerated stories and engaging in farcical behaviour, but such attempts ultimately served only to compound his rejection and isolation. Mr Smith would socially withdraw and ruminate over others' responses, leading to anger and resentment. These ruminations would escalate his anger to the point that he would sometimes act out on more physically and emotionally vulnerable peers. During this period of adolescence he also appears to have developed a pattern of alleviating his emotional distress through compulsive sexual self-stimulation and fantasy relating to themes of aggression and dominance. Such sexual stimulation would strongly reinforce the fantasies of dominance over others as a way of defending against his feelings of rejection and inadequacy, while simultaneously sexualising his violent impulses. This repeated early pairing of sexual and aggressive, retributional drives represents one of the primary risk factors in Mr Smith's sexual offending.

At approximately age 15, Mr Smith began teaching martial arts to younger children within an established Karate Dojo. This experience is reported to have contributed to a sense of social efficacy, as he felt admired and respected by the younger students. However, it is also reported that he would fantasise about offending against his pupils and used his position as teacher to gain sexual stimulation from physical contact with both male and female children during classes. It is reported that he would later masturbate to fantasies of abusing children, again further reinforcing these deviant fantasies.

Reports indicate that Mr Smith left school at age 16 to join the workforce, but that he demonstrated an unstable work history, losing several jobs in his first year out of school. He has reported that he had difficulty interacting effectively with adults, but that another factor in his employment problems was his sense of entitlement, such that he did not like to be told what to do. Such an attitude, if not substantially modified, will also serve as a significant barrier to treatment aimed at reducing his risk of reoffending.

Previous Offending

The most recent sexual offending appears to represent a significant increase in the level of violence in comparison with previous sexual offences committed by Mr Smith. The Police

Summary of Facts for the indecent assault of a 12-year-old four years prior to the index offending suggests that this earlier offence did not involve verbal threats or use of physical violence. However, the Police Summary of Facts for a charge of indecent assault upon a 15-year-old male that occurred two years later (1990) indicates that this incident involved forcing the victim into Mr Smith's car and a threat of physical abuse if the victim attempted to escape. The judge's sentencing notes reveal that the degree of force and coercion used in these earlier cases was disputed, yet it appears clear that Mr Smith imposed himself in a sexual manner upon the victim against the victim's will, while not yet resorting to actual physical assault as in the current index offence.

Prior to these offences in the late 1980s and early 1990s, Mr Smith sexually offended against an 8-year-old boy in 1980, for which he was sentenced to 18 months probation. In 1983 he was again convicted for indecent assault against two boys aged 10 and 12 years, for which he was sentenced to 19 months probation and seven months periodic detention. This offence also involved a conviction for abducting a child, although no further information on the specifics of these offences was found in the available file documentation. In 1987 he was convicted on three charges of sexual offending against a 12-year-old male, for which he was sentenced to six months imprisonment.

Mr Smith thus has a pattern of offending sexually against preadolescent and adolescent males, with six convictions for indecent assault from the age of 18 until his index offence at age 29. In previous reports it is noted that Mr Smith has also acknowledged an earlier onset of offending and a more extensive number and type of offences than those reflected in his criminal convictions. It is noted that his most recent offences have incorporated more violence than his earlier sexual offences. In addition to his sexual offences, Mr Smith has previous convictions for vehicle conversion, making a false statement to police, fraudulent use of a document and theft.

Index Offending

In the offending for which he is currently incarcerated, Mr Smith was driving in a suburb of the city where he lives when he noticed the victim waiting near a bus stop. He induced the victim to get into the car rather than wait for a bus. Mr Smith then drove the victim to a secluded area and became physically assaultive, striking the victim repeatedly across the face. It is reported in the Police Summary of Facts that Mr Smith kept the victim in this parking area for approximately 45 minutes, continuing his verbal threats and intimidation, before driving to another secluded area. At this location Mr Smith fondled the victim's genitals despite the victim's resistance and inserted a foreign object into the victims anus. Mr Smith was again physically assaultive during this time. Following this period of abuse, Mr Smith drove the victim to an area near the victim's home and released him, threatening to have him killed if he reported the incident.

Treatment History

Mr Smith has now completed a specialised treatment program for sex offenders on three previous occasions, beginning in 1990. His response at the completion of his first program experience was judged to be unsatisfactory and he underwent the program a second time during 1991, prior to his release in 1992 after he became eligible for parole. At the end of this second attempt at the program, it was stated that he '… was motivated to address treatment issues. However, his inability to be consistent in his application of therapy and an intermittent return to manipulative and dishonest behaviour restricted the progress he made in treatment.'

Following this 1992 release he then sexually reoffended in a short period of time, and was returned to prison on a sentence of 12 years. He was again referred to a treatment program in 1999, when it was noted that he had undergone a major attitudinal change and was now ready to benefit from treatment. He has again completed the sex offender program. While he appears to have made further progress in the cognitive understanding of the factors contributing to his offences, it has been noted that he has yet to demonstrate a consistent change in behaviour or use of adaptive coping strategies. Prior reports go on to point out that a particular concern is his pattern of dishonesty, which is described as more refined and difficult to detect. Although he had apparently completed the program, there were incidents of rule-breaking behaviour related to his use of a computer and attempting to communicate inappropriately by letter with another inmate. Following these behaviours he was discharged from the program and transferred to the mainline prison population. Mr Smith has thus had an extensive involvement in treatment focusing specifically on his sexual offending. He appears to have gained a significant understanding of the factors related to his offending, but still needs to demonstrate a consistent application of these principles in his daily behaviour and current interpersonal relationships.

Assessment Findings

Intellectual Functioning

One area of inconsistency in Mr Smith's previous assessment reports involves his level of intellectual functioning. This issue is important not as a risk factor per se, but rather as it may represent a barrier to Mr Smith responding adequately to available cognitive–behavioural treatment modalities, and as a limitation to his ability to successfully implement the relapse prevention strategies which such modalities emphasise. The earliest noted assessment of Mr Smith's intelligence is provided by the psychiatric report in 1987. Based on his mother's reports regarding his school performance and Mr Smith's own 'immature diction and mode of presentation', the psychiatrist concluded that he 'probably has an IQ in the low 70s at best, which incidentally would place him in the bottom 4 or 5% of the IQ range …' This conclusion was reflected in at least one subsequent psychologist's report, who stated that, 'his low intelligence is an additional barrier to (treatment) progress'.

In contrast to this assessment, a report in 1992 included results of the Revised Wechsler Adult Intelligence Scale (WAIS-R), which showed a full scale IQ of 86, placing him in the low average range. His verbal IQ score was recorded as 81, while his performance IQ was recorded as 98, which is an average score for his age group in tasks of processing visual information, perceptual organisation, and perceptual–motor skills. His lower verbal score may be understood in part as related to his poor performance in and early departure from formal education. However, a subsequent administration in 2004 of the WAIS-III, showed a full-scale IQ of 98, with a verbal IQ of 95 and a performance IQ of 102, all of which are in the average range.

The variations in assessment results obtained on different occasions highlight the caution with which such results should be interpreted and incorporated into treatment planning, along with the need for carefully standardised assessment by competently qualified clinical practitioners. It is possible that Mr Smith has improved his verbal IQ performance through more recent educational experiences, or that previous assessment performances were influenced by anxiety or other forms of distress or dysfunction. Despite the observed discrepancy in testing results over time, it seems safe to conclude that Mr Smith is currently functioning in the average range of intelligence, so that formal intellectual deficits do not appear to pose a substantial impediment to his capacity to benefit from treatment and thereby reduce his risk of reoffending.

Risk Assessment

Mr Smith's potential to reoffend was evaluated using actuarial risk assessment measures and standardised dynamic risk factors. Specifically, he was evaluated using the Static-99, a risk assessment measure utilising historical offence-related variables, as well as the Psychopathy Checklist Revised (PCL-R), and the Stable-2007, a measure of dynamic risk factors for sexual reoffending.

Static Risk Factors

Actuarial static risk measures such as the Static-99 work by placing an offender in a group of offenders with similar unchanging (static) historical characteristics for whom reoffence rates have been determined over time following their release from prison. On the Static-99, Mr Smith was scored in the high range of risk for sexual reoffending, based on his prior sexual offences, his choice of unrelated, male strangers as victims, and his lack of long-term intimate adult relationships. Large samples of other sexual offenders scoring in this range on the Static-99 have shown sexual recidivism rates of 39% at five years, 45% at ten years, and 52% at fifteen years following release to the community (Harris, Phenix, Hanson, & Thornton, 2003). More recent norms for the Static-99 indicate that Mr Smith' score places him in a group that has a five-year sexual recidivism rate of 28.2% for routine correctional samples and 44.0% for high-risk samples, and ten-year sexual recidivism rates of 39.8% for routine samples and 54.3% for high-risk samples (Helmus, Hanson, & Thornton, 2009). Another way of reporting risk for someone with Mr Smith's Static-99 score is that his relative risk of sexual recidivism is four times higher than the average sex offender.

Dynamic Risk Factors

While risk assessments based on static factors are, by definition unchanging, it is recognised by many experts in this field that risk is influenced by changing emotional, interpersonal and situational variables, referred to as dynamic risk factors. Internationally recognised and empirically founded measures of dynamic risk factors for sexual reoffending include instruments referred to as the Stable and Acute (Hanson & Harris, 2001). These measures assess both stable dynamic factors that contribute to risk but change slowly over time, and acute factors that may be present for a short period of time and contribute to an individual's more immediate risk for sexual offending. A recent revision to the Stable and Acute appeared in 2007 and are referred to as the Stable-2007 and Acute-2007. Earlier and widely used versions of these measures have been available since 2000, and are referred to as the Stable-2000 and Acute-2000.

Stable Dynamic Factors

There is a clear consensus in the field of risk assessment with sexual offenders that best practice standards require the use of standardised measures specifically developed for the assessment of dynamic risk factors. Stable dynamic risk factors are defined by Hanson, Harris, Scott and Helmus (2007) as 'personal skill deficits, predilections, and learned behaviors that correlate with sexual recidivism but that can be changed through intervention' (p. i). The Stable-2007 assesses 13 dynamic risk factors that include significant social influences, capacity for relationship stability, emotional identification with children, hostility toward women, general social rejection, lack of concern for others, impulsivity, poor problem-solving skills, negative emotionality, sexual preoccupation, using sex as coping, deviant sexual preference and cooperation with supervision. Items are scored 0, 1 or 2 according to specified criteria, and then a total score is obtained that places the offender in one of three risk categories labelled low, moderate or high.

The first item on negative social influences assesses the nature of the offender's primary interpersonal relationships. Mr Smith identified several family members as his closest relationships, and the information he provided suggests that none of them represent clearly antisocial influences on Mr Smith's behaviour (e.g., condoning sexual abuse, supporting alcohol or drug abuse, criminal activities, or defiance of the conditions of supervision). The capacity for relationship stability refers to having had a stable intimate relationship of at least two years' duration, which Mr Smith lacks. He showed no signs of emotional identification with children or significant hostility toward women. He did demonstrate evidence of general social rejection and lack of concern for others. Impulsivity is currently less of a problem for Mr Smith than it has been in the past, but he still occasionally displays impulsive behaviour. Similarly, he has shown improvements in his problem-solving skills and negative emotionality, although in recent months he has had episodes demonstrating both of these problems.

Based on the current assessment of Mr Smith's recent functioning, there is little evidence that he continues to experience the high levels of sexual preoccupation and sex drive that was evident in his descriptions of his behaviour when he was younger. The observations of the prison officers also suggest that Mr Smith is not a sexually preoccupied or sexually active prisoner. His self-reported sexual fantasy and masturbatory behaviour do not suggest the use of sex as coping at this point in time. The sexual offences for which he has been convicted suggest the presence of a deviant sexual preference for coercive sexual activity with pre- and post-pubescent males. The presence of deviant sexual arousal is one of the strongest risk factors for sexual reoffending, and will be considered in more detail in a subsequent section of this report.

The final item addresses cooperation with supervision. Ideally, this item is intended to assess the adequacy of compliance and cooperation with supervision in the community, as the Stable-2000 and 2007 were designed to monitor the current risk level of offenders on parole. However, the reports of prison officers familiar with Mr Smith indicate that he is a generally compliant and cooperative inmate, and has been given a position of responsibility in the unit garden. Mr

Smith also reports a willingness to comply with any conditions associated with parole supervision. Results of the current assessment yield a total score on the Stable-2007 that places Mr Smith in the range of scores labelled as *Moderate risk* by the developers of this measure.

Acute Dynamic Factors

Risk assessment with sex offenders also calls for consideration of acute dynamic risk factors, defined as highly transient conditions that would only last hours or days. These factors include 'rapidly changing environmental and intrapersonal stresses, conditions, or events that have been shown by previous research to be related to imminent sexual reoffence' (Hanson et al., 2007, p. i). The Acute-2007 is designed to assess these factors, including items to assess victim access, hostility, sexual preoccupation, rejection of supervision, emotional collapse, collapse of social supports and substance abuse. These items are explicitly designed to monitor an offender's ongoing functioning under supervision in the community, and typically cannot be adequately assessed in a way that can be extrapolated to his functioning in the postrelease environment while the offender remains incarcerated. However, based on information regarding Mr Smith's functioning over the period of his offending, it can be anticipated that he should be particularly cautious in the areas of victim access, collapse of social supports and sexual preoccupation. If he places himself in a situation without appropriate, stable social support, experiences a return of sexual preoccupation, and creates situations that provide potential access to victims, this re-creation of conditions associated with his previous sexual offending will increase the risk of reoffending.

There is no precise formula available for combining the results of actuarial risk measures such as the Static-99 and dynamic risk measures such as the Stable and Acute to arrive at a clearly defined adjusted level of risk for sexual reoffending.

The approach recommended by the internationally recognised expert Karl Hanson and his colleagues (Hanson et al., 2007) suggests that a high level of static risk combined with a moderate level of stable dynamic risk yields what they refer to as a high overall risk.

As previously described, actuarial approaches to risk assessment work by placing an individual offender in a group of offenders with similar characteristics for whom specific sexual reoffending rates over time have been observed. In order to better understand the risk presented by the offender under consideration, an individualised formulation is needed, including other factors known to contribute to increased risk.

Psychopathy

Psychopathy is a severe form of personality disorder defined by a distinctive set of behaviours and personality traits. Highly psychopathic offenders have consistently shown significantly higher rates of sexual recidivism, as well as greater levels of institutional misconduct and poor response to available treatment programs. Especially high rates of sexual recidivism have been observed in offenders who show a combination of high psychopathy and deviant sexual arousal.

Mr Smith has been previously assessed using the Psychopathy Checklist Screening Version (PCL:SV). Results of this evaluation indicated that Mr Smith demonstrates a high level of psychopathic traits. It should be noted that the PCL:SV has demonstrated a relatively high false positive rate, but a consistently low false negative rate. What this means in practice is that if an offender scores highly on the PCL:SV, there is a significant possibility that they are not in fact properly classified as a psychopath (i.e., that the score represents a 'false positive' classification). However, if an offender scores low on the PCL:SV, there is a strong likelihood that they are properly classified as not being a psychopath (i.e., that there is a low likelihood of a 'false negative' classification), and therefore we can be reasonably certain that a low score accurately characterises the individual as not psychopathic.

In cases such as Mr Smith, an assessment with the full PCL-R should be conducted to obtain a more definitive conclusion on the level of psychopathy that is present. Results of the current assessment using the PCL-R found that Mr Smith obtained a score in the moderate range, approximately equal to the mean score for correctional populations. He does not therefore meet the criteria to be classified as highly psychopathic. He does demonstrate certain traits associated with psychopathy, which will bear on his response to treatment and supervision. These characteristics, such as pathological lying, manipulation, lack of remorse and empathy, impulsivity and irresponsibility, may make it more difficult for him to conform to the expectations of a treatment program and to internalise the treatment goals in an enduring manner. However, Mr Smith does not reach the level of psychopathy, as measured by the instrument most commonly used and widely validated in this area, to be included in the class of offenders who have consistently demonstrated the worst outcomes for treatment failure and serious reoffending.

MCMI-III

Considering personality features more broadly as they relate to treatment considerations, results of a Millon Clinical Multiaxial Inventory administered in 2002 provides a profile of Mr Smith's personality features. On this measure, he appears to display prominent avoidant, dependent and self-defeating personality features, marked by a significant level of reported anxiety. Individuals with this profile desperately want to be accepted and involved with other people but this desire is blocked by intense fear of being rejected or ridiculed. They scan their environment for threats to their self-esteem and try to present themselves in a favourable manner, but are seldom successful as they feel a continual sense of uneasiness and anxiety, tending to overreact to minor events. They typically perceive themselves as socially inept, inferior, and inadequate. Because of their fear of social situations and close relationships, they may rely heavily on fantasy to gratify their needs for affection and to cope with their anger. This has the potential to restrict them to a solitary life where they are more likely to reactivate memories of past social rejections, rather than risk forming new, more satisfactory relationships. The dependency traits augment the core avoidant tendencies and add a desire to be supported and guided by others. However, the passive–aggressive elements suggest the presence of moodiness and resentment, with significant difficulty trusting others. Such individuals may vacillate between being friendly and cooperative and then being hostile, followed by apologies to become accepted again. As they are often uncomfortable with their anger, they may resort to covert expressions of hostility, such as passive obstructionism.

Despite remarks regarding a sense of entitlement presented in various earlier reports, Mr Smith had a particularly low score on the scale measuring narcissistic traits, which are often associated with entitlement. It appears that Mr Smith displays entitlement stemming from his overindulgence as a child and his limited capacity to recognise the impact of his behaviour on others or the consequences to himself. Unlike the overtly grandiose sense of self-worth associated with narcissism, Mr Smith in fact struggles with a profound sense of inadequacy and social incompetence, contributing to his anxiety and occasional depression. The potentially positive side of those with essentially avoidant personality patterns is that they can be extremely sensitive to the needs and perspective of others. They can potentially show substantial compassion and understanding and be emotionally responsive, if they can set aside their mistrust and expectation of rejection or ridicule to develop more direct and less reactive interactions with others.

Sexual Deviance

Research has indicated that the presence of deviant sexual arousal is associated with increased rates of sexual reoffending. The generally accepted best standardised procedure for assessing deviant sexual arousal is penile plethysmograph technology (PPG), which measures increases in penile circumference in response to various sexual stimuli, usually including visual and/or auditory stimuli.

Evidence for sexual deviance can be drawn from the pattern of Mr Smith's sexual offending against young males over an extended period of time. Sex offenders with male victims are known, through research conducted on large groups of offenders across a number of jurisdictions, to have significantly higher rates of sexual reoffending than those who have only female victims. Paedophiles with a distinct sexual preference for prepubescent children, especially when this includes males, present a select subgroup of offenders with a particularly high risk of sexual reoffending.

The assessment of sexual deviance warrants close consideration. It appears that risk assessment experts sometimes conclude that deviant sexual arousal must be present, based solely on the presence of convictions for sexual offences. Yet sexual offending alone is not sufficient evidence for the presence of sexual deviance. International experts such as Stephen Hart and Randall Kropp (2009) have stated:

> Mental health professionals should attempt a direct and comprehensive evaluation of sexual deviance, gathering information about normal and abnormal sexual thoughts, urges, images, fantasies, behavior, and physiological arousal. An important corollary of this standard is that assessments of sexual deviance should avoid over-focusing on convictions for sexual offenses. Sexual offenses are neither necessary nor sufficient for a diagnosis of sexual deviance. Many people with sexual deviance never act on their thoughts, images, urges, or fantasies; and many of those who act in a manner con-

> sistent with their sexual deviance do so in a way that may be perfectly legal (e.g., see Marshall, 2006). Also, many — perhaps the majority — of people who commit sexual offenses do not suffer from sexual deviance. Sexual offenses may be the result of many other causal factors, including such things as anger, generalized negative attitudes toward women, poor impulse control, poor heterosexual skills, and inappropriate sexualization of nonsexual needs. Assuming that all sexual offenders have sexual deviance is as illogical as assuming that all thieves have kleptomania or that all arsonists have pyromania. (p. 560)

In the case of Mr Smith, there is sufficient evidence that he experiences deviant sexual arousal. The assessments conducted as part of his treatment program participation included the penile plethysmograph (PPG), which indicated significant levels of arousal to coercive sexual stimuli with pre- and post-pubescent males and females. He also has self-reported sexual arousal to fantasies of dominance and physically coercive sex with adolescent boys.

Clinical Case Formulation

Mr Smith's early life experiences included rejection and ridicule by his peers, combined with an overindulgence by his mother and ineffectual discipline related to his progressively disabled father. These conditions lead to the development of a profound sense of inadequacy and anxiety, social incompetence and isolation, along with a sense of entitlement and the use of manipulation and lying to get his way within the family. Although he had a strong desire to connect interpersonally with others, he did not develop the social skills or interpersonal sensitivity to achieve lasting relationships. When his dependency needs were not met and he experienced instead the teasing and ridicule of his peers, he appears to have begun to comfort himself through sexual stimulation, with fantasies of control, aggression and retribution. His offending thus resulted from a highly sexualised ideation of others, particularly physically and emotionally less mature males with whom he could act out the deviant sexual fantasies that had been repeatedly reinforced through masturbation.

Previous psychological reports have noted that Mr Smith's sexual offences against children have become more opportunistic and predatory in nature. Records indicate that Mr Smith continued to experience difficulties developing and maintaining satisfactory adult relationships, resulting in subjective distress and feelings of isolation. It appears that Mr Smith utilised his previous pattern of sexual preoccupation to mediate stress and regulate his affect, and that fantasies of control and dominance served to soothe his sense of inadequacy while expressing his anger and resentment over the perceived rejections of others. Specifically, in his most recent sexual offending, Mr Smith drove around in his car to locate a potential victim, an adolescent male that he believed he could intimidate and control. He then physically and sexually abused the victim at different times during a period of more than two hours, and induced a significant level of fear both to gain the victim's compliance and to prevent him from reporting the incident. These behaviours seem to manifest Mr Smith's sexualised fantasies of dominance, control and aggression, which serve to facilitate temporary feelings of power and efficacy that Mr Smith otherwise lacks.

Conclusions Regarding Risk

Results of the current assessment indicate that Mr Smith presents a high risk of sexual reoffending. He obtained a score on the Static-99 that places him in the high-risk category for that measure. His score on the Stable-2007 was in the moderate range. The combination of these two measures results in an overall high level of risk according to guidelines from the experts who developed these scales. Although Mr Smith is currently assessed as demonstrating only moderate levels of psychopathy, his pattern of previous sexual offending and the results of PPG assessment following specialised treatment for sex offenders indicate an enduring deviant sexual arousal. This factor is empirically associated with elevated levels of risk for sexual reoffending. The most likely victims of any sexual reoffending by Mr Smith, should it occur, are preadolescent or adolescent males. Based on his pattern of previous offending, such offences are likely to be opportunistic sexual assaults against males previously unknown to Mr Smith during periods of social isolation when he is experiencing negative moods and a sense of being personally inadequate or powerless.

Recommendations

Treatment

Treatment goals at this stage are seen as a continuation of the extensive treatment experiences that Mr Smith has already undergone. He appears to have a solid cognitive understanding of his offence cycle, including the precursors and high-risk situations associated with his sexual offences. He states that he continues to practise the masturbatory reconditioning techniques that he has been taught in order to strengthen his arousal to appropriate adult partners and decrease his interest in young males like those he has victimised. The areas where he needs to demonstrate continuing progress involve applying the skills and insights that he has learned in his current everyday interpersonal relationships. He accurately identifies that he needs to work on being consistently open and honest in his dealing with others and eliminate his use of deceit, manipulation and secrecy, as these behaviours have contributed to the development of situations in which he has offended and interfered with his capacity to benefit from interventions.

Specific treatment goals for Mr Smith have been consistently identified in previous psychological reports. These have included:

- develop an understanding of how he came to offend
- learn how to maintain healthy adult relationships
- replace sexual thoughts of children with appropriate adult fantasies
- replace coercive sexual thoughts with appropriate intimate fantasies
- learn appropriate interpersonal boundaries
- develop alternative coping strategies during time of negative emotions
- learn not to see children as sex objects
- understand the effects of offending on victims and develop empathy
- recognise and challenge cognitive distortions
- learn warning signs to his offending and high-risk situations and how to manage these.

In light of Mr Smith's extensive treatment history, it is anticipated that little more is to be gained from additional intensive residential treatment for his sexual offending. He appears to have acquired, at a cognitive level, an understanding of the precursors to his offending and the factors associated with increased risk of reoffending. He has been taught a variety of cognitive and behavioural techniques for managing this risk. What remains for Mr Smith is the need to further internalise these treatment gains and demonstrate a consistent adherence to candid, honest, prosocial behaviour in his daily interactions.

Planning for Release: Risk Contingencies

Risk is contingent on a variety of personal and environmental factors, and a specific release plan should be developed for Mr Smith. He recognises the importance of a reintegration process that includes the development of a support network in the community. A key factor in minimising his risk will be the adequacy of his close relationships with appropriate adult partners. The distress, isolation and frustration that have resulted from previous situations in which Mr Smith has failed to establish adequate relationships with other adults have directly contributed to his sexual offences. Therefore it is essential that Mr Smith establish and maintain a strong social network of individuals familiar with his offence cycle who will be actively involved in his transition to an offence-free lifestyle in the community.

An adequate release plan for Mr Smith should therefore include consideration of his living situation, with particular attention to the nature of his close interpersonal relationships. Mr Smith also recognises that placing himself in situations where he is alone, especially if he is driving around in a car with access to potential victims, will put him at particularly high risk of reoffending. Having a supportive social network available, and suitable activities accessed through reliable modes of public transportation, will correspondingly reduce his immediate level of risk.

Need for Supervision

The imposition of an Extended Supervision Order following Mr Smith's release from prison is, of course, a matter for the Court to decide. The current assessment indicates that Mr Smith continues to present a high risk of sexual reoffending against young males, especially under circumstances that appear likely to exist in Mr Smith's life in the community without ongoing supervision and support. Some form of monitoring and support services for Mr Smith to assist him in making a successful transition to a productive and offence-free lifestyle outside of prison is therefore recommended.

Jean-Luc Picard, Ph.D. — Registered Clinical Psychologist,
Date April 25, 2006

Commentary on Assessment

Goals of Forensic Risk Assessment and Measures Used

As mentioned in the introductory comments of this chapter, the primary goal of forensic risk assessment is to provide objective information based on current best practice standards to judicial decision-makers. There are a variety of psychometric, ethical and professional practice issues inherent in this area of specialisation, which are beyond the scope of this chapter to address in detail (see e.g., Beech, Craig, & Browne, 2009; Bush, Connell, & Denney, 2006; Campbell, 2007; Craig, Browne, & Beech, 2008; Doren, 2002; LaFond, 2005; Melton, Petrila, Poythress, & Slobogin, 2007; Winick & LaFond, 2003). The main points to be discussed here concern the current state of risk assessment measures, the corresponding need to be specific in reporting about both the strengths and limitations of our risk assessment methods and some of the special considerations about the professional role of the risk assessment expert.

Choice of Measures

The field of forensic risk assessment has seen substantial advances over the past 20 years with the development of empirically validated actuarial measures. Although there is continuing debate over the optimal utilisation of static and dynamic risk factors in risk assessment (see e.g., Quinsey, Harris, Rice, & Cormier, 2006, versus Hanson & Harris, 2001; Craig, Browne, & Stringer, 2004), actuarial measures have consistently demonstrated a significant improvement over clinical judgment for predicting the risk of sexual reoffending. Actuarial measures function by placing individual offenders into groups with known reconviction rates, so that individual risk estimates are based on observed group outcomes. Examples of such measures with research evidence of predictive validity include the Violence Risk Appraisal Guide (VRAG; Harris, Rice, & Quinsey, 1993), the Sex Offender Risk Appraisal Guide (SORAG; Quinsey, Harris, Rice, & Cormier, 1998), the Rapid Risk Assessment of Sexual Offense Recidivism (RRASOR; Hanson, 1997), and the Static-99 (Hanson & Thornton, 2000). Actuarial measures such as these form the foundation of the best-validated risk assessment procedures currently available. Recent risk measures specifically developed for sexual offenders also include the Risk of Sexual Violence Protocol (RSVP; Hart et al.,

2003) and the Risk Matrix 2000 (Thornton et al., 2003). These measures provide promising approaches to utilising static and dynamic risk factors in a comprehensive assessment of risk, but currently have not undergone the same degree of empirical validation of other available measures.

The actuarial measure with the most empirical support is the Static-99 (Hanson & Thornton, 2000). The Static-99 contains 10 items based on historical factors. These include: number of prior sexual offences, number of prior sentencing dates, convictions of noncontact sex offences, nonsexual violence in the index offence, prior convictions for nonsexual violence, having unrelated victims, having victims who are strangers, having male victims, being under 25 years of age and being single (i.e., never having been in a live-in intimate relationship for at least two years). Doren (2004) noted that there had been at least 22 studies of the Static-99's predictive validity beyond the Hanson and Thornton (2000) developmental study, where they originally reported a significant correlation with sexual recidivism and statistics indicating moderate levels of predictive accuracy. Hanson and Morton-Bourgon (2009) cite 63 replication studies, demonstrating the rapid advance in the empirical investigation of this measure.

Recent research on sex offenders has shown that risk predictions made by static actuarial measures can be enhanced by incorporating dynamic variables to give a fuller picture of individualised prediction of risk of this subgroup (Craig, Browne, & Stringer, 2004; Craissati & Beech, 2005). Studies have given empirical support to the hypothesis that including an assessment of dynamic factors can strengthen the predictive ability of static actuarial measures designed to measure sexual recidivism (Beech, Friendship, Erikson, & Hanson, 2002; Thornton, 2002). A recent review of the effectiveness of sexual recidivism risk assessments found that structured clinical judgment, where a clinician makes a prediction of risk guided by an appropriate actuarial measure, combined with dynamic variables specific to an individual offender, showed good predictive accuracy (Hanson & Morton-Bourgon, 2005).

Predictive Accuracy of Risk Measures

Unlike determinate sentences following conviction for a criminal offence, current community protection laws provide for the imposition of legal and civil sanctions such as involuntary civil commitment or extended supervision against sex offenders based on the risk of future offences (Vess, 2009c; Vess & Eccleston, 2009). The primary concerns about human rights in relation to judicial decisions that may curtail an offender's freedom under such laws therefore stem from the current level of accuracy of available measures to predict the likelihood of sexual reoffending. There often appears to be confusion on this issue in the evidence provided to the Court through risk assessment reports and expert testimony, which will make it difficult for the Court to draw clear conclusions about the accuracy of risk assessment findings, and therefore to decide the proper weight to place on the available evidence. Because of the important issues of community safety and individual offender rights involved in assessing and reporting risk, practitioners should be able to clearly communicate the known parameters for the accuracy of the risk measures that they use (Vess, 2009b).

Ethical Concerns

Risk assessment with offenders also introduces special considerations about the limits of confidentiality and informed consent. In such cases, the client is often the Court or other judicial body rather than the individual offender. In many legal contexts involving risk assessment, the assessor is authorised to proceed with the assessment report regardless of whether the offender consents to an interview or declines to participate in the assessment process. The limits of confidentiality, as well as the current and future uses of the assessment report, must be made completely clear to the individual being assessed when seeking their informed consent to engage in the assessment (Vess, 2009a; Vess, Ward, & Yates, in press; Ward, Gannon, & Vess, 2009).

Other ethical considerations in this area involve the clarity of role boundaries. Although the primary client is seldom the offender, we are inviting an individual to engage in a process of self-revelation that will have a direct effect on decisions made about his or her liberty. There is an inherent ethical tension between the trust and rapport that is essential to an optimal assessment process and the utilisation of information in reports to the courts or other state agencies that have the power to determine the offender's freedom. The role of the assessor and the boundaries involved in the assessment process must be made explicitly clear to the offender, even when this may result in more limited disclosure in the assessment process. It is the offender's right to make an informed decision about what he or she discloses, in full awareness of the likely consequences resulting from the use of this information in a risk assessment report (Vess, in press).

Summary

The case of Mr Smith highlights several issues that sometimes arise in forensic risk assessment. Measures must be chosen that are relevant to the individual to be assessed (e.g., the measures were developed and normed on a relevant population sufficiently similar to the current case) and to the legal question to be addressed (e.g., risk of sexual reoffending against children). Where conflicting or inconsistent assessment data are available, attempts should be made to reconcile or explain these discrepancies. Issues of confidentiality and informed consent in the forensic context should be addressed with the individual prior to assessment, regardless of whether their consent is required in order to produce a report. In order to be of optimal utility, the risk assessment should provide an individualised formulation of risk. Such a formulation includes an aetiological, explanatory framework for the individual's offending, and recognises that risk is contingent on internal and external factors that will vary over time. It is only with such an understanding of the case that effective means can be developed for managing risk.

Endnote

1 This case assessment is fictional and is to be used for the purposes of demonstration only. Any resemblance to persons known is entirely coincidental.

References

Beech, A.R., Craig, L.A., & Browne, K.D. (2009). *Assessment and treatment of sex offenders: A handbook.* Chichester, UK: Wiley.

Beech, A., Friendship, C., Erikson, M., & Hanson, R.K. (2002). The relationship between static and dynamic risk factors and reconviction in a sample of U.K. child abusers. *Sexual Abuse: A Journal of Research and Treatment, 14,* 155–167.

Bush, S.S., Connell, M.A., & Denney, R.L. (2006). *Ethical practice in forensic psychology: A systematic model for decision making.* Washington, DC: American Psychological Association.

Campbell, T.W. (2007). *Assessing sex offenders: Problems and pitfalls.* Springfield, IL: Charles C Thomas.

Craig, L.A., Browne, K.D., & Beech, A.R. (2008). *Assessing risk in sex offenders: A practitioner's guide.* Chichester, UK: Wiley.

Craig, L.A., Browne, K.D., & Stringer, I. (2004). Comparing sex offender assessment measures on a U.K. sample. *International Journal of Offender Therapy and Comparative Criminology, 48*, 7–27.

Craissati, J., & Beech, A. (2005). Risk prediction and failure in a complete urban sample of sex offenders. *The Journal of Forensic Psychiatry & Psychology, 16*, 24–40.

Doren, D. (2002). *Evaluating sex offenders: A manual for civil commitments and beyond.* London: Sage.

Doren, D.M. (2004). Stability of the interpretative risk percentages for the RRASOR and Static-99. *Sexual Abuse: A Journal of Research and Treatment, 16*, 25–36.

Hanson, R.K. (1997). *The development of a brief actuarial risk scale for sexual offense recidivism* (User report 1997–04). Ottawa, Canada: Department of the Solicitor General of Canada.

Hanson, R.K., & Harris, A.J.R. (2001). A structured approach to evaluating change among sexual offenders. *Sexual Abuse: A Journal of Research and Treatment, 13*, 105–122.

Hanson, R.K., & Morton-Bourgon, K.E. (2005). The characteristics of persistent sexual offenders: A meta-analysis of recidivism studies. *Journal of Consulting and Clinical Psychology, 73*, 1154–1163.

Hanson, R.K., & Morton-Bourgon, K.E. (2009). The accuracy of recidivism risk assessments for sexual offenders: A meta-analysis of 118 prediction studies. *Psychological Assessment, 21*(1), 1–21.

Hanson, R.K., & Thornton, D. (2000). Improving risk assessment for sex offenders: A comparison of three actuarial scales. *Law and Human Behaviour, 24*, 119–136.

Harris, A.J.R., Phenix, A., Hanson, R.K., & Thornton, D. (2003). Static-99 Coding Rules: Revised — 2003. Retrieved August 23, 2005, from the Public Safety Canada web site at http://www.publicsafety.gc.ca/res/cor/rep/_fl/2003-03-stc-cde-eng.pdf

Harris, G.T., Rice, M.E., & Quinsey, V.L. (1993). Violent recidivism of mentally disordered offenders: The development of a statistical prediction instrument. *Criminal Justice and Behavior, 20*, 315–335.

Hart, S.D., & Kropp, P.R. (2008). Sexual deviance and the law. In D.R. Laws & W.T. O'Donohue (Eds.), *Sexual deviance: Theory, assessment, and treatment* (pp.557–570). New York: Guilford Press.

Hart, S.D., Kropp, R., Laws, D.R., Klaver, J., Logan, C., & Watt, K. (2003). *The Risk for Sexual Violence Protocol (RSVP).* Burnaby, BC: Mental Health, Law and Policy Institute, Simon Fraser University.

Helmus, L., Hanson, R.K., & Thornton, D. (2009). Reporting Static-99 in light of new research on recidivism norms. *The Forum, 21*(1), 38–45.

LaFond, J.Q. (2005). *Preventing sexual violence: How society should cope with sex offenders.* Washington DC: American Psychological Association.

Marshall, W.L. (2006). Diagnostic problems with sexual offenders. In W.L. Marshall, Y.M. Fernandez, L.E. Marshall, & G.A. Serran (Eds.), *Sexual offender treatment: Controversial issues* (pp. 33–44). Chichester, UK: Wiley.

Melton, G.B., Petrila, J., Poythress, N.G., & Slobogin, C. (2007). *Psychological evaluations for the courts: A handbook for mental health professionals and lawyers* (3rd ed.). New York: Guilford Press.

Quinsey, V.L., Harris, G.T., Rice, M.E., & Cormier, C.A. (1998). *Violent offenders: Appraising and managing risk*. Washington, DC: American Psychological Association.

Quinsey, V.L., Harris, G.T., Rice, M.E., & Cormier, C.A. (2006). *Violent offenders: Appraising and managing risk* (2nd ed.). Washington, DC: American Psychological Association.

Thornton, D. (2002). Constructing and testing a framework for dynamic risk assessment. *Sexual Abuse: A Journal of Research and Treatment 14*, 139–153.

Thornton, D., Mann, R., Webster, S., et al. (2003). Distinguishing and combining risks for sexual and violent recidivism. In R. Prentky, E. Janus, M. Seto & A.W. Burgess (Eds.), Understanding and managing sexually coercive behavior. *Annals of the New York Academy of Sciences, 989*, 225–235.

Vess, J. (2008). Sex offender risk assessment: Consideration of human rights in community protection legislation. *Legal and Criminological Psychology, 13*, 245–256.

Vess, J. (2009a). Fear and loathing in public policy: Ethical issues in laws for sex offenders. *Aggression and Violent Behavior, 14*, 264–272.

Vess, J. (2009b). Risk assessment of sexual offenders for Extended Supervision Orders in New Zealand: Basic principles and current practice. *Journal of Child Sexual Abuse, 18*, 174–189.

Vess, J. (2009c). Extended supervision or civil commitment for managing the risk of sexual offenders: Public safety and individual rights. *Sexual Abuse in Australia and New Zealand: An Interdisciplinary Journal, 1*, 70–78.

Vess, J. (in press). Human rights issues in sex offender risk assessment. In D. Boer, L. Craig, R. Eher, M. Miner, & F. Pfafflin (Eds.), *International perspectives on the assessment and treatment of sexual offenders: Theory, practice and research*. Chichester, UK: Wiley.

Ward, T., Gannon, T., & Vess, J. (2009). Human rights, ethical principles and standards in forensic psychology. *International Journal of Offender Therapy and Comparative Criminology, 53*, 126–144.

Vess, J., & Eccleston, L. (2009). Extended supervision of sexual offenders in Australia and New Zealand: Differences in implementation across jurisdictions. *Psychiatry, Psychology and Law, 16*, 271–287.

Vess, J., Ward, T., & Yates, P. (in press). Ethics of risk assessment. In K.D. Browne, A.R. Beech, & L.A. Craig (Eds.), *Assessments in forensic practice*. Chichester, UK: Wiley.

Winick, B.J., & La Fond, J.Q. (Eds.) (2003). *Protecting society from sexually dangerous offenders: Law, justice and therapy*. Washington, DC: American Psychological Association.

CHAPTER 9

Cognitive Assessment of a Patient With Dementia of the Alzheimer's Type

Emma Gould

The case presented in this chapter represents an example of a cognitive assessment conducted for diagnostic purposes and illustrates a number of issues of relevance to cognitive assessment, diagnosis and practice in a rural area. Such cases are typical of those seen by a clinician employed within a public hospital setting, but has the added complexity of being based in a rural area where a clinical psychologist may be required to conduct a more specialised assessment that traditionally falls under the purview of a clinical neuropsychologist. While the eventual diagnosis was one of dementia of the Alzheimer's type (DAT), the referral was made requesting diagnostic impression and an evaluation of the client's competency. This required the clinician to comment on the client's ability to make financial and lifestyle decisions and their ability to live independently. As a high prevalence disorder, DAT cases are often seen by clinicians working within the public hospital system.

Alzheimer's disease is the most common cause of dementia. It is a neurodegenerative disorder of organic origin, with a chronic and progressive pattern of deterioration in cognition, behaviour and activities of daily living (Burns, 2009). Up to 24 million people worldwide were estimated to have suffered from a form of dementia in 2001, with projected estimates of 81 million in 2040 if no effective medical breakthroughs occur in terms of treatment or preventative strategies (Ferri et al., 2005). In Australia, it was estimated that there would be approximately 227,300 cases of dementia by 2008 and 731,000 by 2050 (Access Economics, 2006). With at least 60% of individuals placed in high-care residential facilities and approximately 30% of individuals in low-care facilities having a diagnosis of dementia, it is one of the most common precipitating factors in such placement (Rosewarne et al., 1997).

The *Diagnostic and Statistical Manual* (DSM-IV-TR; American Psychiatric Association, 2000) describes dementia as a progressive impairment in cognitive functioning. It can include such features as: memory decline and problems with new learning; impaired motor coordination; poor communication; deficits in executive functioning, judgment and personality; and emotional disturbances. The DSM-IV-TR details many different dementias with similar symptom presentations differentiated based on aetiology. Dementias can be of cortical, subcortical or mixed variety pathology. DAT is a cortical dementia. Onset of the condition tends to be insidious with gradual decline (Salmon & Filoteo, 2007). Rapid forgetting of new information is considered one of the hallmark features of DAT, with other characteristic cognitive deficits in areas such as executive functioning, working memory and attentional processing (Braaten, Parsons, McCue, Sellers, & Burns, 2006). Aphasia, apraxia and agnosia may also be seen (APA, 2000).

As an assessment primarily aimed at determining decline in cognitive functioning, there are a number of interesting issues highlighted by this case. The client's premorbid intellectual capacity must be estimated in order to determine if there is deterioration. With respect to test selection, it is important to conduct a thorough evaluation of a range of cognitive domains while being mindful of the duration of testing. The length of an assessment and number of sessions are particularly relevant to the assessment of an elderly individual who may fatigue quickly. When conducting a cognitive assessment of an elderly individual, it is also important to consider that some decline in performance may represent expected age-related cognitive deterioration (Maruff & Darby, 2006), thus highlighting the need to use appropriate age-based norms. Another issue illustrated by this case, and of particular relevance to assessment of an elderly individual, is the importance of collecting corroborating information from a reliable source. Due to memory dysfunction, such clients are often poor historians (O'Connor, Brodaty, Chiu, & Ames, 2007). In writing the report it is particularly important to specify clearly where information came from and to compare the client's account with that of another trusted source.

Differential diagnosis is a main focus of this case, driving the selection of appropriate assessment procedures. This required the integration of information from a number of sources and techniques. Such matters are discussed in detail in the second half of this chapter. Particularly important for the clinician to remember is that a diagnosis of DAT is essentially a diagnosis of exclusion. Confirmation of a DAT diagnosis is not possible until autopsy. Other causes of cognitive deterioration that must be ruled out before a diagnosis of DAT can be made include: delirium, substance abuse, a variety of medical conditions, traumatic head injury, vascular disorders, depression and other forms of dementia (Lezak, Howieson, Loring, Hannay, & Fisher, 2004).

As mentioned, this case also depicts a patient admitted to a small hospital located in a rural town. In a small community without access to a neuropsychologist the clinical psychologist asked to conduct the assessment must consider the limited access to neuropsychological tests and their own competence to administer and interpret such tests in relation to brain-behaviour functioning. In addition, the length of a cognitive assessment report in a public hospital setting must be brief and concise as many health professionals within such an environment are too busy to read a lengthy report with detail they may consider superfluous. Issues such as those mentioned above will be discussed in detail following the presentation of the report concerning a fictional client, Ms Iris Reagan.

The client, Ms Iris Reagan, aged 83, had been bought to the Accident and Emergency Department by her daughter, concerned about her considerable recent weight loss, deteriorating mental state and recent failure to cope at home. Upon admission to the hospital, Ms Reagan had a period of confusion and unsteady gait. These resolved after she was treated for a urinary tract infection. The referral was made by Dr E. Kraepelin, a geriatrician at the local hospital, who requested a cognitive assessment to assist with diagnostic clarification and to determine Ms Reagan's competence to make financial and lifestyle decisions.

The Case of Iris Reagan

CLINICAL PSYCHOLOGY ASSESSMENT[1]
PRIVATE AND CONFIDENTIAL

PATIENT NUMBER:	5003481
CLIENT NAME:	Ms Iris Reagan
D.O.B:	July 31, 1926
AGE:	83 years
REFERRAL:	Dr Edward Kraepelin, Geriatrician, Insula Hospital, Daisy Lake
CLINICIAN:	Dr Alexandria Luria, Clinical Psychologist
ASSESSMENT DATES:	August 6, 2009, August 7, 2009, August 11, 2009 and August 13, 2009

Referral and Presenting Problem

Ms Iris Reagan was admitted to Insula Hospital on August 1, 2009 due to deteriorating mental state, failure to cope at home and malnutrition. Upon admission, Ms Reagan's daughter reported that she has a long history of depressive illness, which she believes has been exacerbated by the death of Ms Reagan's husband four months prior. Her daughter further expressed concerns regarding Ms Reagan's recent weight loss and deteriorating memory. Since being admitted to the ward she has appeared confused, with an unsteady gait and periods of wandering. She has also been periodically incontinent, although this appears to have resolved since she was treated for a urinary tract infection. A CT scan on August 4, 2009 showed mild prominence of ventricles and cerebral sulci. No focal lesions were noted. Dr E Kraepelin, a consultant geriatrician, referred Ms Reagan for a cognitive assessment to assist with diagnostic clarification and to determine if she is competent to make financial and lifestyle decisions.

Presentation

Ms Iris Reagan was pleasant and cooperative throughout the assessment, although tired easily and periodically expressed her desire for the sessions to be completed quickly. She ambulated independently, was socially appropriate throughout the assessment and no motor deficits or gait disturbances were noted. Her mood was euthymic, although restricted in range. She described previously feeling very lonely and often 'crying all night', but reported that she had been feeling 'much happier recently'. She denied any suicidal ideation and commented that while she missed her husband very much, she accepted that 'he is now gone and I am comforted by the memory that we had a long and happy life together'. Ms Reagan showed some signs of dysarthria and word-finding difficulties were noted in general conversation. She tended to engage in conversation spontaneously but a paucity of content was noted. With regard to personal history, Ms Reagan's self-report was vague and often contradictory and showed a marked temporal gradient with better recall of events and significant dates from early in her life compared to more recent incidents. She was oriented to person and place, but not to time or day. She was aware that she was in hospital but could not articulate why this was, stating 'I think I had to come to hospital for minor surgery'. Ms Reagan was also uncertain as to how long she had been in hospital but thought it had probably been a 'very long time'. Ms Reagan had little insight into her current deficits, generally unaware that she was performing poorly or unconcerned by her deficits.

History

Information regarding Ms Iris Reagan's personal history was gathered from her medical file and an interview with herself and her eldest daughter (Ms Jane Murdoch). Ms Reagan reported that she had been the youngest of four children, with two brothers and one sister. She is the only surviving sibling.

She was born and raised in the small rural township of Daisy Lake and has lived there all her life. Ms Reagan stated that her mother had died from breast cancer when she was 22 years of age (this was confirmed by her daughter Ms Murdoch) but inaccurately stated this was in 1972 (Ms Reagan was 46 years of age in 1972). Ms Reagan stated she had been very close to her father, who died in 1982 from Alzheimer's disease, caring for him for the last three years of his life.

Ms Reagan was married in 1950 and gave birth to her first daughter, Ms Murdoch, within the first year of marriage. She stated that she has three children, two daughters (Jane and Elizabeth) and her youngest child, a son (Robert), all of whom moved to live in 'the big city' once they completed high school. Ms Murdoch confirmed that she and her siblings all lived in Melbourne and stated that while they tried to visit their mother when they could, none of them felt particularly close to her. Asked about grandchildren, Ms Reagan reported that she had 'four beautiful grandchildren', but was unable to name them, explaining that 'I don't get to see them very often and they have strange names that are hard to get right'. Ms Reagan briefly became tearful when discussing her husband, commenting that she missed him very much and was very lonely since his death. She was confused about how long she had been on her own, at one point stating her husband had died five years earlier, and later in the conversation reporting that he had passed away only two weeks prior. Ms Murdoch stated that her father had died four months earlier after a heart attack.

Asked about education, Ms Reagan stated that she had completed Year 11, but then left school to help care for her mother. She stated she had been disappointed about leaving school as she was 'an excellent student and always enjoyed learning'. Ms Murdoch commented that her mother enjoys watching documentaries and has been an avid reader all her life. After her mother's death Ms Reagan was briefly employed by a local building firm as a bookkeeper, however, she resigned after three years when she gave birth to her first child. She had not been employed since having children, commenting that 'my husband preferred me to stay home and care for our children'. Ms Murdoch stated that her father would have been happy for Ms Reagan to return to work but that she had become withdrawn and isolated, suffering from recurrent episodes of depression throughout her life and this was the reason for her not returning to work.

Ms Murdoch described her mother as 'melancholic and very dependent on my father'. She stated that she and her siblings all had difficult relationships with their mother and felt this was due to her mother's psychiatric history. She recalled two episodes from her childhood where her mother had been hospitalised following suicide attempts, but did not believe her mother had attempted to take her own life since then. Ms Murdoch commented that she was worried that her mother's current state was due to grief and felt that her mother had 'lost the will to live since my father passed away'. Medical records show Ms Reagan has been treated with a series of antidepressants and has been taking sertraline since 2001. Ms Reagan described her health as 'very good', stating that she has never experienced any major health concerns but that she occasionally suffers from headaches. Medical records indicate she suffers from high blood pressure, was hospitalised in 1992 when she had her gallbladder removed, but has otherwise been physically healthy throughout her life. At the time of her current hospital admission she was described as 'seriously malnourished'. Ms Reagan stated that she had never liked the taste of alcohol and her daughter confirmed that she had never drank alcohol or smoked cigarettes.

Ms Murdoch had not seen her mother for three months prior to her admission to hospital. She stated that she arrived to visit with her mother on Saturday (August 1, 2009) and was shocked to see her mother had lost a considerable amount of weight since she last saw her, was untidy and dishevelled in appearance and there was a pile of unpaid utility bills on the kitchen bench. She reported that Mr Reagan had always paid all the household bills, and made financial and social decisions for the couple. Ms Murdoch took her mother to the Accident and Emergency Department of Insula hospital and she was immediately admitted to hospital.

Ms Reagan believes that her memory is not as good as it was previously but does not report any functional difficulties with forgetting information or becoming lost. Ms Reagan said that she enjoys reading and reads the paper every day; however, she was unable to engage in conversation concerning recent news events. She acknowledged that her daughter is concerned about her but stated that she did not believe her son-in-law would like her to live with them. Ms Reagan reported that she would not require extra assistance if she returned home, indicating that she cooks for herself and enjoys ironing. She could not explain why she had lost weight recently and was unconcerned about her daughter's suggestion that she was not coping at home on her own.

Tests Administered

- Wechsler Adult Intelligence Scale–Fourth Edition (WAIS-IV; selected subtests)
- Wechsler Memory Scale–Fourth Edition (WMS-IV; selected subtests)
- Hopkins Verbal Learning Test–Revised
- Controlled Oral Word Association Test (COWAT)
- Trail Making Test
- Geriatric Depression Scale (self-report completed by Ms Reagan)
- Geriatric Depression Scale (informant version completed by Ms Reagan's daughter, Ms Murdoch)
- Hamilton Depression Rating Scale (clinician rating scale)
- Praxis and Naming were assessed informally

Results

While Ms Reagan did not complete high school and has limited work history, she did finish Year 11 and has always shown a keen interest in learning. Based on this, her premorbid intellectual functioning is estimated to have been in the average range.

It is important to note that Ms Reagan fatigued easily during assessment, leading to a number of brief testing session. She persevered with tasks, even when difficult and demonstrated consistently good effort. On the basis of Ms Reagan's test-taking behaviours, the results of this assessment are considered a valid indication of her current level of cognitive functioning.

Attention/Concentration

While Ms Reagan was generally attentive and remained focused throughout the assessment, she showed some impairment in higher order attentional processing, becoming easily overwhelmed by more complex tasks. She was unable to shift attention between task demands, indicating impaired switching of attention. Ms Reagan was able to perform routine mental operations, but had difficulty with more complex mental tracking tasks, making several errors when asked to count backwards from 20. Notable cognitive slowing was also observed, with poor performance on all timed tasks and she was easily fatigued by the assessment.

Memory and Learning

Ms Reagan's immediate memory was in the low average range for her age; however, her working memory was considerably poorer, performing in the moderately impaired range. Working memory is the ability to hold information in mind for a brief period of time while mentally manipulating it. She was able to hold up to five piece of information in mind reliably and repeat them after a short period (several seconds). In contrast, on a working memory task, she was unable to consistently reorganise and manipulate three items of information in her mind.

On both verbal and visually presented memory tasks, Ms Reagan consistently performed well below what is expected for her age, reflecting a severe memory deficit. She showed an inability to retain information, even for short periods of time, indicating rapid forgetting of information presented to her. She was unable to benefit from cues or prompts, showing extremely poor recall of information previously presented even when provided in a recognition format. Ms Reagan did not benefit from the repetition of information, showing poor learning across several trials. Moreover, Ms Reagan's poor performance on memory tasks did not appear to be the result of reduced effort as she was unable to improve her performance even when given encouragement and more time to answer. On a list-learning task where she was required to learn a list of 12 words, she showed no improvement over three trials and frequently gave incorrect answers (providing words not on the list) rather than a poverty of answers.

Executive Functioning

In terms of higher order cognitive functioning, Ms Reagan performed in the moderate to severely impaired range on tasks of executive processing. Ms Reagan exhibited cognitive inflexibility, being unable to switch between concepts and was unable to self-monitor. A tendency to perseverate on cognitive and motor tasks was also noted. While she did not show evidence of disinhibition or impulsivity, her problem-solving ability was considerably reduced compared to her estimated premorbid capacity. She performed poorly on both visually and verbally based reasoning tasks. The severe deficits in her ability to reason through verbally based problems indicate that she is unable to adequately respond to everyday problems or changes in her environment. Furthermore, when asked what she would do if she smelt smoke in her home, she stated she would sit and wait for the 'fireman to come' but did not indicate that she would phone the emergency services. Prompted to explain how the fire department would know to come to her home, she replied 'that is their job, so they should notice it and come to my place'.

Visuo-Spatial and Constructional Praxis and Motor Apraxia

While Ms Reagan showed no obvious motor difficulties and was able to perform basic motor praxis tasks, she did show moderate deficits on tasks of spatial conceptualisation and orientation. She showed considerable difficulty in drawing a clock face, making errors in relation to the positioning of the numbers and the general organisation of the image.

Language

Ms Reagan performed in the severely impaired range on tests of verbal fluency. She had particular difficulty in generating words from a semantic prompt, performing better with a phonemic cue. She performed adequately on a very basic informal test of confrontation naming (able to correctly identify the examiner's watch and various other objects around the room), but some mild word-finding difficulties were noted through the course of the assessment.

Mood

Some variability was noted in the evaluation of depression, based on the source of the information. Ms Reagan's daughter, Ms Murdoch, completed the Geriatric Depression Scale (informant version) with a score of 9/15, endorsing such item as 'she feels that her life is empty' and 'she often feels helpless'. In contrast, Ms Reagan scored only 10/30 on the self-report version of the Geriatric Depression Scale, placing her barely in the moderately depressed range (moderate depression indicated by scores in the range of 10 to 19). Contrary to her daughter's estimates, Ms Reagan endorsed such items as 'I am basically satisfied with my life', 'I feel happy most of the time' and 'I do not feel I have more problems with memory than most'. While scoring in the moderately depressed range, some of Ms Reagan's responses that contributed to this score were age-appropriate, such as 'I do not feel full of energy'.

While several of the items on the Hamilton Depression Rating Scale may lead to inflated scores in an elderly population, Ms Reagan's score of 15 (above the range of 0 to 7 for nondepressed population, but lower than the score of 20 used as a cut-off for moderate severity depression) clearly indicates that her current mood is not of great concern. This score is relatively low, given her past history of depressive illness, and, as with the Geriatric Depression Scale, the score is more reflective of her physical symptoms such as insomnia and weight loss, rather than any evidence of lowered or depressed mood. Furthermore, Ms Reagan did not show any signs of depression during the assessment; becoming appropriately tearful when discussing her husband's death but otherwise exhibiting generally euthymic mood.

Summary and Conclusion

Ms Reagan is an 83-year-old widow who was admitted to Insula Hospital due to deteriorating mental state, failure to cope at home and malnutrition. Medical records showed that upon admission she was described as 'confused, with unsteady gait and periods of wandering'. Incontinence, also first noted early in her admission, had since resolved following treatment for a urinary tract infection, and no obvious gait or motor disturbances were noted during the current examination. While Ms Reagan has a long history of major depressive disorder, her current mood appears only mildly depressed and she denied any suicidal ideation. While her current state of cognitive decline is likely to be exacerbated by the recent death of her husband, both due to the grief associated with this and the sudden change in her home circumstances, the degree of impairment observed on testing is greater than that expected as a result of depressive illness and suggests a more organic aetiology. Ms Reagan showed global impairment on cognitive testing, with her ability to retain new information, verbal fluency and problem-solving capacity being noted as especially impaired.

Strengths

- Ms Reagan showed good social skills
- attention and concentration were intact at a basic level
- no obvious motor difficulties were noted and basic motor praxis was intact
- only mild word-finding difficulties were noted and she performed well on basic, informal confrontation naming.

Weaknesses

- Ms Reagan was unable to switch attentional focus
- she showed considerable cognitive slowing
- her working memory span was moderately impaired
- Ms Reagan showed severe deficits in respect to learning and memory, with rapid forgetting of new information
- prompts and cues did not help with recall of information
- Ms Reagan showed moderate to severe deficits in executive functioning; especially notable were her poor reasoning and problem-solving abilities
- spatial processing was impaired and she had moderate deficits in visuo-spatial construction
- her verbal fluency was severely impaired, with semantic cues considerably poorer than her performance on phonemically cued fluency.

The pattern of performance exhibited by Ms Reagan, along with mild prominence of ventricles and cerebral sulci noted on CT scan, is consistent with a neurodegenerative disorder. While she does appear to be functioning globally at a cognitive level well below her estimated premorbid intellectual level, her rapid forgetting of information on memory tasks, and decreased verbal fluency are strong indicators of impairment resulting from dementia of the Alzheimer's type. A review assessment should be conducted in 12 months to confirm continued cognitive decline.

Ms Reagan also showed impaired insight into her current cognitive status and the impact of these deficits upon her everyday functioning. This and her impaired problem-solving abilities will mean that Ms Reagan will have difficulty with financial planning and making complex decisions regarding her lifestyle. She will be unable to effectively respond to novelty. Ms Reagan's poor problem-solving and reasoning will impact upon her ability to self-care even at the very basic level. She will require considerable care and supervision and returning to independent living is not recommended.

Diagnosis

Axis I:	290.0	Dementia of the Alzheimer's Type (Uncomplicated) (Principle current diagnosis)
	296.36	Major Depressive Disorder (Recurrent, in full remission)
Axis II:		Nil
Axis III:	331.0	Alzheimer's disease
Axis IV:		Death of spouse Poor family and social support
Axis V:		GAF = 31

Recommendations

- Ms Reagan's ability to make financial and lifestyle decisions is severely impaired; a Power of Attorney should be appointed; the administration of finances and guardianship is recommended if the family is unable to make ongoing decisions regarding Ms Reagan's care (these options should be discussed with Ms Reagan and her family)

- A review assessment by a clinical neuropsychologist in 12 months is recommended
- Education regarding DAT, Ms Reagan's current cognitive status and her long-term prognosis should be provided to her family
- Return to living at home is not recommended as Ms Reagan's executive deficits indicate that she will be unable to monitor her activities and attend to basic self-care needs
- Because she has difficulty planning and organising her actions, coordinating daily tasks such as shopping, cleaning and cooking are likely to be problematic. Mrs Reagan should be seen by an occupational therapist for a functional assessment of her daily living skills
- Due to Ms Reagan's poor executive functioning she will benefit from a well-structured environment with a clear routine provided for her
- When information is given to her, it should be broken down into small segments
- Only one or two segments of information should be presented at a time, to avoid overloading and poor concentration
- Strategies such as diaries and reminders on a whiteboard are unlikely to help, she will require explicit prompts and reminders immediately before she is to do a task or attend an appointment
- It is preferable that she deals with only one task at a time, rather than alternating between two or more

---

Dr Alexandria Luria — Clinical Psychologist
August 15, 2009

Commentary

Aims and Techniques Used in Assessment

Dementia of the Alzheimer's type (DAT) is one of 12 different dementia diagnoses listed in the DSM-IV-TR. While the case presented in this chapter represents a relatively 'classic' cognitive profile of DAT, it does illustrate a number of important issues with regard to the assessment of cognitive functioning. The following commentary will address issues such as determining cognitive deterioration or change, differential diagnosis, conducting assessments with elderly patients, working in a rural setting and approaches to report writing.

Prior to discussing the assessment and write up of this case, it is important to highlight that the client was seen in a rural hospital located in a small country town. In a major metropolitan hospital, such a cognitive assessment referral would usually be made to a clinical neuropsychologist. In this fictitious case, the clinical psychologist was experienced in conducting cognitive assessments, having worked in a rural location for many years thus necessitating the need to have a broad range of competencies. If this case had included more complex features posing greater difficulty in distinguishing the probable type of dementia and requiring the use of specialised neuropsychological instruments the clinician was neither trained in nor had access to, the client should have been referred to a clinical neuropsychologist. This may have involved transporting the client to a metropolitan hospital.

A key feature of this case was the focus on a decline in functioning. This was evident from the referral question, and hospital admission notes detailing 'deteriorating mental state' and 'recent weight loss and deteriorating memory'. As a consequence, one of the first objectives of the assessment was to determine deterioration or decline in functioning and to establish the client's current level of cognitive functioning to use as a baseline to compare future results to in order to corroborate further deterioration. With no prior cognitive or intellectual assessment, it is necessary to estimate a client's premorbid intelligence in order to make a judgment on whether the current state represents a change. There are several methods for estimating premorbid intelligence quotient (IQ). One technique is to use a reading test that consists of words of irregular spelling, such as the National Adult Reading Test (NART; Nelson & Willison, 1991). The NART is commonly used in neuropsychological settings as a rough measure of premorbid IQ as the irregularly spelt words are unlikely to be pronounced correctly unless the individual has prior knowledge of them. While a useful technique, due to the advanced age of this client the addition of an extra cognitive test was considered too demanding and unnecessary. Some authors have proposed the use of algorithms based on variables such as educational background, gender, ethnicity and occupation. One example of this is the Barona Index (Barona, Reynolds, & Chastain, 1984). Unfortunately, such algorithms have often been found to overestimate premorbid IQ levels and tend to be less accurate for individuals of extremely low or high functioning (Groth-Marnat, 2009; for a commentary of algorithm estimates of premorbid IQ, see Hawkins, 2006). Given that most of these algorithms yield a considerably decreased premorbid IQ estimate for someone with minimal employment history and would not have given credit to Ms Reagan for her sustained interest in 'learning' and enjoyment of documentaries, the use of an algorithm was also not considered appropriate. Instead, Dr Luria based her estimate of Ms Reagan's premorbid IQ on clinical judgment, informed by information about educational history (noting that completion of Year 11 when Ms Reagan was young was a relatively high level of education for a female), employment history (while brief, Ms Reagan did not find the work too intellectually challenging and cognitively was capable of continued employment) and her interest in the world around her.

Closely associated with the concept of decline in functioning and of relevance to clear and accurate diagnosis, is the establishment of a thorough baseline assessment for use in review investigations. One of the main aims of assessment is to establish a comprehensive baseline of performance (Groth-Marnat, 2009). In possible dementia cases, such as this example, a review assessment can be compared to the baseline results to confirm the progressive deterioration inherent in a diagnosis of dementia. While the case of Iris Reagan includes strong evidence of reduced daily living skills from the history and a clear cognitive profile consistent with DAT (see discussion below), it may often be necessary for a clinician to be more tentative in suggesting a diagnosis of dementia until a review assessment has been conducted.

Given that definitive confirmation of DAT is currently still only possible at autopsy, DAT is a diagnosis based on exclusion. The clinician needs to rule out other possible causes of decline in functioning such as age-related cognitive decline, substance abuse, medical conditions, vascular disorders, delirium, other forms of dementia and depression (Lezak et al., 2004). As discussed above, formal testing showed clear deterioration in cognitive functioning compared to estimated premorbid IQ and this was, as shown by comparison to age-based norms, considerably below expectations for the client's age. As such, age-related cognitive decline was easily ruled out. No history of substance abuse was noted and there were no ongoing medical conditions that could be causally linked to her current state. While Ms Reagan suffered from high blood pressure, she did not have any other major risk factors for vascular disorders, there was no reported history of ischemia and no evidence of infarction on the CT scan. Based on this background information, vascular dementia seemed an unlikely diagnosis and her performance on assessment showed none of the obvious characteristics of vascular dementia, such as more focal cognitive deficits — in comparison to the widespread deficits exhibited by Ms Reagan — and a stepwise deterioration in functioning (Lezak et al., 2004; Sachdev, 2007). With no major motor disturbance noted, and the late age of onset, subcortical dementias such as Parkinson's and Huntington's disease also do not appear to be viable diagnostic options. Delirium is an important possibility to consider when making a potential diagnosis of dementia. While both dementia and delirium can manifest with global, and often severe, cognitive impairment (Rabin, Wishart, Fields, & Saykin, 2006), delirium tends to have an acute onset, reduced alertness, changes in psychomotor behaviour (increased or decreased), disorganised or sometimes incoherent thinking and may include delusions or hallucinations (Sachdev, 2007). While it is possible that Ms Reagan was showing some features of delirium upon her admission to hospital, with an unsteady gait and acute confusion, this had resolved following the effective treatment of a urinary tract infection. Even prior to formal assessment it was apparent that the assessment would focus on distinguishing between the diagnoses of dementia and depression, especially given the patient's history of depressive illness. It should also be noted that these diagnoses are not necessarily mutually exclusive.

The final general issue of note concerns the length and style of the written report. Report format and length can vary due to the setting in which the assessment is conducted, the target audience and the referral question (Groth-Marnat & Horvarth, 2006). Effective reports answer the referral question and communicate the results of the assessment clearly and succinctly and in language that the intended recipient of the report will understand (Smith-Harvey, 1997). Compared to many of the other case examples in this book, the example report written about Iris Reagan is relatively brief. Rather than documenting a formal mental status exam (MSE), many of the elements of an MSE are described in the presentation section of the report. Due to her reported prior history of depressive illness, the client's mood and potential risk for suicidal ideation was obviously of prime concern and is discussed in the report. In line with the referral, the assessment in this case was primarily cognitive and this is the main focus of the report. Furthermore, information from the medical file and other assessment, such as the CT scan, was kept to a minimum as the referral source was employed by the hospital and would have access to this information directly from the patient's general medical file. The referring doctor would also be familiar with medical terms used in the report. Such hospital reports are often brief because doctors with heavy case loads do not have the time to read lengthy reports about every client. It is for this reason the current report also includes a summary section.

Choice of Measures

The following section will focus on why the assessment techniques used in this case were selected and what information they provided the clinician to assist in making a diagnosis and answering the referral question. Conducting a thorough assessment that covers all relevant domains of functioning without administering an unnecessarily long battery of cognitive tests is often difficult to balance in such cases. Elderly clients often fatigue easily, necessitating the administration of a range of tests across several sessions or reducing the number of assessment measures administered. The importance of integrating information from a range of different sources is highlighted and alternative assessment tools commonly used in dementia assessments will also be mentioned briefly.

Assessment is more than just administering psychometric tests. An important part of the information-gathering process involves collecting personal history information about the client (Groth-Marnat,

2009). With respect to the diagnosis of dementia and, more specifically, distinguishing between the various forms of dementia, information about the rate of decline can be invaluable. Vascular dementia is often described as having a 'stepwise' decline in functioning as increasing neurological damage occurs with each successive vascular event, while the deterioration in DAT is generally more gradual and insidious (Rabin et al., 2006). While gradual decline was not obvious from the information provided by the client's daughter, this case highlights its complex nature. The client was recently widowed. The death of a spouse represents a major stressful event, producing profound feelings of loss and grief. In addition, in this case it also left Ms Reagan living independently and was a significant change in circumstances. The gradual decline in functioning of an individual suffering from DAT may often go unnoticed until a considerable change in their environment occurs. Major changes to living arrangements and other lifestyle circumstances require considerable cognitive flexibility and problem-solving skills that may be beyond the capacity of the individual with dementia, leaving them unable to compensate and adapt (Sachdev, 2007). This was apparent in the current case. Moreover, progressive and gradual decline in functioning may have been occurring prior to her husband's death but was unnoticed by others as a spouse often compensates for their partner's inability to cope (Sachdev, 2007). Finally, due to her history of depression and predictable grief over her husband's death, Ms Reagan's children were primed to attribute any difficulty in her ability to cope to mood-related impairment.

The history interview conducted with Ms Reagan also highlighted many of her cognitive and memory difficulties. Observation of Ms Reagan during this time provided valuable information of relevance to her current mental status and questions about her perception of her ability to cope at home yielded useful evidence of her lack of insight. Her inability to discuss anything that she had recently read in the paper suggested memory loss. Ms Reagan was also more accurate in detailing personal information from her younger years than in reporting of more recent events. This temporal nature of her long-term memory decline is characteristic of DAT. Due to poor memory and lack of insight in dementia cases, corroboration of information from other sources is essential (Sachdev, 2007).

Cognitive impairment can result from a myriad of biological and psychological causes. Perusal of the medical file enabled the clinician to rule out a number of medical causes for the deficits seen in this case. Common causes of intellectual dysfunction that should be ruled out include traumatic brain injury, medication toxicity, infection, hypothyroidism and B12 deficiency (Rabin et al., 2006). The CT scan showed no focal lesions as may be expected after a stroke or a traumatic brain injury, instead revealing evidence of general brain atrophy consistent with the global impairment across many domains noted on the formal cognitive assessment.

The WAIS-IV (Wechsler, 2008) is one of the most frequently used measures of cognitive capacity. It has sound psychometric properties and provides useful information to the clinician about their client's cognitive strengths and weaknesses (Groth-Marnat, 2009). While this test battery is often used to provide IQ and composite index scores, there is little need for a clinician to determine the IQ of a patient with dementia. In order to keep the testing to a minimum with an elderly individual who fatigues easily, only selected subtests from the WAIS-IV were administered. Initially, nonverbal subtests tend to be reduced on the WAIS-IV in comparison to verbal subtests. In a sample of individuals with a probable diagnosis of mild DAT, scores on the Processing Speed Index were found to be 10 points lower than the mean Verbal Comprehension Index score (Wechsler, 2008). Deficits are commonly seen on subtests that are unfamiliar, timed or abstract in nature (Lezak et al., 2004). Symbol Search, Coding, Arithmetic and Information are subtests that are particularly sensitive to impairment due to DAT (Groth-Marnat, 2009). Vocabulary was administered to Iris as a useful measure of her current verbal abilities. As one of the subtests most resistant to cognitive deterioration (Groth-Marnat, 2009) it also served as another informal tool to assist the clinician in estimating premorbid IQ. Symbol Search and Coding revealed notable motor and cognitive slowing. Her performance on Similarities was concrete, revealing Ms Reagan has poor abstract verbal reasoning skills. Performance on both Matrix Reasoning and Visual Puzzles indicated the poor problem-solving and reasoning skills extended to nonverbal tasks. Working memory was assessed by Letter-Number-Sequencing and Digit Span. Relatively intact immediate memory span was noted as evidenced by adequate performance on Digit Span

Forwards, while considerable difficulty with the mental manipulation of Digit Span Backwards and Letter-Number-Sequencing was observed. To further reduce assessment duration, Arithmetic was not administered as it was anticipated that Ms Reagan would struggle with this task due to her Working Memory deficits.

Learning and memory was predominantly assessed by the Hopkins Verbal Learning Test–Revised (HVLT-R; Benedict, Schretlen, Groninger, & Brandt, 1998) and the WMS-IV (Wechsler, 2009). While there are many word list-learning test available, such as the California Verbal Learning Test (Delis, Kaplan, Kramer, & Ober, 2000), the Auditory Verbal Learning Test (Schmidt, 1996) and Word Lists from the WMS-III (Wechsler, 1997), Ms Reagan was administered the HVLT-R. The HVLT-R was selected because it is easy to administer, has been validated for use in several neurologically impaired populations, including DAT, and is particularly well tolerated even by individuals with severe memory deficits. It includes 12 words, which is fewer than most of the other list-learning tasks, and they represent four different semantic categories. With only three learning trials it is shorter than other tests of this type (Benedict et al., 1998). Ms Reagan performed on trial one at a similar level to Digit Span Forwards, reflecting her relatively intact immediate memory span. However, she showed little improvement across learning trials and severely impoverished recall after a 25-minute delay, indicative of the rapid forgetting that is a hallmark of DAT. The level of memory impairment seen in this case was more extreme than would be expected of an individual suffering from depressive illness. Observation of the client's performance on this task also helped distinguish between memory disturbance due to DAT or major depressive disorder. Individuals suffering from depression often believe their memory is poor but with praise and encouragement can often improve their recall of information. Poorer performance is often reflected in recall of fewer words but with few intrusive errors. In contrast, individuals with DAT often appear unaware or unconcerned by their poor performance and often make numerous errors, providing many words at recall that were not on the original list (Sachdev, 2007).

Subtests from the WMS-IV administered to Ms Reagan included Logical Memory, Visual Reproduction and the optional Brief Cognitive Status Exam. Performance on Logical Memory revealed that retention of verbal information was no better for meaningful, story-based information than it was on the HVLT-R. Visual Reproduction showed that memory deficits were not confined to verbally presented information. The Brief Cognitive Status Exam is a new addition to the WMS-IV and provides useful information with respect to a client's orientation, inhibition, incidental recall and mental control (Wechsler, 2009). Furthermore, it includes a clock drawing task that has long been considered a useful task for assessing dementia patients (Lezak et al., 2004).

Additional cognitive tests administered to Ms Reagan included the Controlled Oral Word Association Test (COWAT; Eslinger, Damasio, & Benton, 1984) and the Trail Making Test. COWAT is a verbal fluency task that has been shown to be useful in the assessment of DAT. Verbal fluency is often reduced in patients with DAT and semantic fluency is often more impaired than phonemic fluency (Salmon, Heindel, & Lange, 1999), as was seen in this case. Furthermore, performance on verbal fluency tasks is considerably lower in individuals with DAT compared to individuals with a diagnosis of major depressive disorder (Braaten et al., 2006). Performance on Part B of the Trail Making Test, a measure of complex mental tracking (Lezak, et al., 2004), revealed that Ms Reagan was unable to switch attentional focus.

While many other formal tests of cognition are useful in the assessment of DAT, these can add considerable time to an already lengthy assessment process and are less likely to be readily available to a clinician practicing in a rural area. Particularly in patients with profound cognitive deterioration, many informal techniques will provide sufficient information. Confrontation naming is a skill that is often impaired in DAT (Bowles, Obler, & Albert, 1987) and can be effectively measured by the Boston Naming Test (Goodglass & Kaplan, 2000). In this instance, the clinician did not have access to this task, so simply pointed to items in the room and asked Ms Reagan to name them. Praxis was also evaluated by asking Ms Reagan to pantomime various motor actions such as brushing her teeth and waving goodbye. Difficulty with such tasks has been reported in individuals with DAT (Schwartz, Adair, & Raymer, 2000) and such problems with conceptual apraxia have been found to correlate with the ability of patient's to perform everyday activities (Derouesné, Lagha-Pierucci, Thibault, Baudouin-Madec, & Lacomblez, 2000). Reasoning and problem-solving was further investigated informally by asking Ms Reagan what she would do if she smelt smoke in her home. This technique is particularly useful as it gives the clinician a clear indication of risk when considering whether a patient should return to independent living.

The severity of deficits noted on testing clearly suggested that Iris suffered from dementia rather than reduced cognitive functioning as a result of depression. While the quantitative and qualitative pattern of her results on formal tests also strongly suggested DAT, it was important to assess her current mood given that she has a long history of major depressive disorder and the two diagnoses are not mutually exclusive. The results of the assessment in this case illustrate many of the difficulties with assessing depression in the elderly. Several self-report measures of depression have been shown to have good utility with elderly populations, including the Beck Depression Inventory (BDI-II; Beck, 1987) and the Geriatric Depression Scale used in this case (GDS; Yesavage et al., 1983). While self-report measures are inherently problematic when administered to an individual with cognitive impairment and poor insight, the GSD was selected for use in this case as it was specifically developed for use with older individuals and is easy to administer, even to individuals with cognitive impairment (O'Hara, Coman, & Butters, 2006). Furthermore, this measure is freely available on the internet, along with a recently developed Informant Version. While the use of these two sources was useful, Ms Reagan may have underrated her current level of depression due to her lack of insight and her daughter, Jane Murdoch, may have overestimated her mother's level of depression due to her negative childhood experience with her mother's mood disturbances and her initial belief that her mother's current deterioration was a consequence of grief. To compensate for some of these difficulties, The Hamilton Rating Scale for Depression (HRSD; Hamilton, 1967) was used. The HRSD is an interview-based measure that allows the clinician to evaluate depression severity even in hospitalised or cognitively impaired clients. Careful interpretation is required, as many of the items may be symptoms of other conditions such as dementia and delirium (e.g., sleep disturbances) or are not relevant to elderly individuals (e.g., menstrual disturbance).

Finally, the results of the above assessment were written in a formal report to the geriatrician who made the initial referral.

Recommendations were made concerning the care and treatment that the client would require. Based on the probable diagnosis of DAT, the geriatrician would then need to consider whether Ms Reagan was a suitable candidate for pharmacologic treatment. In follow-up sessions the clinician would discuss with the family Ms Reagan's care needs and emphasise that she is unable to return to independent living. Education of the family thus becomes of paramount importance in cases such as this. Aspects of the assessment can be useful in this regard, enabling the clinician to highlight some of the problem-solving difficulties that would place the client at risk if they were unsupervised and highlighting the severity of memory deficits. The family would need to make decisions regarding whether they were able to care for Ms Reagan themselves, with relevant supports in place, or consider placing her in an appropriate aged care facility. If the client did not have any family, or the family was in dispute about the client's care, the report may be required for an application for guardianship under the *Guardianship and Administration Act (1986).*

Endnote

1 This case assessment is fictional and is to be used for the purposes of demonstration only. Any resemblance to persons known is entirely coincidental.

References

Access Economics. (2006). *Dementia in the Asia Pacific region: The epidemic is here.* Canberra, Australia: Alzheimer's Australia.

American Psychiatric Association. (2000). *Diagnostic and statistical manual of mental disorders* (Revised 4th ed.). Washington, DC: Author.

Barona, A., Reynolds, C., & Chastain, R. (1984). A demographically based index of premorbid intelligence for the WAIS-R. *Journal of Consulting and Clinical Psychology, 52*(5), 885–887.

Beck, A.T. (1987). *Beck depression inventory.* San Antonio, TX: Psychological Corporation.

Benedict, R.H.B., Schretlen, D., Groninger, L., & Brandt, J. (1998). Hopkins verbal learning test–revised: Normative data and analysis of inter-form and test-retest reliability. *The Clinical Neuropsychologist, 12,* 43–55.

Bowles, N.L., Obler, L.K., & Albert, M.L. (1987). Naming errors in healthy aging and dementia of the Alzheimer's type. *Cortex, 23,* 519–524.

Braaten, A.J., Parsons, T.D., McCue, R., Sellers, A., & Burns, W.J. (2006). Neurocognitive differential diagnosis of dementing diseases: Alzheimer's dementia, vascular dementia, frontotemporal dementia, and major depressive disorder. *International Journal of Neuroscience, 116,* 1271–1293.

Burns, A. (2009). Clinical review: Alzheimer's disease. *British Medical Journal, 338*, b158.

Delis, D.C., Kaplan, E., Kramer, J.H., & Ober, B.A. (2000). *California verbal learning test*–2nd ed. *(CVLT-II) manual*. San Antonio, TX: Psychological Corporation.

Derouesné, C., Lagha-Pierucci, S., Thibault, S., Baudouin-Madec, V., & Lacomblez, L. (2000). Apraxic disturbances in patients with mild to moderate Alzheimer's disease. *Neuropsychologia*, 38, 1760–1769.

Eslinger, P.J., Damasio, A.R., & Benton, A.L. (1984). *The Iowa screening battery for mental decline*. Iowa City: University of Iowa.

Ferri, C.P., Prince, M., Brayne, C., Brodaty, H., Fratiglioni, L., Ganguli, M., et al. (2005). Global prevalence of dementia: A Dephi consensus study. *Lancet, 366*, 2112–2117.

Goodglass, H., & Kaplan, E. (2000). *Boston naming test*. Philadelphia: Lippincott Williams & Wilkins.

Groth-Marnat, G. (2009). *Handbook of psychological assessment* (5th. ed.) Hoboken, NJ: Wiley.

Groth-Marnat, G., & Horvath, L.S. (2006). The psychological report: A review of current controversies. *Journal of Clinical Psychology, 62*(1), 73–81.

Hamilton, M. (1967). Development of a rating scale for primary depressive illness. *British Journal of Social and Clinical Psychology, 6*, 278–96.

Hawkins, K.A. (2006). Limitations to the validity of the Barona Regression Formula and similar demographically based methods of estimating preinjury intellectual functioning. *Behavioral Science and the Law, 13*(4), 491–503.

Lezak, M.D., Howieson, D.B., Loring, D.W., Hannay, H.J., & Fisher, J.S. (2004). *Neuropsychological assessment* (4th ed.). New York: Oxford University Press.

Maruff, P., & Darby, D. (2006). Age-related memory impairment. In P.J. Snyder, P.D. Nussbaum, & D.L. Robins (Eds.), *Clinical neuropsychology: A pocket handbook for assessment* (pp. 155–182). Washington, DC: American Psychological Association.

Nelson, H.E., & Willison, J. (1991). *The National Adult Reading Test (NART): Test Manual* (2nd ed.). Windsor, UK: NFER Nelson.

O'Connor, D., Brodaty, H., Chiu, E., & Ames, D. (2007). Psychiatry of old age. In S. Bloch and B.S. Singh (Eds.), *Foundations of clinical psychiatry* (3rd ed., pp. 457–481). Melbourne, Australia: Melbourne University Press.

O'Hara, R., Coman, E., & Butters, M. (2006). Late-life depression. In P.J. Snyder, P.D. Nussbaum, & D.L Robins (Eds.), *Clinical neuropsychology: A pocket handbook for* assessment (pp. 183–209). Washington, DC: American Psychological Association.

Rabin, L.A., Wishart, H.A., Fields, R.B., & Saykin, A.J. (2006). The dementias. In P.J. Snyder, P.D. Nussbaum, & D.L Robins (Eds.), *Clinical neuropsychology: A pocket handbook for assessment* (pp. 210–239). Washington, DC: American Psychological Association.

Rosewarne, R.C., Opie, J.R., Bruce, A.M., Ward, S., Doyle, C., & Sach, J. (1997). *Care needs of people with dementia and challenging behaviour living in residential facilities: Commonwealth and State service systems.* Aged and Community Care Service Development and Evaluation Reports, Working Paper 4. Canberra, Australia: Australian Government Printing Service.

Sachdev, P. (2007). Neuropsychiatric disorders. In S. Bloch & B.S. Singh (Eds.), *Foundations of clinical psychiatry* (3rd ed., pp. 356–383). Melbourne, Australia: Melbourne University Press.

Salmon, D.P., & Filoteo, J.V. (2007). Neuropsychology of cortical versus subcortical dementia syndromes. *Seminars in Neurology, 27*(1), 7–21.

Salmon, D.P., Heindel, W.C., & Lange, K.L. (1999). Differential decline in word generation from phonemic and semantic categories during the course of Alzheimer's disease: Implications for the integrity of semantic memory. *Journal of the International Neuropsychological Society, 7*, 692–703.

Schmidt, M. (1996). *Rey auditory verbal learning test: A handbook.* Los Angeles, CA: Western Psychological Services.

Schwartz, R.L., Adair, J.C., & Raymer, A.M. (2000). Conceptual apraxia in probable Alzheimer's disease as demonstrated by the Florida Action Recall Test. *Journal of International Neuropsychological Society, 6*, 265–270.

Smith-Harvey, V. (1997). Improving readability of psychological reports. *Professional Psychology, Research and Practice, 28*(3), 271–274.

Wechsler, D. (1997). *Wechsler memory scale.* 3rd ed. San Antonio, TX: Psychological Corporation.

Wechsler, D. (2008). *WAIS-IV administration and scoring manual.* San Antonio, TX: Psychological Corporation.

Wechsler, D. (2009). *WMS-IV administration and scoring manual.* San Antonio, TX: Psychological Corporation.

Yesavage, J.A., Brink, T.L., Rose, T.L., Lum, O., Huang, V., Adey, M.B., & Leirer, V.O. (1983). Development and validation of a geriatric depression screening scale: A preliminary report. *Journal of Psychiatric Research, 17*, 37–49.

CHAPTER 10

The Educational and Clinical Assessment of a Child With Learning Difficulties

Marina Haywood

The case reported in this chapter is of a 15-year-old male referred for a cognitive assessment. The case raises a number of issues that the clinician is frequently confronted with when assessing children in the educational or clinical context. If these issues are not adequately addressed, the ability of the clinician to provide a systematic and comprehensive assessment and written report will be in question and the quality of the recommendations and interventions will suffer accordingly. These issues are: (1) the clarity of the referral question, (2) the ability–achievement discrepancy model used in diagnosing learning disabilities, (3) the usefulness of the (often brief) assessments usually conducted by mental health teams and (4) the choice of assessment tools. The first two issues are discussed here and the final two issues are in the Commentary section at the end of this chapter.

The referral from the child's local mental health team was a request for an assessment of the child's cognitive strengths and weaknesses, a common enough request that should automatically raise suspicions. The request is vague. The questions that immediately jump into the clinician's mind should be the five big Ws:

- Who is involved with the child and the request for an assessment? (Was the referral made at the request of the local mental health team, the child's parents, the school the child attends or all of these? Who should the report be directed to?)
- What has happened for the request to be made? (What has the child been doing to precipitate an assessment?)
- Why has the request been made? Why is it necessary to know the child's strengths and weaknesses?
- Where is the child placed? What school does the child go to?
- When is the request taking place (i.e., how old is the child? What grade is the child currently in?)

Before commencing the assessment, the clinician must seek answers to these questions in order to be able to shape the assessment, as well as the report. Throughout the report, the referral question needs to be answered and if the initial question is inadequate or unclear, the answers the clinician provides will also be inadequate. Of course, the clinician may address other questions that arise during the assessment, however the assessment and report writing process will be easier if as much information about the client is gathered before the assessment takes place.

On initial interview with the child and his mother, it became apparent that the child's future at school was in question. The child had been seen five years previously by an audiologist who diagnosed an 'auditory processing deficit' (a controversial term that is not included as a diagnosis in DSM-IV and tends not to be used by psychologists). At the time, he also underwent a psychological assessment and was diagnosed with dyslexia on the basis of his results on the Wechsler Intelligence Scale for Children — Third Edition (WISC-III) together with results on a reading test. The child had also received a diagnosis of attention deficit hyperactivity disorder (ADHD) by a paediatrician who prescribed Ritalin®, which the child took for about six months. The child ceased taking the medication partly because, according to his mother, the drug did not seem to change his behaviour and partly because she did not agree with the diagnosis.

Before an assessment is conducted, the first step should be to obtain permission from the child's parents to speak to any professionals involved with the child and to obtain any previous reports or details of assessments. This aids in gathering sufficient background information on the child to address the five big Ws. The second step should be to formulate hypotheses based on the information gathered. These hypotheses may take the form of possible diagnoses (in the present case, for example, ADHD, dyslexia, and/or reduced working memory, among others). Clinicians may consult the DSM-IV for the types of diagnoses that may be made and that have been suggested previously. In the case reported here, the clinician familiarised herself with the criteria for ADHD as well as for learning disabilities. It is important for the clinician not to assume the veracity of previous assessments, as is evident in the case report here.

Once an 'intellectual disability' has been precluded (in Australia this is classified as a Full Scale IQ equal to or less than 70 and called 'mental retardation' in DSM-IV) the type of learning disability (if any) needs to be diagnosed. Briefly, DSM-IV classifies 'learning disorders' into 'reading disorders', 'mathematics disorders', 'disorders of written expression', and 'learning disorder not otherwise specified'. In all cases, according to DSM-IV, the disorder is diagnosed if, on a standardised test measuring the particular ability, the child falls 'substantially below that expected given the person's chronological age, intelligence and age-appropriate education'. In other words, the child has normal IQ but displays a discrepancy between performance on an IQ test and a measure of achievement.

What constitutes 'substantially below' is a controversial issue, and varies from country to country and, indeed, from state to state within Australia. DSM-IV defines 'substantially below' as a discrepancy of more than two standard deviations, and between 1 and 2 standard deviations when the child's IQ may be affected by an associated cognitive or medical disorder. The usefulness of this ability–achievement discrepancy model, frequently used to determine whether a child may be classified as having a learning disorder, has been questioned. The issue is important because governments generally will not provide educational aid or funding to a child if they do not meet the discrepancy cut-off. First, children have been reported with a learning disability but without an ability–achievement discrepancy (see Kavale & Flanagan, 2007 and Meyer, 2000, for reviews). Second, scores on ability tests may be affected by (pertinent to the case reported here) reduced working memory and other factors, including mood, but it is difficult (if not impossible) to objectively segment that portion due to an 'associated cognitive disorder'. One can, of course, hypothesise that, for example, a child has reduced performance on a given ability subtest because of (say), reduced working memory, but the extent of that reduction cannot be easily quantified. It is essential that the clinician working with children in an educational setting is acutely aware of these issues, as well as the ability–achievement discrepancy in their particular state or country that is applicable to the child they are assessing.

The style of the report and what to include is partially determined by the clinician's preferences, the referral source and the relevancy of the comment. The manner in which scores are reported is important. For example, scaled scores are understandable by either other clinicians or by someone who is aware that many tests are standardised with a mean of 100 and a standard deviation of 15, but this is not common knowledge. However, it is my feeling that the most understandable types of information are classifications and percentiles. Age- and grade-appropriate levels are unreliable, given the high variability in children's performance, particularly pre-puberty.

I have included some brief recommendations that I considered to be suitable for the client in this case study. I cannot emphasise enough that any recommendations that are to be made should be made AFTER consulting with the people who are involved in the child's welfare (e.g., the mother and their teacher). Children with learning difficulties compensate differently for their disorder, depending on their particular strengths and weaknesses, what they have been exposed to at home and at school, and a myriad of other factors. This means that a recommendation must be made according to the profile of the individual child. For example, a child who forgets routine activities will require different strategies from a child who forgets novel activities. An organised child will differ from a disorganised child. A child who has a preference for functioning in the verbal domain, but not the nonverbal, will also require a set of uniquely designed strategies.

The Case of William

CLINICAL EDUCATIONAL AND PSYCHOLOGICAL ASSESSMENT[1] — PRIVATE AND CONFIDENTIAL

NAME:	William
ADDRESS:	27 Princes Road, Belgolla, Whoop Whoop.
DOB:	January 4, 1990
AGE AT TESTING:	15 years 9 months
CLINICIAN:	Dr Anna Livia Plurabelle
DATES ASSESSED:	September 8 and 26, 2005
DATE OF REPORT:	October 7, 2005

William is a 15-year-old youth referred by the Belgolla Child and Adolescent Mental Health Service (CAMHS) for a full assessment of his strengths and weaknesses. William had been seen previously by various learning specialists in the Belgolla area as throughout his schooling he has had problems concentrating.

On interview, William and his mother, Rosemary, reported that his main problem is with concentration. William said he loses focus easily and gets distracted; that in exams and when he is copying from the board, he has to think how to spell things and that slows him down. Rosemary said, for example, that if she asks him to make his bed she will have to remind him two or three times because he will get distracted on the way and forget what he was asked. William was originally intending to go through to Year 11 and 12 but now wondered whether he should enrol in his local TAFE, which runs an equivalent Year 11–12 stream that is apparently more practically oriented than the traditional school system (as well as teaching literacy and numeracy subjects) and appears to be designed for students who want to work in a trade after high school. William said he likes working with his hands and is interested in becoming a plumber and working with his father, who is a builder.

Background

Family History

William lives with his mother, Rosemary, and his younger sister (aged 9). William's parents are divorced and Rosemary has primary custody of him, although he and his sister stay with their father (Alan) every second weekend and on one or two nights every week. William said he has a good relationship with both his parents and his younger sister. William is also in regular contact with his maternal and paternal grandparents. Rosemary works part-time as a legal secretary, and Alan is a builder.

Medical History

William's hearing and sight were reportedly normal on assessment. Rosemary reported that there was no familial history of learning difficulties with the exception of William's father, who she said was poor at spelling and used to find reading difficult. Significant medical issues included asthma that developed when William was around 8 years of age and has been well managed since that time. No other medical complications were reported.

Developmental History

Rosemary reported an uneventful pregnancy with no birth complications, that William achieved his developmental milestones in infancy and early childhood appropriately, and had no major illnesses as a child.

Educational History

William commenced school at age 5 at Bellgola Primary School. He participated in reading recovery in Grade 1 on a weekly basis for two terms, on the recommendation of the special education teacher at the school, who was concerned about his level of distractibility and ability to follow instructions. William moved to Mullambimbii High School in Year 7 and where he is now in Year 10. His National Assessment Program — Literacy and Numeracy (NAPLAN) results from 2004 when he was in Year 9 indicate he was below the national average for reading comprehension, but in the average range for writing, spelling, grammar and punctuation and numeracy. Comments from William's school reports indicate that he displays poor organisation in writing, a lack of understanding of complex questions, struggles to submit work in time and that he is distractible. These comments were confirmed on interview with his current Year 9 teacher, Mrs Pam Verbosity, who also said that William was a delightful young man who always tried his best. When asked, Mrs Verbosity commented that she did not think, despite William's level of distractibility, that he was particularly impulsive in class.

Previous Assessments

William was referred for speech pathology when he was 5 years old because he was stuttering and not finishing his words when speaking quickly. This reportedly resolved within about nine months of therapy at Mullambimbii Hospital. In 1999, when William was in Grade 4 (at 9 years 3 months), he was seen by Dr Noel Chomsky, psychologist with the Child and Adolescent Mental Health Service (CAMHS) at Mullambimbii, who administered the WISC-III, a measure of intellectual functioning, on which William performed in the high average to superior range for verbal and nonverbal abilities and mental processing speed (82nd, 75th and 73rd percentiles respectively), but below average on a task measuring working memory (at the 25th percentile for his age). Dr Chomsky also administered subtests from the Woodcock

Diagnostic Reading Battery (WDRB), and reported that William performed at an age equivalent of 8 on identifying single words and 11 on reading pseudowords. In contrast, on the Neale Analysis of Reading Ability, William performed at an age equivalent of 7 at reading accuracy. Dr Chomsky reported that the discrepant results between word and nonword reading occurred because of the 'successful training' William received in his Prep year in word decoding skills. On the basis of his reading performance on the Neale, and on reports from his teacher that William underwent reading recovery in Grade 1, Dr Chomsky concluded that William was suffering from a 'specific learning disability that some would call dyslexia'. Dr Chomsky also concluded that William's performance was similar to that of children with ADHD and consequently recommended that he be seen by a speech pathologist and a paediatrician.

William was then referred to Ms Phyllis Phoneme, speech pathologist and audiologist, when he was 8 years 1 month, because of concerns that he was not 'processing sounds efficiently'. The available report (undated) suggested that William had an 'auditory processing deficit' (as measured by the digit span backward task) and difficulty listening in the presence of background noise.

William was then assessed by Dr Sarah Sunshine, paediatrician, who commenced William on a trial of Ritalin®. Rosemary reported that it did not seem to have much of an effect and William stopped taking the medication approximately six months later.

Tests Administered

- Wechsler Intelligence Scale for Children — 4th edition (WISC-IV)
- Wechsler Individual Achievement Test — 2nd edition: selected subtests (WIAT-II)

- Working Memory Test Battery for Children (WMTB-C)
- Children's Memory Scale (CMS) — selected subtests

Results

Presentation

William was casually but appropriately dressed. He was friendly and articulate during the assessment, with a broad smile. There were no obvious signs of receptive or expressive language difficulties and affect was appropriate. He willingly discussed his past and current concerns. He discussed feeling somewhat 'lost' at school, but denied depression and said he was well supported by his teachers and the school generally and said he had a good peer group. William frequently problem-solved aloud and appeared aware of when he was failing a task because of being overloaded with information. He did not appear to be particularly impulsive in his responses. He worked well through the testing session, responding well to feedback and displaying humour when he was obviously failing a task, although he visibly tired both during and at the end of the four-hour assessment. William gave the frequent impression during test administration that he would have a 'burst of energy' and then flag. His performance is viewed as a generally accurate reflection of his capabilities.

General Ability

Overall, William's performance on the WISC-IV fell in the average range for his age (50th percentile) with commensurate verbal and perceptual skills, but with considerable variability. Hence, his performance across domains is reported separately. His full-scale IQ is currently significantly lower than when he was seen in 1997 when he performed overall in the high average to superior range.

Verbal Skills

William performed in the average to high average range for his age (61st percentile) on tasks measuring verbal word definition, conceptual reasoning, and understanding general and social knowledge. His relative weaknesses were in verbally defining words and doing mathematical problems mentally (average range). His performance is significantly lower than when he was seen in 1997, when he performed in the high average to superior range on these latter two tasks.

Nonverbal Skills

William's nonverbal problem-solving abilities also fell in the average to high average range (71st percentile) but, in contrast to his verbal performance, his performance was similar to when he was seen in 1997. His relative strength was on a task requiring synthesising perceptual material (choosing a piece from a number of distractors that fit a geometric design) (superior range). He performed in the average range on tasks requiring him to choose conceptually similar pictures from several distractors and make 3D block arrangements out of 2D pictures.

Speed of Information Processing

William's mental and motoric processing speed fell within the low average to average range for his age (42nd percentile). He did better on a task matching one of two symbols with a corresponding row (average range) and less well on a task requiring transcription of digits to symbols (low average range). I note that this latter task involves working memory as the individual can perform considerably faster if the digit–symbol pairs are memorised. His performance is below expectations, and is also lower than when he was seen in 1997.

Short-Term Working Memory and Attention

William was only able to 'hold' simple verbal information mentally for four digits forwards reliably, and three digits backwards reliably and his performance was in the borderline-impaired to low average range on both tasks (at the 18th percentile). His performance is similar to his 1997 assessment.

William performed similarly on more complex tasks of working memory (the WMTB-C). When he was required to hold and either repeat or match verbal information, he performed in the borderline to low average range for his age (9th percentile). He performed with similar difficulties on tasks requiring him to hold visuo-spatial information (reproducing a maze route and on a measure of spatial span). On more complex tasks requiring the ability to hold and manipulate information, William also performed at the low average range. For example, one task required him to listen to a list of phrases (such as 'scissors cut paper' or 'oranges play music'), make a judgment about their semantic veracity and, after completion of the list, recall the last word of each sentence. While William was correct on his semantic judgments, he was only able to demonstrate reliably a recall span of two words (i.e., listen to two sentences, make judgments about their meaningfulness and then recall the last word of each).

Memory and New Learning

William's immediate and delayed recall was below expectations and variable, but consistent with his reduced working memory. While his recall of meaningful verbally presented information in the form of short stories was at the average level, he recalled considerably more of the first story than the second (e.g., on immediate recall 23/44 compared with 11/44 elements). He was able to retain this information after a 20-minute delay, but appeared confused in his recognition of the material as he scored in the borderline range when asked directly about whether elements of the stories were present. This latter performance suggests the amount of material he had to remember was overwhelming to him.

William's initial recall was reduced and, although he benefited from repetition, the rate at which he learned was below expectations. On a task that required him to learn 14 unrelated word pairs (e.g., cabbage-school), and then recall the second when cued from the first word, he recalled only one pair on the first trial and seven by the third trial. Similarly, on a list of 14 unrelated words, he initially recalled only four words and after four repetitions improved to nine words, which dropped to seven after an intervening task. It was apparent that it was effortful recall that was difficult, as, after a 20-minute delay, William performed in the borderline to low average range on recall of these unrelated words, but at the average range for recognition (i.e., was 'x' in the list?), an easier task for this material.

Academic Achievement

William was administered the WIAT-II to measure his academic achievement. He performed with considerable variability on the reading composite index. While he performed in the high average to superior range for his age on reading single words (97th percentile), in contrast, his reading comprehension was a relative weakness (13th percentile), as was his pseudoword decoding (37th percentile). His written spelling was also a relative weakness (34th percentile). He was able to spell words such as 'beginning', 'subsidise' and 'patients' but spelt 'doubt' as 'dowt', 'ceiling' as 'seeling', 'accept' as 'axcept', 'they're' as 'thear' and 'excitement' as 'excitment'. These errors indicate a lack of knowledge of sound-to-letter rules.

He performed more consistently on the mathematics composite index: maths reasoning (84th percentile) and mathematics calculations (75th percentile). While William made some calculation errors on complex problems and on solving algebraic equations, he generally displayed an awareness of maths rules and strategies. He was able to interpret grids and graphs, use patterns to solve problems and use quantities less than a whole. However, he frequently requested that questions be repeated. He also performed well on the oral language composite: listening comprehension (82nd percentile) and oral comprehension (91st percentile). This latter task involves measures of word fluency (number of words produced in a given time interval) and making up stories to pictures. These stories are scored according to their grammar, punctuation, level of detail, clarity, logical sequencing and originality. His performance on the mathematics composite index and on oral and listening comprehension constitutes a relative strength for William.

Summary of Test Results

William's general level of intellectual functioning was in the average range but with noncommensurate performance across domains. He was in the average to high average range for verbal and nonverbal abilities, and in the low average to average range for mental processing speed and working memory. In comparison to his overall IQ, he demonstrated a number of relative strengths on formal cognitive testing:

- verbal conceptual or inferential knowledge
- expressing social and general knowledge
- perceptual synthesis of material (i.e., piecing together geometric puzzles)
- written maths reasoning
- single word reading
- word reasoning and oral comprehension.

When compared with the previous assessment, William demonstrated some reductions in performance. On these tasks, and on others not given to him on that occasion, his performance is consistent with his current level of intellectual functioning:

- visual conceptual or inferential knowledge
- listening to and repeating short stories
- knowledge of word definitions
- nonverbal problem-solving
- mentally calculating maths problems
- speed of mental processing in a task involving an element of working memory.

William demonstrated relative weaknesses on:

- reading comprehension, written spelling, and reading nonwords
- effortful recall of complex verbal material
- recalling lengthy meaningful material when he found it overwhelming
- initial learning
- learning with repetition
- any task requiring holding or manipulation of visuospatial and verbal information, that is, any task requiring short-term and working memory.

Formulation

William is a young man of 15 years 3 months who was referred by his local CAMHS for an assessment of his cognitive strengths and weaknesses following longstanding concerns about poor concentration and being distractible. When William was approximately 8 years old, he received a diagnosis of ADHD. However, this diagnosis was subsequently disputed by his mother, Rosemary, and by his current school teacher. Moreover, there was no indication during the current assessment that William met any of the DSM-IV diagnostic criteria for this disorder.

When William was assessed in 1997 by Dr Chomsky at CAMHS, his overall level of intellectual functioning was in the high average to superior range, but at the current assessment he performed in the average range. This reduction was on measures of verbal abilities and mental processing speed. In 1997, he performed in the average to superior range on verbal tests and in the average to high average range on mental processing speed. On the current occasion, he performed in the average to high average range on verbal subtests and the low average to average range on mental processing speed tasks. At both assessments, William's working memory was well below expectations, and in the borderline to low average range. In his report, Dr Chomsky concluded that William was suffering from dyslexia. There was no indication in the results of the current assessment that William struggles with reading. His mild difficulty at the current assessment in reading nonwords is most likely a residue of his earlier difficulties in reading, which he now appears to have overcome. Reading nonwords is similar to reading words in a foreign language (or new vocabulary), and in the future William may find it difficult to learn new languages. William's remaining weaknesses (in reading comprehension, written spelling, recall and initial learning), together with the reduction in his intellectual functioning, are most likely due to his reduced working memory. William's reduced working memory may also have impacted on his mental processing speed. He may have learned to partially compensate for reduced working memory by slowing down and becoming more careful in his work (and indeed he made no errors on the tasks measuring mental processing speed).

In the classroom, William's reduced working memory may manifest by him struggling with tasks that combine mental processing demands with storage of several items. He may find it difficult to follow instructions or to keep up with classroom activities, appear inattentive and lose his place. He will also require more time to complete tasks in order that he may monitor the quality of his work, check his work for mistakes, re-find his place when reading and overall attempt to become more organised in his written work.

Moreover, the working memory demands of the classroom increase with increasing age. For example, if a child with poor working memory capacity has found it difficult to learn their times-tables or the mapping of individual sounds to letters or letter groups, once that child reaches a grade at which higher performance is required, the child is likely to fail. There is a strong correlation between working memory and academic achievement. It is not so much that William's intellectual functioning has reduced, but that the gap between his performance on tasks of academic achievement and that of age-matched peers has increased.

The aetiology of working memory deficits is complex and not clear. Working memory is associated with the prefrontal cortex of the brain and the development of the executive functions, but can be reduced independently of the other executive functions (planning, organisation, abstract or conceptual thinking, goal-directed behaviour and impulse control). There may either be a developmental impairment or a developmental delay. If the latter, then the child may be expected to 'catch-up', but if the former, the child's working memory capacity and length of time that material can be held in working memory will be reduced compared with his or her age-matched peers. It is this shortened capacity and duration that William will need to compensate for.

In regard to whether William is entitled to any government funding for his learning difficulty, a diagnosis of a 'learning disorder' according to DSM-IV criteria, would need to be made. While William has real learning difficulties as a result of his reduced working memory, given there is little discrepancy between his level of academic achievement and his overall IQ, such a diagnosis cannot be made.

Recommendations

Rosemary and William are concerned that William is currently in Year 10 and needs to make decisions about the next step in his education. Whatever educational program William decides to take in the next two years, he will require considerably more time than other children to compensate for his reduced working memory. This will be very important when he is sitting exams or doing any time-limited assessment. William is certainly capable of sitting exams but I cannot anticipate the level of his results. Moreover, he would need more time than other children if he undertook any examination process.

In terms of strategies that may be useful to ameliorate reduced working memory, the following suggestions may be useful:

1. When William is attempting to learn something (or even reading a book or watching a DVD), he needs to make himself aware of when his working memory is failing (when he is feeling overwhelmed) and stop at that point in order to consolidate what he has already learned. This is really important because it will give him time for incubation of learning.
2. Not only is it important for William to become aware of when his working memory is failing, but he should also try to become aware of the types of situations that exceed his working memory capacity or overwhelm him. For example, is he good with routine activities (apparently not, given that he consistently forgets routine instructions) or does his working memory fail only when he is doing a novel task? If it is routine instructions that William forgets, he may find it useful to have a short list placed on the fridge that he can regularly check (e.g., photos of a made bed, a tidied room, a cleaned bathroom, etc.).

3. William should keep a notepad with tear-off pages and get into the habit of regularly checking it at least four times a day: before he leaves for school in the morning, as soon as he gets to school, before he leaves for home in the afternoon and when he arrives home. What he writes on the notepad depends on what failures he experiences (see point 2 above). For example, if he remembers to do routine activities but forgets novel ones, such as changing homework, excursions and so forth, he should write the novel tasks on the notepad.
4. When William is reading, he should try the following strategies in order to better comprehend the material. These strategies apply equally to narrative and factual information:

   (a) Pre-reading. Looking through a chapter for subheading, sub-subheadings, key words and italicised words, in order to get an idea of what the chapter is about.

   (b) After each couple of sentences, or after a paragraph, William should try to form an image of what he is reading.

   (c) An alternative method to (b), when the information is not easily imageable, is to paraphrase what he is reading — put it into his own words. Either method will help to get the information into long-term memory and thereby avoid keeping the material in his current (and temporary) working memory. William might also use the notepad to jot down key points in the text (this does NOT involve directly transcribing the text).

   (d) Looking ahead, that is, attempting to guess what will be in the next paragraph.

   (e) Be aware of when his working memory is failing and stopping and re-reading if he doesn't remember what he has read.

These strategies may initially take time and hence seem laborious and time-wasting but if William puts them into practice until they become more or less automatic, it will save considerable time in the future. It may be useful for him to practise with Rosemary approximately 2–3 times per week, by William reading aloud to Rosemary and implementing the steps while he does so.

5. When giving William instructions at home, ask him to repeat them. While this will not prevent him from being distracted and not completing the task, it may at least help him to remember what he had to do if he temporarily forgets.

I hope William finds this report and its recommendations useful. Please do not hesitate to contact me (by phone or email) should you wish to discuss anything further.

Dr Anna Livia Plurabelle — M. Clin. Neuro., PhD.
March 4, 2008

Commentary on the Assessment

Choice of Assessment Tools

In the past, William had been diagnosed as having ADHD, an auditory processing deficit and dyslexia. He was also reportedly disorganised, had difficulty understanding and responding to complex questions and was distractible. These comments should provide you with sufficient detail to form hypotheses about any possible disability so you may determine the type of assessment tools you will use. Hence, William was assessed via measures of IQ, academic achievement, working memory and memory generally, and criteria for ADHD were qualitatively examined during the assessment.

The choice of assessment measures is often largely determined by what is available in the place of assessment. The experienced clinician will realise, however, that it is not the test itself that is important but how it is used combined with the qualitative information that comes from the assessment itself. Obviously, when children are being assessed, measures of IQ and academic achievement are necessary. The choice of other tools should be determined largely on the basis of the historical aspects of the case and whether the child in question has suffered from an acquired or developmental disorder. If the former, the choice of tests will partly be determined by the type and extent of brain damage suffered. With developmental disorders, however, where there is no known brain aetiology, all types of learning disorders should be considered.

Measure of IQ

The minimum assessment tool normally used (and often the only tool) in community assessment centres will be an IQ measure (generally the WISC-IV). Indeed, it is essential for most appraisals, particularly with children, to begin with an examination of intellectual functioning in order to obtain a measure of what the child is capable of doing. The problem arises when it is assumed that WISC-IV performance measures whether the child has a learning disability, instead of the results acting as a baseline against which other test performance may be compared.

The WISC-IV is an excellent tool for providing an estimate of overall intellectual functioning, as well as functioning in the verbal and nonverbal domains. Moreover, subtest scatter may also be clinically meaningful. However, perfectly average (or normal) WISC-IV scores may be obtained by children who nevertheless have quite significant learning difficulties. The scales do not adequately address working memory, phonological processing ability, or whether the child can comprehend adequately. The scales do not measure the executive functions. Moreover, each subtest measures a myriad of abilities and hence reduced performance may be due to different aetiologies.

Working memory acts as a building block for 'higher-level' cognitive processes. If working memory is reduced in a child such as William, performance on any task requiring manipulation of information may also be affected. The Picture Concepts subtest, for example, includes a working memory component. This subtest is thought to be the visual equivalent of the Similarities subtest, both measuring conceptual reasoning, and hence a child should perform similarly across both subtests. However, the presentation of material is very different. In Similarities, only two concepts are presented. In Picture Concepts, eight or even 12 concepts are presented at any one time and the child needs to hold all concepts in mind while sorting out which are similar. If the child has reduced working memory, they may perform poorly on the latter subtest simply because of difficulties holding all concepts in mind, rather than because of reductions in the ability to reason conceptually. An alternative tool to the WISC-IV is the Stanford-Binet Intelligence Scales, Fifth Edition.

Academic Achievement

A measure of academic achievement should give the clinician some knowledge of how the child is functioning at school and whether a discrepancy exists between ability and achievement. As mentioned in the introduction to this case, the 'discrepancy' model is the current model used in Australia to determine whether a child is eligible for government funding, although the amount of the discrepancy varies from state to state.

The WIAT-II, used to assess William, is commonly used in Australia and comprises four component scores: Reading, Mathematics, Written Expression and Oral Expression, with individual subtests within each component that may yield valuable information about how a child is performing in school-based subjects. The combination of the Reading and Oral Expression composite scores will be most useful when diagnosing a reading disorder, for example. A child with dyslexia should, for example, display weaknesses at Reading Single Words, and hence Reading Comprehension, as well as Pseudoword decoding. Conversely, the dyslexic child's strengths will frequently be in oral expression and listening comprehension, although reduced working memory may counter against good listening comprehension, as was seen in the case reported here.

One difficulty with the WIAT-II is that it is lengthy to administer, particularly if the child has difficulty reading or writing. Moreover, it does not measure all types of potential learning difficulties such as difficulties with working memory or language. Hence, it may be best to select the subtests to be administered based on your hypotheses and the child's difficulties. For example, if the clinician has already established that the child is slow at handwriting, and struggles with reading, it would be simpler, and more appropriate, to administer the oral expression subtest instead of the written expression subtest. An alternative to the WIAT-II is the Woodcock-Johnson Test of Achievement (3rd edition).

Working Memory, Memory and Language

The choice of a measure of working memory was determined by the anecdotal descriptions given by William and his mother, the descriptions of his performance at school and the previous diagnosis of an 'auditory processing deficit'. This latter term is frequently used by audiologists and speech pathologists to refer to a difficulty processing speech (and other) sounds and hence may lead to dyslexia, specific language impairment or even working memory difficulties. As is apparent, the difficulty with the term is that it is both all-encompassing and not specific enough. In any event, it should alert the clinician that a given child may indeed have a learning difficulty.

The CMS was chosen to obtain a measure of listening comprehension (story recall), initial learning (word pairs and word lists) and learning with repetition (both word pairs and word lists). These subtests on the CMS most closely 'mimic' learning in the classroom which is largely verbal and repetitive. To the author's knowledge, there is currently no complete alternative to the WMTB-C, although the alternatives to the CMS are the *Wide Range Assessment of Memory and Learning* (2nd edition), the *Test of Memory and Learning* (2nd edition), and the NEPSY-II.

Endnote

1 This case assessment is fictional and is to be used for the purposes of demonstration only. Any resemblance to persons known is entirely coincidental.

References

Adams, W., & Sheslow, D. (2003). *Wide range assessment of memory and learning* (2nd ed.). Camberwell, Australia: ACER.

Cohen, M. (1997). *Children's memory scale.* Marrickville, Australia: Harcourt Assessment

Kavale, A.K., & Flanagan, D.P. (2007). Ability-achievement discrepancy, response to intervention, and assessment of cognitive abilities/processes in specific learning disability identification: Towards a contemporary operational definition. In S.R. Jimerson, M.K. Burns & A.M. Vanderheyden (Eds.), *Handbook of response to intervention: The science and practice of assessment and intervention* (pp. 130–147). New York: Springer Science.

Meyer, M.S. (2000). The ability-achievement discrepancy: Does it contribute to an understanding of learning disabilities? *Educational Psychology Review, 12*(3), 315–337.

Korkman, M., Kirk, U., & Kemp, S. (2007). *NEPSY* (2nd ed.). San Antonio, TX: Pearson Assessment.

Pickering, S., & Gathercole, S. (2001). *Working memory test battery for children.* Marrickville, Australia: Harcourt Assessment.

Reynolds, C.R., & Bigler, E.D. (2007). *Test of memory & learning* (2nd ed.). San Antonio, TX: Pearson Assessment.

Roid, G. (2003). *Stanford-Binet intelligence scales* (5th ed.). Melbourne, Australia: ACER.

Wechsler, D. (2003). *Wechsler intelligence scale for children* (4th ed.). Australian Standardised edition. Sydney, Australia: Harcourt Assessment.

Wechsler, D. (2007). *Wechsler individual achievement test* (2nd ed.). Sydney, Australia: Harcourt Assessment.

Woodcock, R.W., McGrew, K.S., & Mather, N. (2001). *Woodcock-Johnson test of achievement* (3rd ed.). Rolling Meadows, IL: Riverside Publishing.

CHAPTER 11

The Clinical Assessment of a Patient with Schizophrenia

Linda Byrne

Young people presenting with psychotic symptoms pose a myriad of challenges for the clinician. Often there can be concomitant drug and alcohol abuse, poor family relations and a long period of untreated psychosis. All of these factors can result in poorer prognosis for the client. This case highlights the importance of thorough assessment of mental state, symptoms and cognitive functioning in an adolescent patient with a recent diagnosis of schizophrenia, the most common psychotic disorder. While this case has a neuropsychological focus, understanding the cognitive profile of this type of patient can lay the groundwork for development of an appropriate treatment plan.

Schizophrenia is the most common psychotic disorder. With a lifetime prevalence of approximately 4 people in 1000 (Saha, Chant, Welham, & McGrath, 2005), it is a relatively rare disorder. However, it has a high burden of disease. Based on the number of years a person will live with their disorder, it is one of the ten leading causes of disability worldwide (Fleishman, 2003). The age of onset for males is typically between the ages of 17 and 25, for women it is usually in the mid- to late-twenties. Because it affects people at such a young age, often people with schizophrenia do not have the opportunity to finish their education, form relationships or find and maintain meaningful employment. With symptoms ranging from the classic 'positive' indicators of hallucinations and delusions, to 'negative' symptoms including poverty of speech content and impoverishment of emotion and motivation, it is a disorder that can be difficult for the individual and the family to understand. With such a varied presentation, it is clear that schizophrenia is an imperfectly understood group of disorders that affect the brain and behaviour.

There are three key inclusionary features to a diagnosis of schizophrenia, according to the *Diagnostic and Statistical Manual* (DSM-IV-TR; American Psychiatric Association [APA], 2000). The first are the characteristic symptoms of the disorder that include delusions, hallucinations, disorganised speech, grossly disorganised or catatonic behaviour and finally, negative symptoms. At least two (or more) of these symptoms must be present for a *significant* portion of time during a one-month period, or less, if successfully treated. The second necessary feature is social or occupational dysfunction. Work, interpersonal relations or self-care all are included in this category and must be below the level achieved prior to the onset of the disorder. If the affected individual is an adolescent, as in the case presented here, then educational attainment is considered in this category. The third feature to be included for diagnosis is that of duration. There must be a period of at least six months where there are continuous signs of the disturbance. In addition to the inclusionary criteria, as with most DSM-IV diagnoses, there are a series of disorders that must be excluded and these include schizoaffective and mood disorder, substance/general medical condition and relationship to a pervasive developmental disorder. These 'rule-out' diagnoses will be revisited in the commentary section of the case.

A thorough assessment in a case such as this is vital to both the clinician and the client. The first stage is detailed assessment of the client's mental state and symptoms. Once the client's symptoms have been stabilised to some degree by medication and, in this case, electroconvulsive therapy (ECT), the focus can shift to his cognitive capacities. As an adolescent not yet finished schooling, a thorough understanding of his current level of functioning is necessary to assist in educational, and at some point, vocational planning. In addition, the high burden of care for the family in these cases requires the involvement of the caregivers in the assessment process wherever possible. Psychoeducation for the family plays a large role in intervention, but this process commences during the assessment. So too does the establishment of a working relationship with the case manager and the primary health providers once the client returns home. The assessment here is a thorough neuropsychological examination of cognitive abilities with careful attention paid to both the client's mental state and symptom presentation. Particular attention is paid to those areas known to be compromised in schizophrenia. As well as charting deficits, it is important to clearly chart any personal strengths for the client. Mapping what is cognitively possible assists in developing a treatment plan. It is also vital that this information can be fed back to the client's teachers to allow them to help modify aspects of the curriculum as necessary.

There are circumstances under which a clinical psychologist might undertake an assessment of similar scope and depth. Many of the assessment tools used in this case form part of the curriculum in the master's and doctoral courses in clinical psychology and, as such, most clinical psychologists would have the necessary skills to administer and interpret them. While the clinician must remain mindful of not going beyond their level of competence, clinicians located in regional and rural areas without access to specialist neuropsychology services may find themselves undertaking a broader range of testing than in some other settings.

The case presented here follows the fictional case of an 18-year-old youth, Tom Bryant, who was an inpatient in an acute psychiatric ward in a large city hospital at the time of the assessment. Tom lived in a rural setting and had a 20-month history of psychosis. He had recently undergone ECT to treat severe catatonic symptoms. The referral was made by one of the consulting psychiatrists, Dr Maryann Comerford, as Tom's symptoms appeared to be stabilising. The assessment was requested ahead of Tom's likely discharge and return to his parent's home.

The Case of Tom Bryant

REPORT OF NEUROPSYCHOLOGICAL ASSESSMENT1
PRIVATE AND CONFIDENTIAL

NAME:	Tom Bryant
DATE OF BIRTH:	August 10, 1991
ADDRESS:	17 Hillside Crescent, Golden Heights
SOURCE OF REFERRAL:	Dr Maryann Comerford, Consultant Psychiatrist
CLINICIAN:	Dr Marcus Welby, Clinical Neuropsychologist
AGE AT TESTING:	18 years 2 months
DATE OF TESTING:	October 5, 2009, October 6, 2009, October 8, 2009

Presenting Problem

Tom is an 18-year-old youth in his final year of high school. Tom was referred for neuropsychological assessment in order to determine his current level of functioning following recent (4 months previous) electroconvulsive therapy (ECT) treatment. The primary purpose of the assessment is to assist in recommendations to allow Tom to return to school to complete his final year of study.

History of Presenting Problem and Previous Treatment

Tom has a 20-month history of psychosis. He was first seen by his GP, Dr Jason Bateman, following an incident where he wandered away from his home and was found in a confused state. Prior to this incident his parents report some concerns with his behaviour including laughing for no apparent reason, appearing perplexed and fixated on a classmate, with whom he had little previous contact, suspected auditory hallucinations and altered motor behaviour (remaining motionless for long periods of time). These behavioural changes were noticed over an estimated period of two months. His parents also suspect that Tom had started to smoke marijuana just prior to the onset of his problems.

Dr Bateman recommended admission to his local hospital and Tom was commenced on a low dose of rispiridone. No improvement was seen over a two-day period and he was subsequently transferred to the acute psychiatric ward at City Hospital on July 15, 2008. At this time he was unable to follow simple commands and remained confused. During his fifteen-day admission he improved slightly, becoming less confused, but remaining introverted and shy. He was referred to a local psychiatrist (Dr Roberta Green) and was seen periodically over the following months after his return home. During the next 12 months Tom's mental state further deteriorated, he experienced continued auditory hallucinations, prominent negative symptoms and vagueness. During this period his psychiatrist switched his medication to olanzapine. However, given his poor response to treatment, he was readmitted to City Hospital on July 30, 2009. Upon readmission he had minimal response to pharmacological treatment and continued to exhibit marked negative symptoms, including posturing, rigidity and extreme negativism. Symptom evaluation at this time using the Positive and Negative Symptom Scale (PANSS) indicated high levels of positive symptoms and general psychopathology (80th percentile and 75th percentile respectively) and extreme levels of negative symptoms (99.9th percentile). In addition, on the Catatonia Rating Scale, Tom was exhibiting 14 of the 21 catatonic behaviours measured, most at moderate or severe levels. As a consequence, he underwent 12 sessions of ECT and was also placed on small doses of benzodiazepines as required for agitation.

Tom has experienced some improvement in his symptoms in the four months following ECT; however, he still has frequent auditory hallucinations and displays distinct negative symptoms. His spontaneous speech is limited and he needs encouragement to complete tasks at home. Tom also still exhibits some abnormal posturing. At the time of assessment his diagnosis was schizophrenia, catatonic subtype. At the time of assessment he was still taking olanzapine and diazepam.

Family History

Tom lives with his parents on a small, rural property in Golden Heights. He has one maternal half-sister who is 15 years older and three paternal half-brothers (20, 18 and 16 years his senior). Tom's parents are estranged from all of their other children. Tom's mother reported that her pregnancy with him was unexpected and unwanted. Once she came to terms with the pregnancy, she said that she had wanted a daughter. When Tom was born she developed postnatal depression that lasted for approximately three months.

Tom's father has a history of mental health problems with several hospitalisations for depression and anxiety during Tom's preschool and primary school years. Tom's paternal uncle has a history of schizophrenia.

According to Mrs Bryant, the emotional climate in the home was often tense. Communication between the parents was often characterised by conflict. Tom's mother reports that she was disappointed and angry by her husband's frequent hospitalisations and inability to maintain his role as breadwinner. There were also significant unresolved issues of grief and loss surrounding the estrangement of their other children. This was particularly true of Tom's mother who indicated that at times she felt reluctant to show Tom love for fear of him leaving her.

Tom's father admits that he was often 'tough' on his son. He frequently criticised Tom's efforts at school and was particularly disappointed by what he perceived as his son's lack

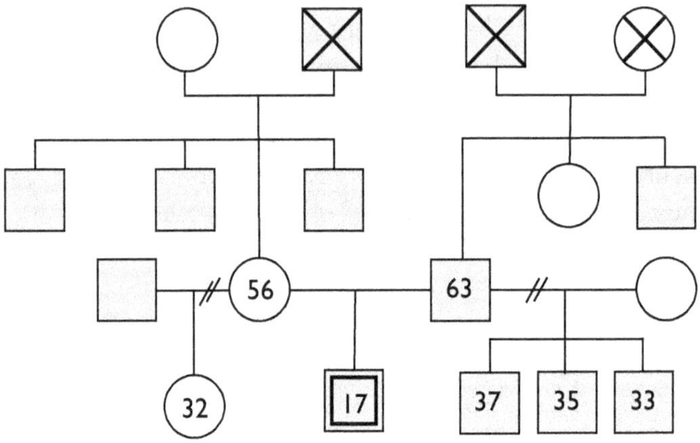

Figure 11.1
Genogram for Tom Bryant.

of sporting prowess. Tom's father reported that he felt that three other sons from a prior marriage were 'ungrateful' and 'always took their mother's side'. He said that he had been a good provider for them and that it 'didn't make any difference' and he believed that they hated him. He has not seen his other children for many years.

Both parents appear unsure of how to assist their son, they both expressed concern that he would be 'just like Jimmy' (Tom's paternal uncle), who has been accommodated in a long-term facility for the mentally ill for over 30 years. They are also concerned about the amount of time that Tom has been out of school and are worried that he may not be able to finish his education. Tom's mother reported that she is unsure of her capacity to care for him at home.

Medical History

Tom's medical history is unremarkable aside from the removal of his appendix at the age of 11. There is no significant neurological history.

Developmental History

Tom was born following a normal pregnancy and vaginal delivery. Tom's mother was a somewhat vague historian, but she believed that he achieved his developmental milestones at a normal rate. Socially, Tom's mother said that he has always only had a few friends.

Educational History

School reports for Tom indicated that in primary school he was an average student and there was no indication of disciplinary problems. This pattern continued at high school. His secondary school home-room teacher indicated that, prior his illness, Tom was an average student in most subjects. He generally performed a little below average in maths. In contrast, he had strengths in music and social sciences. His teachers described him as being quiet and withdrawn, but with a close group of friends. Until around August 2007, his teachers report that his behaviour was normal. Sometime in the latter part of 2007 his teachers reported that his written work was frequently punctuated with profanities. His behaviour also became problematic, swearing at other students, wandering off from classes and appearing to respond to sounds that were not there. The principal of Tom's school has indicated that if at all possible, they would like to have him return to complete his schooling. He is very interested in receiving information regarding the outcome of the assessment in relation to Tom's ability to complete his final year.

Behavioural Observations

Tom presented as an overweight, right-handed male of above-average height. He was dressed in casual clothing. During the first assessment Tom appeared to be withdrawn. He was cooperative with the testing procedure, however, his affect was flat and he demonstrated abnormal body posturing.

Tom's posturing appeared to become worse when he found items difficult. He was extremely softly spoken and had to be asked to repeat some answers in order to be heard. Throughout the assessment he mumbled to himself and would at times respond with repetitive echolalic responses (e.g., 'yeah, yeah, yeah'). On occasion he brought his face very close to the stimulus material on the table as if he had difficulty seeing the items. However, upon questioning he reported that he could see the material. On subsequent assessments, Tom's presentation improved slightly. He was able to maintain eye contact briefly on one or two occasions and even demonstrated some spontaneous speech. His concentration appeared to be sound, as he was able to work for over an hour without a break. Tom's verbal responses to questions were brief. It appeared that if he found a task too difficult, he would not attempt an answer.

Tom was alert and oriented to time and place. However, his behaviour during testing suggested that he was at times responding to auditory hallucinations. For example on a card-sorting task when asked about the strategy he was using, he indicated he was making choices based upon what his voices said. As a result, the current assessment may underestimate his true cognitive abilities.

Tests Administered

- Catatonia Rating Scale (CRS)
- Positive and Negative Symptom Scale (PANSS)
- Wechsler Test of Adult Reading (WTAR)
- Wechsler Adult Intelligence Test–4th Edition (WAIS-IV)
- Wechsler Memory Scale–3rd Edition (WMS-III)
- Wechsler Individual Achievement Test–2nd Edition (WIAT-II)
- Rey Auditory Verbal Learning Test

- Connors Continuous Performance Test
- Rey Complex Figure Test
- Wisconsin Card Sort Test
- Trail Making Test
- Controlled Oral Word Association Test
- Tower of London
- The Awareness of Social Inference Test (TASIT).

NOTE: High Average (74–99%); Average (26–73%); Low Average (10–25%); Borderline (5–9%); Impaired (1–4%). For example if an individual was performing at the 60th percentile this indicates that he is performing at a level that is better than 60% of individuals his age.

Assessment Results

Symptoms

CRS. Tom demonstrated 10 of the 21 symptoms on the CRS including stereotypies, posturing, rigidity, motor inhibition and mutism. Most of these symptoms were rated as minimal, but he demonstrated moderate levels of rigidity, exaggerated responsiveness and mutism. This represents a reduction in catatonic symptoms compared to the assessment prior to commencement of ECT.

PANSS. When compared to other people with a diagnosis of schizophrenia, Tom's current level of positive symptoms is in the average range (55th percentile) with the most prominent positive symptoms being his active hallucinatory behaviour and conceptual disorganisation. In contrast, his level of negative symptoms is extreme (95th percentile). He exhibits the full range of negative symptoms including extreme blunted affect, severe emotional withdrawal, poor rapport, difficulty in abstract thinking, social withdrawal and a lack of spontaneity. His level of general psychopathology as measured by the PANSS is average (65th percentile), with the most prominent features being his posturing, preoccupation and disturbance of volition. Overall, there has been a slight decrease in his symptoms as measured by the PANSS compared to those documented prior to ECT.

Attention, working memory and speed of information processing. Tom was alert and oriented at the time of testing. Tom's performance on a task of sustained attention indicates that he has difficulties with both attention and arousal. He was slow to respond and this was particularly evident as the length of time between stimuli increased. He made a large number of errors on the task suggesting, that he had difficulty attending and that he also had problems inhibiting his responses. Tom's performance on tasks of working memory was variable. On less demanding tasks such as manipulating digits he performed within the normal range for his age. However, on more demanding tasks, he performed poorly. He had difficulty holding and mentally manipulating information. Tom's speed of information processing was also variable. On some tasks he performed within the normal range and on others he performed in the below average range when compared with others of his age.

Intellectual ability. Based on a test of reading, Tom's estimated premorbid level of intellectual functioning was in the average range. In contrast, Tom's current overall level of intellectual functioning is in the well below average (5th percentile) for his age. His verbal ability was in the low average to average range. Nonverbal (performance) ability fell in the impaired to borderline range. There was no significant difference between his overall performance on verbal and nonverbal tasks. Tom demonstrated a relative strength (average range) on a task of general knowledge and a constructional task. His vocabulary was also in the average range. Therefore, some skills that have been well learned appear to remain intact in the context of an overall diminution of abilities.

Learning and memory. Tom demonstrated difficulties on tasks of learning and memory. Tom's immediate recall of visual material was impaired for someone of his age. Following a delay, Tom's performance was below average. However he was able to retain some of the information that he acquired after the immediate trial, indicating that he has difficulty encoding information for later retrieval. Tom's immediate recall of verbal material was also impaired. He demonstrated difficulty in recalling prose passages and in the acquisition of word lists over repeated learning trials. Repetition of material did not improve Tom's performance. His performance on recognition tasks of previously presented material was also impaired for both verbal and visual information. Together these results suggest a significant difficulty with encoding information initially, which is likely to be related to poor attention.

Executive abilities. On tasks of executive ability he demonstrated impairments in planning and organisation, conceptual problem-solving and set shifting.

Visual-spatial skills. On visual-spatial tasks, Tom's performance was varied. His copy of a complex geometric design was intact and his performance on a task of constructional ability was in the average range. However, on other tasks of visual-spatial copying, his performance was impaired when compared to others of his age.

Academic achievement. Tom has good single-word and nonword reading skills (high average). His spelling is in the average range for his age. However, Tom's performance on a task of written computational problems was in the low average range. His performance on tasks of mathematical word problems was in the very low average range for his age. It was noticed during the written computational part of the task that he sometimes rushed the task and made errors because he did not consider what he was required to do (e.g., adding a problem that was actually required subtraction).

Social and emotional functioning. Tom's ability to discriminate between facial expressions was poor. He had difficulties recognising faces displaying anger, disgust and fear. This may result in problems with peer relations if he fails to pick up on the nonverbal indicators in his social interactions with others. He also had difficulty understanding the social inference in conversations where people might say one thing, but mean another.

Summary and Formulation

Tom is an 18-year-old male with a 20-month history of schizophrenia for which he received ECT and is currently taking antipsychotic and anxiolytic medication. Tom displays active hallucinatory behaviour and has marked negative symptoms, including catatonic motor behaviour. Although his current symptomatology is reduced compared to the level he exhibited prior to commencement of ECT treatment. Formal neuropsychological assessment revealed a reduction in intellectual functioning relative to Tom's average estimated premorbid level of functioning. His performance also indicated specific deficits in attention, learning, memory and on tasks of executive functioning, consistent with those seen in individuals with a psychotic illness. He needed encouragement to attempt and complete tasks, especially those he perceived as difficult. Tom also demonstrated marked impairment on tasks of social and emotional functioning. Tom's family life is characterised by high expressed emotion (EE), with confusing and conflicting communication patterns.

Recommendations

Tom will need considerable assistance in order to continue with his schooling this year. He will need assistance with ongoing rehabilitation and school reintegration. It is recommended that Tom undertake cognitive remediation to assist with his difficulties. With encouragement, Tom can attend to a given task; however, his attention is variable. He will need an environment where distractions are kept to a minimum so that he can focus his attention on the task at hand. Tom will benefit from a structured environment where clear routines are established. Given his difficulties with memory, he needs to be taught how to use memory aids such as diaries. Tasks need to be presented in small steps with clear instructions to ensure that he can understand and remember what is expected. Presenting him with too much information, or too many choices, will be overwhelming.

Reassessment is recommended in 12 months time to review Tom's progress. Psychoeducation is recommended for both Tom and his parents as the starting point for a broader therapeutic approach. In addition, referral for family therapy in their area may assist in changing communication patterns that may interfere with Tom's recovery.

Diagnosis

Axis I	295.20	Schizophrenia Catatonic Type
Axis II		Nil
Axis III		Nil
Axis IV		Difficulties with primary support, problems accessing psychiatric care
Axis V	GAF	25 (current)

Treatment Plan

Ongoing Treatment Plan

The overall ongoing management of Tom needs a multi-disciplinary approach, including:

- psychoeducation for Tom's parents
- psychoeducation for Tom

- it is recommended that this material be presented to Tom in a relatively simplistic way, taking into consideration his limited concentration at this time
- psychiatric management and liaison with crisis and community services
- family therapy to treat high EE communication
- cognitive rehabilitation to focus on Tom's current difficulties particularly focusing on attention, memory and executive control.

Dr Marcus Welby, Clinical Neuropsychologist
October 15, 2009

Commentary on Assessment

Aims and Techniques Used in Assessment

Schizophrenia is a relatively uncommon in the general population; however, clients with this diagnosis are frequently seen in acute and outpatient settings. DSM-IV-TR currently lists five subtypes of schizophrenia; paranoid, disorganised, catatonic, undifferentiated and residual. The case presented in this chapter represents one of the most uncommon subtype of schizophrenia, catatonic. Indeed there has been a recommendation that all subtypes are removed under DSM-V (APA, 2010). However, while the diagnosis given to Tom is rare, his cognitive profile is not uncommon in young patients with psychotic illnesses. Particularly where there has been a long duration of untreated psychosis and prominent negative symptoms. His case highlights important considerations when assessing young people with psychotic illnesses, particularly in regard to adequately assessing cognitive functioning. The following commentary will discuss issues surrounding determining symptom levels, differential diagnosis, mapping cognitive change and deciding which cognitive domains to assess. In addition, it will also address considerations when conducting assessments with young people who may have not yet completed their education, treatment planning for this type of client and the size and scope of the report.

Assessment of a young person such as Tom would typically be undertaken by a neuropsychologist. The breadth of testing covered here would ordinarily be beyond the training of most clinical psychologists. As mentioned in the introduction, many of the tests used in this assessment form part of the training curriculum of clinical psychology programs. With additional speciality training, clinical psychologists, particularly those working in areas without access to a neuropsychologist, may feel equipped to undertake similar assessments.

Tom's case clearly is supportive of the biopsychosocial model of the development of schizophrenia. His family history (paternal uncle with schizophrenia) suggests a genetic vulnerability, coupled with the environmental stress of a high EE environment potentially providing the necessary 'double-hit' suggested by the stress–vulnerability model (e.g.,Walker & Diforio, 1997). His behaviour in the early stages of the onset of his disorder raise the spectre of the role of illicit substances, in this case possibly marijuana, in the development of his symptoms. This of course raises the issue of differential diagnosis. Can we rule out a substance-induced psychotic disorder? There are two important issues here; first of all, we have no evidence, just a suspicion that Tom has used marijuana at sometime in the past. According to the DSM-IV-TR criteria for diagnosis of a substance-induced psychotic disorder, there must be *evidence* from 'the history, physical examination or laboratory findings of dependence, abuse, intoxication or withdrawal' (p. 342). Second, Tom's presentation and course of his disorder are better accounted for by the criteria for a primary diagnosis of schizophrenia. As for other possible diagnoses, there is also no evidence from Tom's history or current presentation, that there is a mood component to his disorder, effectively ruling out schizoaffective or mood disorder. Finally, Tom's developmental history does not give any hints of any pervasive developmental disorder.

Carefully charting Tom's symptoms serves a number of purposes. Administering symptom rating scales prior to his ECT treatment and again some months after, allows us to examine the resolution (or not) of symptoms across time. Tom's presentation with the catatonic subtype of schizophrenia is very rare. Only an estimated 1% of cases in developed countries received this diagnosis (Bhugra, 2005). However, higher rates have been reported elsewhere (Bräunig, Krüger, Shugar, Höffler, & Börner, 2000). The rarity of catatonia, and the use of the CRS pre-ECT prompted the clinician to administer this tool in conjunction with the PANSS. Negative symptoms can be particularly resistant to treatment and certainly antipsychotic medication seems to have had limited effectiveness in Tom's case. ECT combined with benzodiazepines has been shown to be the most effective treatment for catatonic symptoms of schizophrenia (Tharyan & Adams, 2005).

As in any disorder where there is the suspicion of cognitive decline, it is important to have some estimate of how the client was functioning before the onset of their difficulties. Emma Gould, in the chapter on cognitive assessment of a patient with dementia of the Alzheimer's Type (DAT), presents an excellent discussion on the various methods of estimating premorbid ability and so a full recap is unnecessary here. The method adopted by Dr Welby was administration of the Wechsler Test of Adult Reading (WTAR; The Psychological Corporation, 2001). The WTAR takes only five to ten minutes to administer and was co-normed with the WAIS-III and the WMS-III. Similar to the National Adult Reading Test (NART; Nelson & Willison, 1991), it is a reading test of words with irregular pronunciation. Given that Tom's schooling has been interrupted by his illness, relying on years of education may produce an inaccurate estimate of his abilities. The difference between his estimated premorbid IQ and his obtained WAIS-IV IQ was marked and indicated a significant drop in his overall level of functioning.

One area of functioning that is sometimes overlooked with young people that present with psychiatric difficulties is academic achievement. Any young person that has not yet completed their education should be assessed with an assessment tool specifically targeting this area. In Tom's case, the referral question explicitly revolves around Tom's capacity to return to school. Dr Welby's administration of selected subtests from the Wechsler Individual Achievement Test–2nd Edition (WIAT-II; Wechsler, 2001) allows for an understanding of the basic level of academic skills he has acquired up until the onset of his illness.

The role of the clinical and neuropsychologist in assessing and treating clients with schizophrenia is multidimensional. While medication remains the first line of treatment for symptom management, psychoeducation, cognitive–behavioural therapy, family therapy and cognitive remediation all have a valuable role to play in improving functional outcome in this group. In addition, there is an emerging literature suggesting that there is a functional significance of social cognition in schizophrenia (Couture, Penn, & Roberts, 2006) and that social cognitive interventions may improve functional outcomes (Horan, Kern, Green, & Penn, 2008). In the case of Tom, Dr Welby acknowledges in his recommendations that a combination of these treatment options may assist Tom and his family.

While cognitive remediation is usually the domain of neuropsychologists, multidisciplinary management of the client can lead to superior outcomes. This is particularly the case when the client is young and there are still many opportunities to assist them in the transition back to their studies. Supportive therapy, especially when it is targeted to address specific deficits and achieve goals set in collaboration with the client, is likely to improve such things as future compliance with medication, ongoing contact with mental health professionals and improve family relations. Moreover, understanding the cognitive strengths and limitations of the client can add in treatment planning.

One final issue relates to the length and general style of the report. Dr Welby has administered a neuropsychological battery that is not atypical in many psychiatric inpatient settings. Testing was lengthy and very comprehensive, and yet the report is relatively brief. As has been noted in other chapters, the style and length of reports will vary depending upon the setting. What should be clear from this case is that reporting of a client's cognitive abilities as measured by a wide variety of tests need not be complicated. Reporting scores for the most part is unnecessary. There are some aspects of this report that are not typical of that written by a neuropsychologist. Developing an ongoing treatment plan is unusual in a neuropsychological report. The inclusion of this section is due to Dr Welby working in a setting where a team of professionals work together to assist Tom's transition back to the community. The brevity reflects an acknowledgment by Dr Welby that many of these treatment options are not the realm of the neuropsychologist. Overall, the goal of this report is to answer the referral question by clearly documenting Tom's current functioning, note any changes and recommend how this information may be best used to assist Tom's return to school.

Choice of Measures

Symptom Assessment

It is clear from the assessment that Tom's symptoms are not properly controlled and are having a detrimental impact on his level of functioning. The application of the PANSS allows for mapping of his current symptom level, which will assist in tracking the resolution (or otherwise) of symptoms over time. The Positive and Negative Symptom Scales (PANSS) contains 30 items and is administered in a semistructured interview format over a period of 30–40 minutes. Additional information provided by hospital staff and family members is sometimes drawn upon for completion of the PANSS. Each item on the PANSS is rated on a seven-point scale (1 = *Symptom is absent*, to 7 = *Symptom is present to an extreme degree*). The PANSS has demonstrated reliability and validity (Kay, Opler, & Lindenmayer, 1988) and is widely used as a method of assessing positive and negative symptoms in schizophrenia.

The inclusion of the Catatonia Rating Scale (CRS) was based upon the relative rarity of the symptoms. Once again, the inclusion of a baseline measure allows for a tracking of the resolution of symptoms. The CRS (Bräunig et al., 2000) is a 21-item clinician-administered rating scale. It comprises 16 catatonic motor symptoms and five catatonic behaviours. The presence and severity of the symptoms are rated during a semistructured examination. It can be administered in conjunction with the PANSS as there are overlapping areas on both scales. The rationale for including an additional rating scale for a subset of psychotic symptoms is that the CRS provides a comprehensive, specific and quantifiable measure of the rare phenomenon of catatonia.

Cognitive Assessment

Cognitive deficits are a core feature in schizophrenia and are present early in the onset of the disorder (Gonzalez-Blanch et al., 2007). There had been some speculation that cognitive deficits would feature in the new criteria for schizophrenia in the DSM-V; however, the taskforce have acknowledged the importance of this area, but specifically excluded them from the new manual (APA, 2010). There has been a large body of research identifying key cognitive deficits and this work has been relied upon by clinicians working with individuals with schizophrenia. As a result of the research, they have typically selected a large, comprehensive battery of tests in order to capture the full range of cognitive domains. Recently the National Institute of Mental Health (NIMH) in the United States undertook an initiative called the Measurement and Treatment Research to Improve Cognition in Schizophrenia (MATRICS). One of the many outcomes of this research has been the development of a consensus cognitive battery, specifically for use in clinical trials (Nuechterlein et al., 2008). This research is important, as key researchers in the area have come together to systematically review the literature, identify the best measures to capture cognitive difficulties in this population and then evaluate their use. The relevance to the practitioner is that this research provides the gold standard for evidence-based practice. Seven key domains were identified as being fundamental in an assessment of schizophrenia; speed of processing, attention/vigilance, working memory, verbal learning, reasoning and problem-solving and finally, social cognition.

So the clinician needs to be guided by the relevant literature when embarking on an assessment of functioning in a given population. However, this case demonstrates how the clinician must go beyond those areas recommended by the research in order to provide the best possible assessment for the individual needs of the client. While assessment should clearly incorporate the seven key domains outlined above, in the context of the referral question, additional assessment is required.

As a result, a comprehensive neuropsychological test battery was selected in order to establish his current and premorbid level of intellectual functioning as well as assessment of academic achievement. This is vital for educational and vocational planning.

The Wechsler Test of Adult Reading (WTAR;The Psychological Corporation, 2001), can be used as an estimate of premorbid ability. Word reading is an ability that remains largely intact in the presence of many other cognitive changes (Lezak et al., 2004). The advantage of the WTAR is that the manual provides tables for direct comparisons with WAIS IQ and WMS-III memory scores.

The WAIS-IV is relatively new and, according to the test publishers, represents an improvement over the WAIS-III in a number of key areas including the size and scope of normative sample and inclusion of more special populations (Wechsler, 2008). It is a comprehensive test of cognitive functioning across four key domains: Verbal

Comprehension, Perceptual Reasoning, Working Memory and Processing Speed. As mentioned above, two of these four domains, Working Memory and Processing Speed are explicitly mentioned by the MATRICs consortium as being fundamental to an assessment of cognition in schizophrenia. Further, administering a complete WAIS-IV to a client such as Tom allows a clear recording of his current intellectual abilities. This is vital if one is to explore change.

At the time of testing, the new WMS-IV (Wechsler, 2009) was not yet released in Australia and so the WMS-III (Wechsler, 1997) was administered. This test, like the other suite of Wechsler tests, has very good psychometric properties and is well used in psychological practices in Australia and overseas. It provides a comprehensive assessment of immediate and delayed recall in both verbal and visual modalities. The Rey Auditory Verbal Learning Test (RAVLT; Lezak, 1983) is a list-learning task that allows for exploration of acquisition of new material, the influence of repeated exposure to learning and recall and how sensitive the client may be to interference. In addition, it also contains a recognition trial. Recognition is easier than free recall and including this measure can allow the clinician to tease out whether a memory deficit may be due to encoding, storage or retrieval difficulties.

The importance of assessing academic achievement in a young person was outlined above. Given that the WTAR, WAIS-IV and WMS-III were all administered, the choice of test for this domain was obvious. The WIAT-II allows the clinician to directly compare a client's academic performance to their intellectual ability. Only selected subtests of the WIAT-III were administered to Tom. Even when such a comprehensive assessment takes place, the clinician needs to remain mindful of the difficulties for the client in completing such a lengthy assessment. Restricting the achievement tests to the core areas of reading, spelling and mathematics provided sufficient information for Dr Welby to address the referral question.

Disruption to attentional processes can be measured in a number of ways. The Continuous Performance Test provides information on the ability of a client to sustain attention. In addition, it also provides information on errors, including omissions (failure to respond) and commissions (responding in error). The CPT has been touted as a potential genetic marker for schizophrenia (Chen et al., 1998). Tom's performance on this test was markedly atypical.

Problem-solving and planning were identified as two of the seven domains that should be examined in schizophrenia. These two types of ability fall under the umbrella of executive functioning. The Wisconsin Card Sort Test, Tower of London and Controlled Oral Word Association test (COWAT) were all selected to exam Tom's executive abilities. Executive functioning relates to higher-order cognitive abilities and these are thought to be mediated by the frontal lobes. The WCST is a classic measure of set-shifting and inhibition. The Tower of London allows for examination of planning and the COWAT test, which is typically included in larger aphasia batteries (see Strauss, Sherman, & Spreen, 2006) measures verbal generativity and can be useful for eliciting preservative responses.

The inclusion of an additional perceptual reasoning task such as the Rey Complex Figure test is typical in a neuropsychological assessment and Tom's performance on this task was one of the few areas of relative strength.

Tom's cognitive profile displays many of the classic findings in the neuropsychological functioning in schizophrenia. He has poor attention, executive control and verbal memory. He has experienced a decline in functioning from his premorbid state. His symptoms, both negative and positive, impacted upon his performance. Despite the severity of his symptoms and the recently exposure to ECT, there are several areas of cognitive ability that remain at least in the average range. It is to these areas that the clinician must look when designing an appropriate intervention.

One final note on the assessment tools used in Tom's case. The Awareness of Social Inference Test (TASIT; McDonald, Flanagan, & Rollins, 2002) is a relatively new test developed in Australia to assess and treat deficits in social perception. It was originally developed to assess and treat these deficits in clients who had suffered a head injury. There are few tests with good psychometric properties that have been developed to measure social cognition. There are fundamental deficits in several areas of social cognition in schizophrenia including emotional perception, social information processing and theory of mind and, as previously mentioned, these deficits are linked to poor functional outcomes (Couture et al., 2006). While this is a relatively new instrument, it is gaining traction in the schizophrenia literature as a useful tool in measuring these important domains (e.g., Chung, Mathews, & Barch, 2010).

Choice of Treatment

There are a number of options available for the clinician when treating a client with schizophrenia. Psychoeducation for both Tom and his family would be the first step. Evidence from trials indicates the effectiveness of this approach as part of any treatment program for people with schizophrenia (Pekkala & Merinder, 2002). Cognitive–behavioural therapy (CBT) has been found to be efficacious in improving both overall mental state and global functioning in randomised control trials (Hodgkinson, Evans, O'Donnell, Nicholson, & Walsh, 2000; Sensky et al., 2000). Clinicians interested in this approach are directed to several excellent resources by Douglas Turkington, David Kingdon and their colleagues (Kingdon & Turkington, 2008; Wright, Turkington, Kingdon, & Basco, 2009).

Two other critical areas focus on remediation of cognitive deficits and social cognitive deficits. The latter was not recommended in Tom's case. This is mainly due to the fact that while there is evidence emerging as to the effectiveness of social cognitive remediation (Horan et al., 2008), as yet this type of program has not found its way into mainstream practice. There has been a body of work generated by Alice Medalia in the United States using an individualised approach to cognitive remediation that has shown some positive outcomes (Medalia, Revheim, & Casey, 2002; Medalia, Revheim, & Casey, 2000). She advocates an approach known as the Neuropsychological Educational Approach to Rehabilitation (NEAR; Medalia & Freilich, 2008). This is a comprehensive, manualised approach that emphasises the cognitive and educational aspects of remediation. This type of intervention has been adopted here in Australia by some clinical neuropsychologists and the outcome of randomised control trial found significant improvements in verbal and visual memory, sustained attention and executive functioning (Redoblado-Hodge et al., 2010).

Endnote

1. This case assessment is fictional and is to be used for the purposes of demonstration only. Any resemblance to persons known is entirely coincidental.

References

American Psychiatric Association. (2010). American Psychiatric Association: DSM-5 development. Retrieved from http://www.dsm5.0rg/Pages/Default.aspx

American Psychiatric Association. (2000). *The diagnostic and statistical manual of mental disorders* (4th ed. — text revised). Washington: Author.

Bräunig, P., Krüger, S., Shugar, G., Höffler, J., & Börner, I. (2000). The Catatonia Rating Scale I: Development, reliability and use. *Comprehensive Psychiatry, 41*(2), 147–158.

Bhugra, D. (2005). The global perspective of schizophrenia. *PLoS Medicine, 2*(5), e151.

Chen, W.J., Hsiao, C.K., Hsiao, L.L., & Hwu, H.G. (1998). Performance of the Continuous Performance Test among community samples. *Schizophrenia Bulletin, 24,* 163-174.

Chung, Y.S., Mathews, J.R., & Barch, D.S. (2010). The effect of social processing on different aspects of social cognition in schizophrenia. *Schizophrenia Bulletin,* doi:10.1093/schbul/sbq012

Couture, S.M., Penn., D.L., & Roberts, D.L. (2006). The functional significance of social cognition in schizophrenia. *Schizophrenia Bulletin, 32*(1), 44–63.

Fleishman, M. (2003). Economic Grand Rounds: Psychopharmacosocioeconomics and the global burden of disease. *Psychiatric Services, 54,* 142–144.

Gonzalez-Blanch, C., Crespo-Facorro, B., Álvarez-Jiménez, M., Manuel Rodríguez-Sáncheza, J., María Pelayo-Terán, J., Pérez-Iglesias, R., et al. (2007). Cognitive dimensions in first-episode schizophrenia spectrum disorders. *Journal of Psychiatric Research, 41,* 968–977.

Hodgkinson, B., Evans, D., O'Donnell, A., Nicholson, J., & Walsh, K. (2000). *The effectiveness of individual therapy and group therapy in the treatment of schizophrenia: a systematic review. No. 5.* Adelaide, Australia: Joanna Briggs Institute for Evidence Based Nursing and Midwifery

Horan, W.P., Kern, R.S., Green, M.F., & Penn, D.L. (2008). Social cognition training for individuals with schizophrenia: emerging evidence. *American Journal of Psychiatric Rehabilitation, 11,* 205–252.

Kay, S.R., Opler, L.A., & Lindenmayer, J. (1988). Reliability and validity of the positive and negative syndrome scale for schizophrenics. *Psychiatry Research, 23,* 99–110.

Kingdon, D.G., & Turkington, D. (2008). *Cognitive therapy of schizophrenia.* New York: Guilford Press.

Lezak, M.D. (1983). *Neuropsychological assessment* (2nd edition). New York: Oxford University Press.

Lezak, M.D., Howieson, D.B., Loring, D.W., Hannay. H.J., & Fisher, J.S. (2004). *Neuropsychological assessment* (4th ed.). New York: Oxford University Press.

McDonald, S., Flanagan, S., & Rollins, J. (2002). *The Awareness of Social Inference Test.* Bury St Edmonds, UK: Thames Valley Test Company.

Medalia, A., & Freilich, B. (2008). The neuropsychological educational approach to cognitive remediation (NEAR) model: Practice principles and outcome studies. *American Journal of Psychiatric Rehabilitation, 11*, 123–143.

Medalia, A., Revheim, N., & Casey, M. (2002). Remediation of problem-solving in schizophrenia: Evidence of a persistent effect. *Schizophrenia Research, 57*, 165–171.

Medalia, A., Revheim, N., & Casey, M. (2000). Remediation of memory disorders in schizophrenia. *Psychological Medicine, 30*, 1451–1459.

Nuechterlein, K.H., Green, M.F., Kern, R.S., Baade, L.E., Barch, D.M., Cohen, J.D. et al., (2008). The MATRICS Consensus Cognitive Battery, Part 1: Test selection, reliability and validity. *American Journal of Psychiatry, 165*, 203–213.

Pekkala, E.T., & Merinder, L.B. (2002). Psychoeducation for schizophrenia. *Cochrane Database of Systematic Reviews, 2.*

Redoblado-Hodge, M.A., Siciliano, D., Withey, P., Moss, B., Moore, G., Judd, G., Shores, E.A., & Harris, A. (2010). A randomized control trial of cognitive remediation in schizophrenia. *Schizophrenia Bulletin, 36*(2), 419–427.

Saha, S., Chant, D., Welham, J., & McGrath, J.J. (2005). A systematic review of the prevalence of schizophrenia. *PLoS Medicine, 2*, c141.

Sensky, T., Turkington, D., Kingdon, D., Scott, J.L., Scott, J., Siddle, R., O'Carroll, M., Barnes, T.R.E. (2000). A randomized controlled trial of cognitive-behavioral therapy for persistent symptoms in schizophrenia resistant to medication. *Archives of General Psychiatry, 57*, 165–172.

Strauss, E., Sherman, M.S., & Spreen, O. (2006). *A compendium of neuropsychological tests* (3rd ed)*: Administration, norms and commentary.* New York: Oxford University Press.

Tharyan, P., & Adams, C.E. (2005, Apr 18). Electroconvulsive therapy for schizophrenia: a review. *Cochrane Database of Systematic Reviews*, (2).

The Psychological Corporation. (2001). *The Wechsler Test of Adult Reading (WTAR) manual.* San Antonio, TX: The Psychological Corporation.

Walker, E.F., & Diforio, D. (1997). Schizophrenia: A neural diathesis-stress model. *Psychological Review, 104*(4), 667–685.

Wechsler, D. (2009). *The Wechsler Memory Scale* (*WMS-IV*, 4th ed.). San Antonio, TX: The Psychological Corporation.

Wechsler, D. (2008). *The Wechsler Adult Intelligence Test* (*WAIS-IV) manual* (4th ed.). San Antonio, TX: The Psychological Corporation.

Wechsler, D. (2001). *The Wechsler Individual Achievement Test* (*WIAT-II*, 2nd ed.). San Antonio, TX: The Psychological Corporation.

Wechsler, D. (1997). *The Wechsler Memory Scale* (*WMS-III*, 3rd ed.). San Antonio, TX: The Psychological Corporation.

Wright, J.E., Turkington, D., Kingdon, D.G., & Basco, M.R. (2009). *Cognitive–behavior therapy for severe mental illness: An illustrated guide.* Washington, DC: American Psychiatric Association.

APPENDIX A

Test Administration Frequency, Mean Duration of Administration, Scoring and Interpretation

Most used			Longest to administer	
Rank	Test	*N*	Test	Mean minutes
1	Wechsler IQ Scales	130	Halstead-Reitan	270.69
2	Rorschach	102	Woodcock-Johnson	77.12
3	TAT	97	Wechsler IQ Scales	75.62
4	MMPI	92	Stanford-Binet	74.73
5	WRAT	90	MMPI	66.18
6	BVMGT	89	Rorschach	49.41
7	Sentence Completion	85	PIAT	47.5
8	Human Figure	68	WMS	44.22
9	H-T-P	64	Vineland	41.6
10	BDI	64	TAT	40.41
11	WMS	58	MCMI	30.65
12	Kinetic Family	57	MAPI	29.89
13	PPVT	55	WRAT	28.22
14	VMI	41	PPVT	24.64
15	Stanford-Binet	38	CBCL	23.83
16	BVRT	32	Sentence Completion	19.74
17	MCMI	31	H-T-P	15.97
18	CBCL	30	BVRT	15.41
19	Halstead-Reitan	29	VMI	14.88
20	CBRS	29	BVMGT	13.94
21	PIAT	28	Kinetic Family	12.63
22	Vineland	28	Human Figure	12.31
23	MAPI	27	CBRS	11.55
24	Woodcock-Johnson	26	BDI	11.13

continued over

APPENDIX A (CONTINUED)

Test Administration Frequency, Mean Duration of Administration, Scoring and Interpretation

	Longest to score		Longest to interpret	
Rank	Test	Mean minutes	Test	Mean minutes
1	Halstead-Reitan	54.3	Halstead-Reitan	65.82
2	Rorschach	46.09	Rorschach	50.14
3	Stanford-Binet	25.42	TAT	29.95
4	Woodcock-Johnson	24.31	MMPI	28.15
5	TAT	24.07	Stanford-Binet	25.22
6	MCMI	23.41	Wechsler IQ Scales	24.97
7	Wechsler IQ Scales	21.61	Woodcock-Johnson	24.60
8	MMPI	20.33	MCMI	22.78
9	Vineland	20.18	MAPI	21.21
10	Sentence Completion	17.1	Sentence Completion	17.96
11	Wechsler Mem Scale	16.53	Vineland	17.85
12	PPVT	16.53	Wechsler Mem Scale	17.14
13	MAPI	15.47	PPVT	17.14
14	PIAT	14.75	PIAT	16.37
15	CBCL	14.34	H-T-P	14.05
16	WRAT	12.16	CBCL	13.00
17	H-T-P	11.75	WRAT	12.30
18	BVRT	10.9	Human Figure	11.25
19	VMI	10.46	BVMGT	10.47
20	BVMGT	10.02	Kinetic Family	10.41
21	Human Figure	9.82	CBRS	9.77
22	CBRS	9.1	VMI	9.54
23	Kinetic Family	8.55	BVRT	8.84
24	BDI	6.4	BDI	8.33

From 'Time requirements of psychological testing: A survey of practitioners' by J.D. Ball, R.P. Archer & E.A. Imhof, *Journal of Personality Assessment, 63*(2), 239–249. Reprinted by permission of the publisher (Taylor & Francis Group, http://www.informaworld.com).

www.ingramcontent.com/pod-product-compliance
Lightning Source LLC
LaVergne TN
LVHW052254200926
848481LV00002B/361